JAPANESE CAPITALS

is a practical guidebook to the three successive capitals of the country, Nara, Kyoto, and Tokyo, showing how to derive the greatest possible enjoyment from the brilliant civilization of ancient and mediaeval Japan and the invigorating modern cities, without spending a fortune.

You can find air fares to Tokyo much cheaper than those quoted for scheduled services. The overnight bus to Kyoto is another great bargain. Cheap accommodation can be found on arrival (between £3 and £7 for a single room) and low-cost meals are available everywhere, if one steers clear of fashionable areas like Tokyo's Ginza. Buses and trains are frequent, clean, cheap and punctual. Toilets are numerous, well-signposted and spotless. Vending machines for soft or alcoholic drinks are ubiquitous, and the water is not only drinkable (it tastes wonderful) but is provided free as an alternative to expensive coffee or soft drinks. Streets are clean. Passers-by are courteous and almost obsessively keen to practise English by helping you if you are lost. Tourist attractions are well served by public transport, open at reasonable hours and often free or open at small charges, because the Japanese themselves are inveterate travellers: they love to tour their own country. During the last twenty years, when violent crime has increased everywhere else, in Japan it has actually decreased. Women may walk city streets in safety. Guidebooks, maps and leaflets are usually obtainable in English. Japan is today's ideal travel destination.

PHILIP WARD, F.R.S.A., A.L.A., has spent much of his life in Africa and Asia, from Morocco to Indonesia. Because of his long-standing sympathy with Japanese spiritual and artistic values, he is an ideal companion. His previous travel books include *Bangkok, Across Saudi Arabia, The Aeolian Islands, Touring Lebanon, Touring Iran, Touring Cyprus, Tripoli, Albania,* and most recently *Ha'il: Oasis City of Saudi Arabia.*

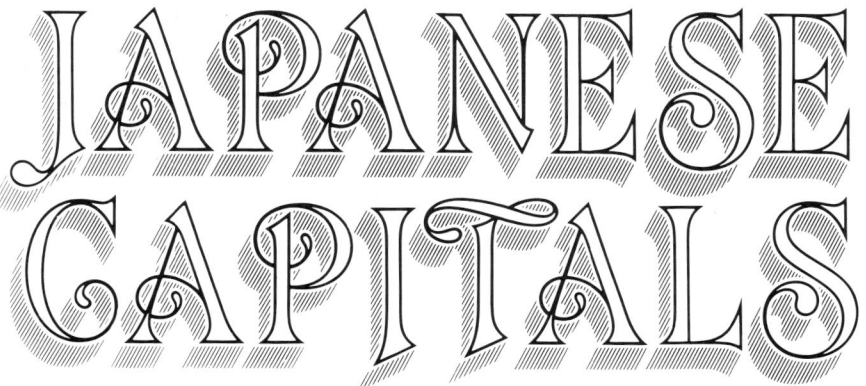

JAPANESE CAPITALS

*a cultural, historical and artistic
guide to Nara, Kyoto and Tokyo,
successive capitals of Japan*

PHILIP WARD

THE OLEANDER PRESS

The Oleander Press
17 Stansgate Avenue
Cambridge CB2 2QZ

The Oleander Press
210 Fifth Avenue
New York, N.Y. 10010
U.S.A.

British Library Cataloguing in Publication Data
Ward, Philip
   Japanese capitals: a cultural, historical and
   artistic guide to Nara, Kyoto and Tokyo,
   successive capitals of Japan.—(Oleander travel
   books; v. 11)
   1. Capitals (Cities)   2. Japan—Capital
   I. Title
   952'.009'732   DS807

ISBN 0–906672–88–0
ISBN 0–906672–89–9 Pbk

Typeset, printed and bound in Great Britain

CONTENTS

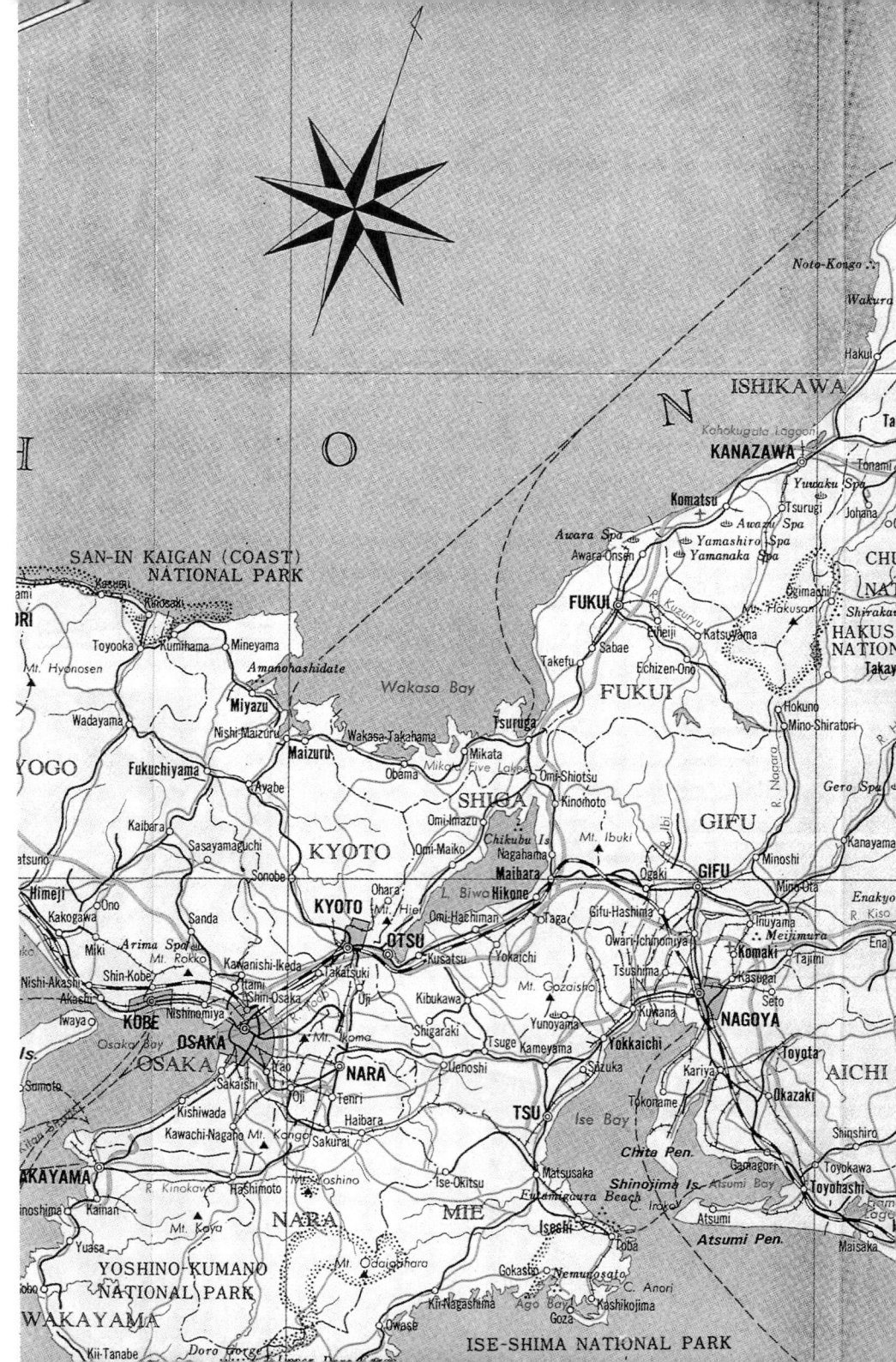

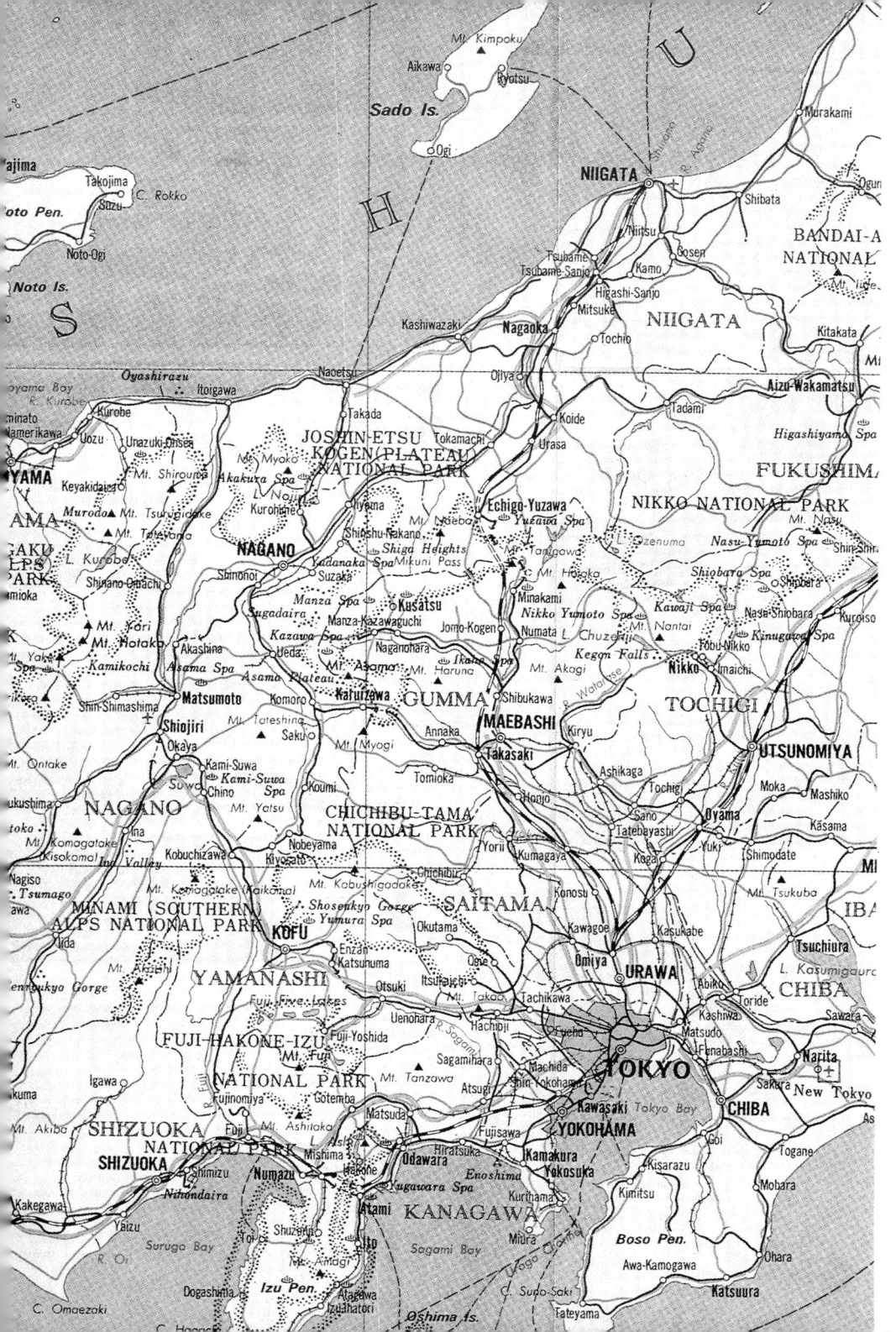

ACKNOWLEDGEMENTS

First and foremost I thank Mr Shoichi Maekawa of Tokyo, his charming family, and Mr S. Tanaoka of Wakeijuku, for their kind hospitality and thoughtful arrangements which enabled me to enjoy experiences not always available to the casual visitor.

In Cambridge my family and I enjoyed the friendship of Kihei and Keika Maekawa, who helped with preparations and potential language problems.

I owe my customary infinite debt of gratitude to my wife, Audrey, and to my daughters, Angela and Carolyn, for allowing me the time and space to write in peace.

In London, Mrs Hutchinson and her colleagues at the Japan National Tourist Organisation gave a great deal of help with illustrations and supplementary reference material to ensure that the practical information was brought up to date.

In Kyoto, Mrs Yoshida of Ryokan Shichijyoso and Mr Yoichi Takamura of Osaka University of Foreign Studies made even keener my enjoyment of one of the world's loveliest cities.

In Nara, I acknowledge with respectful thanks the hospitality of the Chief Abbots of Todaiji and Toshodaiji; of the Chief Abbot and Mrs Nakata of Shin Yakushiji, who allowed me the privilege of evenings, nights and dawns in a Buddhist temple; the friendship of Mr Hiroshi Yamamoto; and the courteous assistance of Mr Takashi Hamada, Director-General of Nara National Museum.

To men and women in the street, everywhere in the present and former capitals of Japan, I express my deep appreciation of their unvarying courtesy.

LIST OF ILLUSTRATIONS

Except where indicated, the illustrations were kindly provided by the Japan National Tourist Office, to whom acknowledgement is hereby gratefully extended.

BEFORE I START

Before I start to write, I close my eyes, listening to Goro Yamaguchi's shakuhachi playing *Koku-reibo*: a bell ringing in the empty sky, one of the three oldest pieces for bamboo flute in the Fuke shakuhachi tradition, composed by a Zen priest called Kyochiku and arranged by Kinko Kurosawa (1710–71) into a tranquil solo which wends a path as if through a shrine, such as Kasuga at Nara.

I open my eyes, and before me hangs a sumi bamboo drawing by Shibutsu (1766–1837), telling the truth in nervously assured black and white. My fingers tighten over a smooth pine votive plaque bought at the Kamigamo Shrine in Kyoto.

Green tea from Uji warms my throat as the bowl warms my hands. Shadows, I recall, flitted across the paper-covered sliding door of my room in Shin Yakushiji, Nara, between the hovering moon and my room facing a bamboo grove. Beyond and within sounded the temple gong.

> *One stroke,*
> *I am alive.*
> *Second gong,*
> *I am awake.*
> *Third note,*
> *I am aware.*
> *Fourth gong,*
> *Nothing is even aware.*
> *The fifth gong,*
> *Ah, the fifth gong!*

QUICK ITINERARIES IN NARA

Nobody should plan to stay fewer than two days in Nara. The recommended stay is five days as a minimum. But for those who *must* stay for a shorter period, here are suggested quick itineraries. As in Kyoto, the length of time that you are prepared to spend in a place will correspond to the enjoyment you can derive from its various facets.

ONE DAY
In the morning, take 'bus 60 from Bay 10 oppposite Kintetsu Nara railway station to Horyuji, seeing also Chuguji, and if possible also Horinji and Hokkiji.

In the afternoon, return to Nara from Hokkijiguchi 'bus stop via Yakushijimae, stopping at Yakushiji and Toshodaiji.

TWO DAYS
Day 1. As above.
Day 2. Take the ring road 'bus from Kintetsu Nara station to Todaiji. Visit Todaiji, Kasuga Shrine, Nara National Museum (or on Mondays, when it is closed, Shin Yakushiji), Sarusawa Pond and Kofukuji. If time allows, Saidaiji (from Saidaiji rail station) or (from Gakuenmae rail station) Yamato Bunkakan Museum (closed on Mondays).

THREE DAYS
Days 1 and 2. As above.
Day 3. Hannyaji, Prefectural Museum, Isuien Garden, Hokkeji, Daianji, Gangoji and Araike Pond.

See the selection of major festivals listed under 'Useful Information' to determine extent of changes. From late October to early November some major treasures from Shosoin are displayed in Nara National Museum, and these should not be missed on any account.

NARA

As we shall spend much of our time reversing Western concepts, it is as well to begin by rejecting the notion of a long-established capital city in Japan, on the model of Lisbon, Paris, or Copenhagen. Tokyo, the most populous city in the world, has been the capital of imperial Japan only since 1868, and it thus forms only the right-hand side panel of the metropolitan triptych. From 794 until that date, Heian-kyo – the modern Kyoto – was the cultural and administrative capital of the country, occupying the central panel of our triptych. The other side belongs to Nara, forty kilometres south of Kyoto, which was called Heijo when it held supremacy as the religious and imperial capital for much of the period between 710 and 794. If Angkor Wat or Prambanan or Ayudhya in South-East Asia are religious centres without a major contemporary rôle, Nara by contrast is still vibrant with the past even as the modern inhabitants go about their daily lives.

Since this book is devoted to capitals, however, it is necessary to understand what the Japanese mean by *miyako*. Now 'capital', originally it signified the site of an honourable dwelling and, as the Emperor's dwelling was the most honourable of all, it came to mean the site of the imperial residence. In the West, the ruler is traditionally enthroned in the capital. In Japan, the capital is wherever the Emperor chooses to be enthroned, and because a new Emperor – avoiding the ritual uncleanness of a place contaminated by death – invariably chose to be installed in a new palace, by definition the site of the capital also moved. In 646, the Japanese imported the idea of a capital, with administrative and military undertones, from China, but the notion of the *miyako* did not disappear. The wooden mansions and temples were quickly dismantled and, using the grid system adopted by Ch'ang-an, T'ang capital of China, and subsequently by North American cities such as New York, reconstructed in an equivalent part of the fresh site.

Kotoku, the thirty-sixth Emperor, adopted many T'ang customs, including the use of *nengo* or 'era' system of dating. He decreed that the first year of his reign (645–6) should be the first year of the Taikwa era; on receiving the gift of a white pheasant (*hakuchi*) he changed the era to Hakuchi in the year 650, and although his successors Saimei and Tenchi abolished the *nengo* system, it was reinstated by Temmu and remains in effect today.

Kotoku made the first Chinese-style 'capital' at Naniwa, in present-day

Osaka, in 646, but in 651 Saimei transferred it to Asuka (or Totsu-Asuka), south of Nara. Tenchi moved in 668 to Omi (modern Otsu) but in 673 Temmu reverted to a different part of Asuka and a few years later Empress Jito changed the capital site to Fujiwara, also south of Nara. There too reigned Mommu (697–707), grandson of Tenchi, and Empress Gemmyo, a daughter of Tenchi. She reigned from 708, but it was not until 710 that she transferred her capital to Nara, which expanded rapidly to become the most important city in Japan. It was she who minted the first Japanese copper coinage, and she who caused the historical records *Kojiki* and *Fudoki* to be compiled from 712 and 713.

Even so, however, the *miyako*-style wandering, inherent in the Japanese mode of ruling, compelled the Emperor Shomu (son of Mommu) who reigned from 724 to 748, succeeding his aunt Gensho, to move his capital from Nara to Kuni (north of Nara) in 740, to Shigaraki (north-east of Nara) in 742, back to Naniwa in 744, and back again to Nara in 745. We should not read too much into these peregrinations, however. Nara was not outshone in secular power or eclipsed in religious domination, as can be seen from the fact that Shomu's reign saw the construction of Nara's Todaiji, and the main hall of the pilgrim-age temple of Hasedera, south of Nara.

In 784, Emperor Kammu moved his headquarters to Nagaoka in Yamashiro Province, but in 794 he decided on the site not far from Lake Biwa to the east, Osaka and the sea to the west, and Nara to the south. This he called Heian-kyo, and it is this city which grew into the cultural capital of Japan, succeeded so recently by the commercial drive of Osaka and the massive urban sprawl of Tokyo–Kawasaki–Yokohama.

Nara today has a population of a quarter of a million, roughly a sixth as many as Kyoto (1·5 million), which is seven times smaller than Tokyo (10·5 million), the greatest megalopolis on earth. It therefore makes a quiet prelude or a calming postlude to your stay in Tokyo or Osaka, and anyone choosing to skirt Nara will see a Japan artificially and unevenly urban, sprawling, and devoted to economic and industrial goals.

The history and culture of Japan are centred on Nara and the Yamato Plain. 'Nara' means 'level land', a commodity precious for ricefields, and for building temples, mansions, towns and cities. Nara, Nagaoka, Kyoto and the huge industrial city of Osaka all owe their consecutive significance to their position clustered on a fertile inhabited plain in a country essentially mountainous.

Most travel agents and holiday companies underestimate the significance of Nara so crucially that they do not even plan for most visitors to spend the night there, and this has led to a shortage of accommodation in Nara at all price levels, compared with Kyoto or Tokyo.

Nara Hotel is very close to Kofukuji, an ideal location. For those on a budget, Ryokan Seikanso, 29 Higashi Kitsuji-cho, Nara City, Nara Pref. 630 is just a ten-minute walk south from the Kintetsu Nara station, beyond Sarusawa Pond. Slightly to the east, and a little dearer, is Ryokan Matsumae, 28–1 Higashi Terabayashi-cho, Nara City, Nara Pref. 630. Also within a ten-minute walk from the Kintetsu Nara station are the Ryokan Sakae, 46 Higashi Kitsuji-cho, Nara City, Nara Pref. 630 and the Ryokan Osakaya, Nishi Kitsuji-cho. More expensive are the business hotels: People's Inn Hanakomichi, 23 Konishimachi, and Business Hotel Shoroku, 1288 Kita 2-chome, Horen-cho, both a couple of minutes' walk from Kintetsu Nara station. Or you might prefer a youth hostel, such as Naraken Seishonen Kaikan, 72 Ikenokami, Handahiraki-cho, Nara City, Nara Pref. 630, ten minutes by bus from JNR Nara Station, or the much larger Nara Youth Hostel, Sogoundoken, 64 Handahiraki-cho, Nara City, Nara Pref. 630, about five minutes by bus from JNR Nara station.

Temple Breakfast

My alarm-clock trilled me awake at six-twenty on a bright spring morning. I slid wooden doors apart to enjoy the early sun dappling through the bamboo grove; birds twittered and monkeys clattered and chittered among protecting trees. I folded away futon and pillows.

> *Sandals weight beyond the sliding paper door.*
> *Gong dawn.*
> *Nervous monkeys chatter in the bamboo grove.*
> *One two drops of rain three.*
> *Appetites revive.*

A communal wash-basin area stood partly open to the sky, bamboo gutters visible just above my head. 'Mind your head' everywhere in Japan, even if notices to that effect are absent, for doorways and ceilings are those cramping Alice in Wonderland. I shaved in cold water, as I have done all over the Far East, but here I sensed that thousands of priests had stood on the same spot, and a shiver of history tickled my spine.

On returning to my room, I shook off my house slippers and closed the paper door behind me. My low table had been laid with breakfast. A new pot of tea and bowl, flakes of seaweed in a cellophane pack (that concession to contemporary fads), hot soup made with onions and seafood, a bowl of plain boiled rice, a tiny cake of fish and seafood, a tiny bowl of beans, a saucer of soy sauce, a hardboiled egg and chopsticks. A fine start to any day.

I exchanged my *yukata*, a wide-sleeved kimono used as a dressing-gown, for my western suit, took my breakfast tray back to the kitchen, and set out to walk downhill into Nara.

Kofukuji

'The Temple Providing Happiness' started life as a hall in Yamashina to house sculptures ordered by Kamatari Fujiwara (614–669) for Shitennoji. They found their way instead to a private chapel in Yamashina established in Kamatari's honour by his widow in 669. When the capital was transferred to Fujiwara, the building moved too, with the new name of Umayasakadera. The final step was

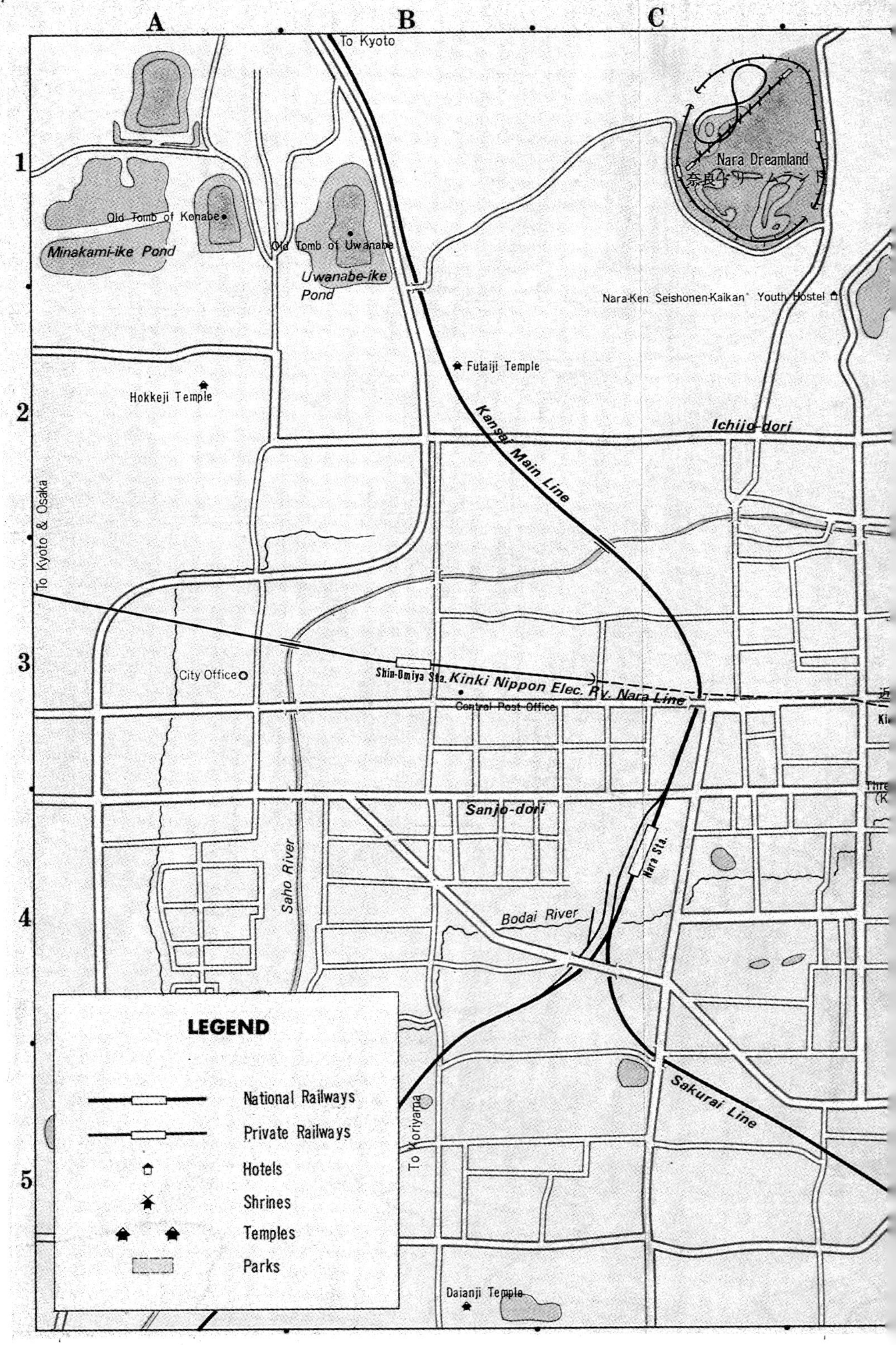

A B C

1

Old Tomb of Konabe ·

Minakami-ike Pond

Old Tomb of Uwanabe ·

Uwanabe-ike Pond

To Kyoto

Nara Dreamland
奈良ドリームランド

Nara-Ken Seishonen-Kaikan Youth Hostel 🏠

♠ Futaiji Temple

2

Hokkeji Temple ♠

Ichijo-dori

Kansai Main Line

To Kyoto & Osaka

3

City Office ○

Shin-Omiya Sta. **Kinki Nippon Elec. Rly. Nara Line**

Central Post Office

Sanjo-dori

Saho River

Nara Sta.

4

Bodai River

To Koriyama

Sakurai Line

5

LEGEND

——————— National Railways

——————— Private Railways

🏠 Hotels

★ Shrines

♠ ♠ Temples

▭ Parks

Daianji Temple

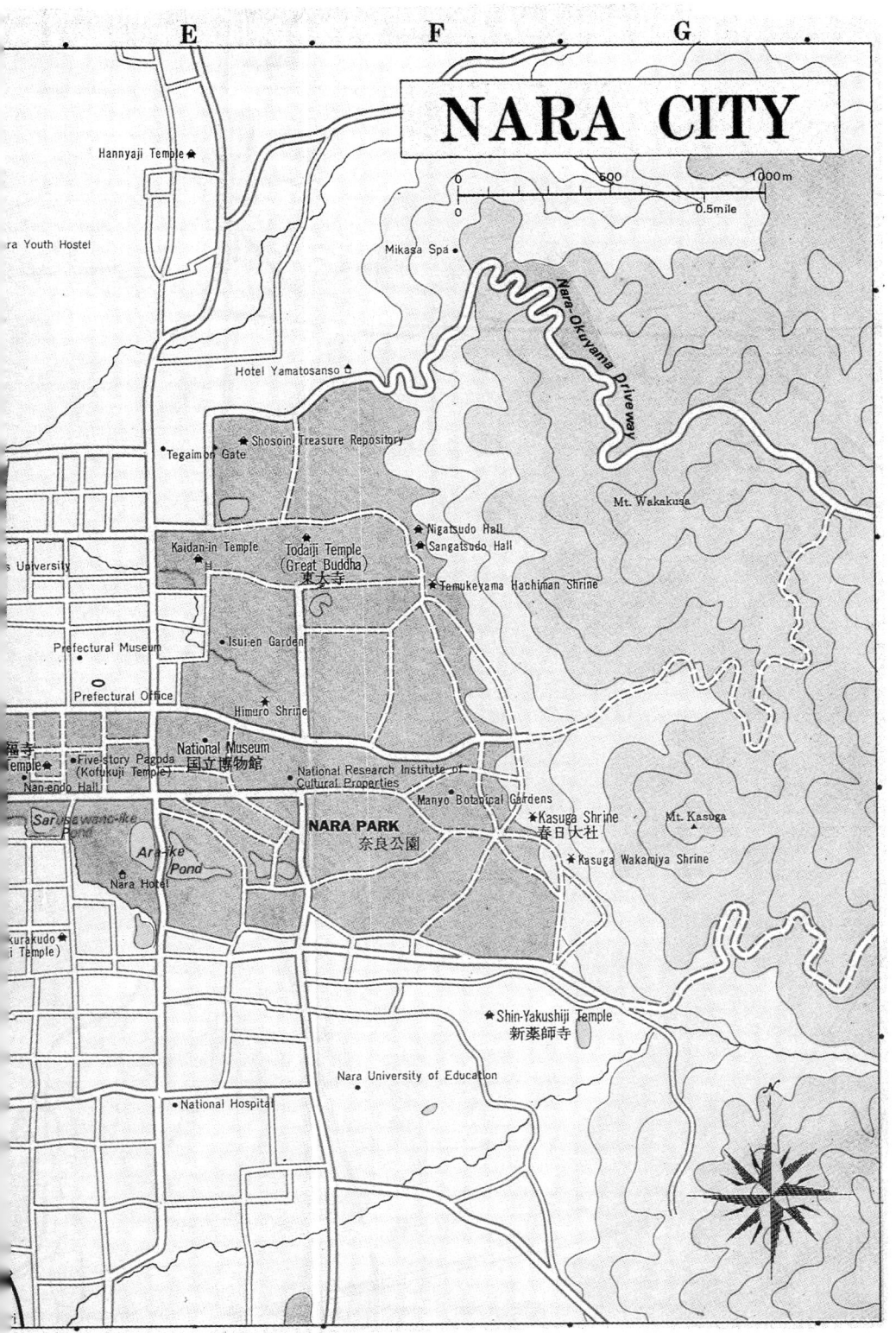

NARA CITY

E   F   G

0   500   1000m
0   0.5mile

Hannyaji Temple

ra Youth Hostel

Mikasa Spa

Nara-Okuyama Driveway

Hotel Yamatosanso

Shosoin Treasure Repository

Tegaimon Gate

Mt. Wakakusa

Kaidan-in Temple

Nigatsudo Hall

Sangatsudo Hall

Todaiji Temple
(Great Buddha)
東大寺

s University

Temukeyama Hachiman Shrine

Isui-en Garden

Prefectural Museum

Prefectural Office

Himuro Shrine

福寺
Temple
Nan-endo Hall

Five-story Pagoda
(Kofukuji Temple)

National Museum
国立博物館

National Research Institute of
Cultural Properties

Manyo Botanical Gardens

Kasuga Shrine
春日大社

Mt. Kasuga

NARA PARK
奈良公園

Sarusawano-ike
Pond

Ara-ike
Pond

Nara Hotel

Kasuga Wakamiya Shrine

kurakudo
Temple)

Shin-Yakushiji Temple
新薬師寺

Nara University of Education

National Hospital

taken with the establishment of Nara as capital in 710, when the temple became closely connected with the Kasuga Shrine and hence known as Kasugaji until it received its 'modern name' in 721, when declared an official temple a year after the death of Fubito Fujiwara, the period to which the original North Octagonal Hall (Hokuendo) dated. Its present reconstruction dates from 1208–10. Fubito was responsible for the Chukondo (Main Hall), immediately to the north of the site of the Great Southern Gate (Nandaimon), and this too fell victim to the devastation caused by power struggles in the late twelfth century: in fact none of the original hundred and seventy recorded buildings of this, one of the Seven Great Temples of Nara, survived that era. Kofukuji was, with Nanji (also called Genkoji), headquarters of one of the two branches of the Hosso Buddhist sect which stressed enlightenment through the powers of the mind, a doctrine associated with Vasubandhu and the Chinese pilgrim Hsüan-tsang. The other two chief sects of Nara Buddhism were Kegon ('Flower-Wreath'), emphasising the metaphysics of the harmonious whole, and Sanron ('Three Treatises'), a doctrine of the dialectics of negation associated with Nagarjuna and Kumarajiva.

Unifying these apparently dissimilar ideas was the central Buddhist doctrine of change, as opposed to the Confucian concept of stability generally accepted in Han China. Hsüan-tsang viewed the whole world as illusory, not existing outside our own minds. The Nara period saw the first roads and bridges made in Japan, the use of irrigation, peregrination of the countryside by missionary Buddhist monks, public baths, and the institution of cremation. When, in his excellent *Japan* (Revised ed., 1952), Sir George Sansom wrote that the Japanese 'have a plentiful vocabulary to denote specific virtues like piety, faithfulness, loyalty, benevolence, and so on; but their language is deficient in words to express such ideas as are represented by sin, conscience, repentance, forgiveness or atonement, in the sense in which they figure in Christian doctrinal and devotional works', one might think that that is hardly surprising, since Japan has never been a Christian country. But in fact what he says is quite untrue for Nara Buddhism. During the ascendancy of the 'Six Sects' – and even later – it was quite common for court ceremonies to include *keka*, which means the open confession of sins, closer perhaps to public confessions in Communist China than to the private confession to a priest practised by Roman Catholics, but still quite clearly the confession of sin.

Though all religious history and doctrines are disputed and disputable, the buildings in which the religion was pursued manage to survive fire and civil war. Kofukuji, aligning itself with its band of warrior monks on the side of the Genji against the Heike clans, was destroyed by the army of Shigehira of the Heike in 1180, but gradually and painfully, at great expense, restored under the ultimately-victorious Genji to something of its former glory, but a massive fire in 1717 reduced most of the compound to rubble. The military rulers of the Edo period neglected a temple founded by the Fujiwaras, and the Meiji Restoration did not bring with it restoration of Kofukuji; on the contrary, some

Kofukuji. The guardian Ashura from the Saikondo (c.734) now in the Temple Museum.

of the temple's lands were converted into Nara Park, and buildings (such as the refectory and Central Hall) were secularized.

The latest stage in the long and eventful life of the Temple Providing Happiness was the construction in 1958 of a Museum (ask for *Kokuhokan*) just east of the Main Hall. The razed Saikondo has provided the two small devils by Koben (1215); two vigorously muscular gate guardians also of the early Kamakura period and repaired in 1288; a wonderful T'ang cast bronze gong stand (with later Japanese gong); six from the original standing 'Ten Great Disciples' (734) in dry lacquer, each individual yet all wonderfully spiritual, particularly perhaps Furuna (in Sanskrit, Purna), the eldest and most eloquent; and finally, the extraordinarily beautiful 'Eight Supernatural Beings' as described in the Lotus Sutra. Contemporary with the disciples, and also of dry lacquer, they are roughly equivalent too in height, but the sensitive execution allows each figure to speak with its own voice. Ashura, for instance, wears a loose skirt of Cambodian type, and has three faces and three pairs of arms, with a sweet face that was clearly made separately from the body. The bird face of Garuda (in Japanese, Karura) has a poignant humour above its conventional suit of armour. Both sets of figures were commissioned by General Mampuku, and obviously encircled a central Shaka image.

The earliest bell recorded in Japan is that dated 689 at Myoshinji, Kyoto, but the one here from the former Kanzenin was cast in 727, and is thus the second oldest.

From the Tokondo (East Main Hall) there are a number of masterpieces. The wooden 'Twelve Heavenly Generals', each bearing an animal of the zodiac, were carved in 1207. The Manjusri (Monju Bosatsu) is created in the 'assembled wood-block' or yosegi style, with a sacred casket denoting wisdom resting on his top-knot, and dates from the late twelfth century. A cast bronze head of Yakushi Nyorai dated 686 is all that remains from an image 2½ metres tall otherwise destroyed in the fire of 1411. 'Four Heavenly Guardians' of the ninth century are carved from single blocks of wood in the ichiboku style. The sturdy protectors stand, brandishing their weapons, on squirming demons. Even more vigorous are the small low-relief wooden figures, carved in the twelfth century, of the 'Twelve Heavenly Generals', where the energy and movement is carefully individualised, so that Mekira throws one arm and one foot aloft in one swift vertical movement, while Shotora, squat and earth-bound, forms a diagonal thrust from hair to his right down to his left: anyone who thinks that Buddhist sculpture lacks humour, variety or originality need only examine these brilliant Juni shinsho to discover his mistake. Even the gargoyles thought unique to Western Gothic have their counterparts in these grimacing 'generals' or elsewhere in the hapless demons trapped underfoot.

Direct portraits include the standing figures of Muchaku (the Indian Asanga) and Seshin (Vasubandhu), two teachers revered by the Hosso sect carved in the early thirteenth century by Unkei, who was also responsible for the very different Miroku Bosatsu, combining realism, classicism, and spiritual beauty in both face and gesture.

South of the Museum stands the latest Tokondo (1415), the fifth on the site, and south again the Five-Storey Pagoda (1426), at 55 metres the highest pagoda in Japan after that of Toji in Kyoto. With the Tokondo it is considered a peak of Muromachi wayo-style architecture.

Balancing it in neat asymmetry is the Three-Storey Pagoda restored shortly after the fire of 1180 and charmingly situated at the top of steps leading down to Sarusawa Pond, with its age-old carp and turtles. An elderly lady opened her shopping-bag nearby, and took out a paper-bag full of empty pea-pods, which she scattered before two grazing deer. They sauntered gracefully up to her, and began to munch on their daily feed.

Due west of the Five-Storey Pagoda stands the Nanendo (South Octagonal Hall), a structure dating to 1741, on the site of the original Nanendo of 813. It was here that the most vigorous stamp in my stamp book was made, the swirling calligraphy somewhat spoilt by the inscription in English and date below. Our predictable, even monotonous, alphabet must seem very primitive to the Japanese, whose kanji, katakana and hiragana combined make even Chinese look static and square. The organic flow of Japanese calligraphy blends like rivers, streams, brooks and waterfalls over the page, resulting in great energy and harmony over hand-made paper whether white or flecked with gold and grasses.

Gangoji

In the second decade of the eighth century, Gangoji (like Daianji, three blocks to the west) was removed column by column and bracket by bracket on ox-carts to the new capital of Heijo-kyo, now Nara. It was so prominent at that time, with Main Hall, Lecture Hall, refectory, belfry and two pagodas, that it was an official temple, with lands in the provinces to provide an adequate income. Of the original structures, only the Zendo remains. Sanron Buddhism made Todaiji ever more dominant, relegating Gangoji to insignificance. The eighth-century priest Chiko, having received a vision of the Pure Land, painted a mandala to show the Western Paradise of Buddha. His Paradise Quarters (Gokurakubo) then prospered as a separate part of Gangoji, and a Main Hall survives from the Kamakura period, as does the replica now shown of the Jodo Mandala, and the Main Hall of Jurinin, once another part of Gangoji.

Daianji

'Great Peace' Temple was transferred to Nara's Sixth Street (Rokujo) in 711. Built like a Chinese temple, just as the city of Heijo itself (and Heian-kyo, or Kyoto, after it) derived its plan from the Chinese capital of Ch'ang-an, Daianji was so important that it possessed its own scriptorium for the copying of sutras. Frequently the victim of fire, it possesses no original building, and only nine of the sculptures from the late Nara period. My favourite is Bato Kannon, a bodhisattva shown in Hindu iconography as horse-headed. Buddhist art is not quite so exuberant, however, and here the equine aspect is confined to a tiny horse-face above a human head. The bell at Daianji is dated 858.

Horyuji

In 572, the wife of the Emperor Yomei gave birth to her second son in the Imperial stables (umaya) since birth pangs came on her as she was walking near them, and this son, Umayado, was named heir to the throne, or Taishi, on the accession of his aunt Suiko in 593. It was he, known as Shotoku Taishi after his death, who consolidated the power of Buddhism, and brought Japan into a degree of conformity with Chinese government and administration. He formed the bureaucracy in 604, and converted the calendar from Japanese to Chinese. He stressed the importance of history to a nation's civilization, and decreed a Constitution, the first legal document in Japan, which defined the relationship of sovereign and ruled as that between heaven and earth. Confucian in government and moral principles, Shotoku nevertheless promoted Buddhism as the national religion, building forty-six monasteries with 820 monks and 560 nuns. After his death, a further 360 temples were constructed during the Nara period alone.

The most important temple in Japan as regards antiquity and evocative atmosphere deserves half a day at least, and you should start out early to arrive at eight a.m. There is a connecting bus at Horyuji from JNR Nara Station, taking 5 minutes and a 30-minute bus-ride from the terminal at the Kintetsu Nara rail station (ask for Horyujimae) which also passes close by Toshodaiji and Yakushiji. I suggest that you do not attempt to see all three in one day, because they are too similar, but devote the second half of each day to museums or shrines.

Horyuji was built by Shotoku outside Nara, at the village of Ikaruga, as the third major Buddhist temple in Japan, following the Shitennoji (now in Osaka) heavily damaged in 1945 by air raids and the Asukadera, largely destroyed. Horyuji was founded in 607 as Ikarugadera, to provide the followers of Prince Shotoku with a place for their physical and spiritual needs, and as his following grew, so did the temple, with sixty-two buildings now extant from the Asuka period spanning the close of the sixth century to the Momoyama period which ended in 1598. In 607 Shotoku commissioned the sculptor Tori to carve the image of Yakushi, the Healing Buddha, for the Kondo, where it became the main object of veneration, and sent his first embassy to China, explaining how he had introduced Chinese concepts of law, religion, government, town-planning, architecture and philosophy into Japan. He brought over Chinese and Korean monks to teach Buddhism, and artisans to bring mainland traditions of building and craftsmanship. The Japanese genius for integrating foreign concepts into their own world-view without compromising their integrity or individuality has remained with them to the present day, achieving consensus by discussion, so avoiding direct confrontation and destructive conflict. Horyuji stands not only as the oldest surviving wooden building in the world, but as the oldest Japanese temple still virtually intact, yet the principles on which it was built were largely Chinese, and the workers who created it were mainly Korean. Horyuji received its name ('Temple of the Prosperity of the Buddhist Law') at its inauguration in 616 by the Korean priest Eji, who had arrived in Japan in 595.

You approach Horyuji through the Nandaimon (Great South Gate) to the Saiin Garan (Western Precinct, though the leaflet provided in English translates it 'Westminster') which was rebuilt in 1439. It leads to the principal sector, or Western Precinct, which was built up around the Kondo and Five-Storey Pagoda, through the Chumon (Inner Gate) with its two temple guardians carved in 711, but restored as recently as 1964.

The Kairo (Corridor) extends left and right from the Chumon, offering a variety of views of the Five-Storey Pagoda and the Main Hall or Kondo. The Chumon itself dates from the year of the temple's construction, and its four-bay façade with two doorways is as unusual as the three-bay side, the only

Horyuji. Temple guardian (c.711).

Horyuji. Main Hall (7th century).

similar example being that of the razed Asukadera. Since the upper storey is clearly smaller than the lower, it gives the appearance of a hall rather than that of a gate.

The Main Hall is probably the oldest wooden building extant, with twenty-eight massive tapering pillars. Two-storeyed, its plan is five bays by four, the lower storey surrounded by a mokoshi, an additional wooden roof or 'lean-to'. It contains sculptures of cardinal importance for the history of Japanese art: another reason to start your exploration of the country here in Nara.

The central trinity is of Shakyamuni (in Japanese Shaka) and attendant bodhisattvas, who remained voluntarily on earth, though they had attained enlightenment, in order to save other beings. All three bronze figures were cast in 623 by Tori, grandson of one Shiba Tatto, who had reached Japan from

China or Korea in 522. The bodhisattvas are the earliest known surviving of this subject, and derive in style from Northern Wei China by way of Korea, but with the first traces of a Japanese delicacy and inwardness, combining austerity with humanity. Look too for the earlier Yakushi Nyorai (dated on the back of the halo to 607), which formed the principal object of veneration until the rebuilding of the Kondo in 670; the attendant bodhisattvas are at least fifty years later than Yakushi. The wooden Shitenno figures (Four Heavenly Guardians) are of late Asuka date, and again the oldest specimens of the subject in Japan. All twelve walls of the Kondo were once decorated with frescoes, but most were destroyed by fire in 1949 and are being restored only slowly and painstakingly.

The Five-Storey Pagoda was dismantled for safety during World War II and has been reassembled using many of the original timbers; its elegant proportions from the lowest roof to the highest are 10:9:8:7:6. Each side of the ground floor has a grotto, so heavily barred as to be hardly visible, with clay figures of 711 (with many others later in date) in the earliest known dioramas: they show the division among disciples of Shakyamuni's ashes, on the west; Buddha's death and entry into Nirvana (in Sanskrit, Mahaparinirvana), on the north; the

Horyuji

13

Bodhisattva Manjusri's visit to the sick lay-disciple Vimalakirti, on the east; and the Coming Buddha (Maitreya in Sanskrit, and Miroku in Japanese) flanked by bodhisattvas and guardians, on the south.

Due north of the Inner Gate stands the Kodo, or lecture hall, where the priests study. Destroyed by fire in 925, the founding lecture hall was replaced in 990 by a hall brought from Kyoto. The sculptures too are of Heian date: Yakushi Nyorai flanked by Nikko and Gakko (respectively Suryaprabhasa and Candrabha in Sanskrit), protected by the Four Heavenly Guardians.

The Library of the Sutras (Kyozo) and Belfry (Shoro) are of late Nara and early Heian age respectively. The Kyozo is a repository for Buddhist teachings and a sculpture of Shotoku Taishi in the act of lecturing on the Tripitaka.

I emerged from the nucleus of the ancient Horyuji with a growing appreciation of the extreme antiquity of Japanese architecture and sculpture: a sense that one feels keenly on observing Saharan rock art or Machu Picchu, Pasargadae or the Western Han excavations uncovered in 1968 at Mancheng, Hopei Province. This nucleus is so significant that, in Tomoya Masuda's *Living Architecture: Japanese*, the author limits his plan of Horyuji to this small sector. In fact there is much more to see even in the western precinct: the western rotunda, or Saiendo, which I found deserted up steps beyond the Sangyoin. Lay Buddhists in the Sangyoin were listening to a sermon being relayed over a microphone; pines outside were hung with paper wishes. I found the Shoryoin closed, and thus was unable to see the images of Shotoku and those of his circle, but the Treasury, or Daihozoden, was fortunately open, and its English captions made a welcome relief from the monolingual captions more usual in Japanese museums. Leading masterpieces here include the earliest known portrait painting of Shotoku, an early Nara Yumechigai Kannon ('Dream-Transforming Kannon') of exquisite beauty, and a slender Kannon named for Kudara (the Korean kingdom of 'Paekche) from its supposed origin – it is certainly very different from the contemporary Japanese works of the Asuka period in the Kondo. The Tamamushi Zushi (Iridescent Miniature Shrine) is believed to have been the shrine for the tutelary icon of Empress Suiko, Shotoku's aunt. Equally fine is the so-called 'Zushi of Lady Tachibana', the lady being mother to the Empress Shomu, though this attribution is not found earlier than the Kamakura period, and the bronze Amida trinity with its shrine can be dated to about 700. The large central figure is Amitabha Buddha in his Western Paradise, seated on lotus flowers with his attendants Kannon and Seishi.

More than three hundred of the choicest items from the Horyuji treasury found their way to the Imperial Household in 1876, when the temple needed funds for restoration. A special gallery was built to house them in the Tokyo National Museum with its own bilingual illustrated catalogue, and should be the second gallery you visit there, after the gallery devoted to archaeology and prehistory, for most of the objects date from Asuka times (552–644) and Early Nara (645–709), while the selection of objects from Shosoin associated with

Todaiji, changed every year at Nara National Museum, date chiefly from Late Nara (710–794).

From Horyuji's own treasury we pass the Todaimon (Great East Gate) to the Toin Garan, which is the site of the Ikaruga Palace of 601. In 739 the abbot Gyoshin (d. 750) built the octagon later known as the Hall of Dreams (Yumedono), and other buildings such as the priests' quarters or Sobo, and the lecture-hall named for the Transmission of the Law, Denpodo. The finest sculptures in the Eastern Precinct are the Kuze Kannon (Saviour of the World) in gold-leaf covered camphor-wood of the early 7th century, and two images of priests: Gyoshin himself in dry lacquer, an awesome figure with a face not unlike a stage Mephistopheles, and Dosen (d. 876) in clay. The Kannon is recorded in an inventory of 761 to have been 'of the height of the Prince of the Upper Palace', or Shotoku Taishi, who must have been much taller than the average Japanese if that was true. Next we come to the Shariden (Hall of Relics) and Eden (Hall of Pictures); in the latter can be found Edo-period copies from paintings of scenes from Shotoku Taishi's life, the originals having been presented to the Imperial Household. The Denpodo, where Lady Tachibana originally lived, was donated to the temple in 739.

Virtually independent of Horyuji, at its eastern end, is the nunnery of Chuguji. Initially sited about a mile to the east as a palace of Shotoku's mother, Anohobe no Hashibito, it was transformed after her death into a temple dedicated to her memory, and even today the abbess is connected with the Imperial family, so that Chuguji is a monzeki, or imperial temple. Its main hall was renovated in 1968 and preserves the oldest known Japanese embroidery, woven by court ladies shortly after Shotoku's death in 622 to commemorate his passing to the Land of Heavenly Longevity (Tenjukoku), after which the mandala embroidery is named. Clearly drawn from Chinese models, the subject is the paradise enjoyed by Shotoku after death, with numerous tortoises symbolising longevity, lotuses and bodhisattvas. The original mandala was 4.8 metres long, but the surviving fragment measures 1.1 metre x 91 cm. During the Kamakura period these fragments were rearranged and mounted by the nun Kotoku Shinnyoni and have been preserved at Chuguji ever since.

The camphor-wood bodhisattva (or according to some scholars Nyoirin Kannon) dates from the mid-seventh century, whereas the cult of Nyoirin Kannon in hanka pose did not reach Japan until the ninth century. It has been suggested that the figure may even represent the young Gautama Buddha, taking the hint from the double *ushnisha*, or top-knot, but if one thinks of the Coming Buddha, Miroku in Japanese or Maitreya in Sanskrit, as the half-smile incarnate, then this is the apotheosis of Asuka-age Maitreyas. Graceful waves in the folding robes; delicate locks of hair overlapping the shoulders; informal left hand resting lightly on the crossed right leg; pensive asymmetry of the right hand rising to touch the smooth chin: each of these features produces a stunning effect individually, but collectively this masterpiece makes a Western counterpart such as Rodin's *Penseur* seem simplistic and prosaic.

In the small but meticulously maintained garden I picked up a fallen leaf as a souvenir, and placed it in my set of postcards of the Tenjukoku embroidery. Everywhere I went in Japan I found a fleeting, anonymous death like this leaf, and preserve each in its own envelope, cheating the oblivion to which it seemed predestined.

Horinji

At Chuguji you will be given a free map to help in finding Horinji and Hokkiji, and bus and train routes. Though in Japanese, the map is arrowed, and the temple attendant will kindly circle whatever you wish to mark. In ten minutes you will have walked the quiet country lanes leading to Horinji, founded in 621 by Prince Shotoku's eldest son Yamashiro, who prayed here for his father's recovery from a serious illness.

Horinji is a tiny temple by comparison with the overpowering Horyuji, but in a way I believe it is more characteristic of the Japanese genius for the intimate displayed in the tea ceremony or the miniature tree, the swift calligraphic page complete in itself or the tray landscape. The garden is enchanting, as is the smiling Yakushi Nyorai, a life-size wooden sculpture of the seventh century attributed to the Tori Busshi school, which forms the central object of veneration in the Kondo. Later images there include Bishamon, Sho Kannon and Kichijo, all of the late Heian era. The Kodo possesses a coloured wooden figure of Eleven-headed Kannon, 4.8 m. in height and others of Jizo and Kokuzo 1.6 m. high, the latter at least of the mid-seventh century.

Hokkiji

Continuing north-east, you suddenly turn a corner and come into view of the elegant three-storey pagoda of 685, which makes all Christian spires except those of Ulm and Salisbury seem coarse and heavy. It was founded by a priest named Fukuryo in 638, on the dying command of Shotoku, with a fine image of Miroku, the coming Buddha. The little temple was almost deserted, and I tiptoed round to avoid disturbing turtles sunning themselves on the bank of their pond. But I scared them nevertheless, and they flopped into the pond and swam lazily, confidently to refuge on their crowded islet in the centre of the pond, unaware of their symbolism – Japanese turtles patiently enduring close contact on islets too small for comfort.

There is a short cut allowing you to walk straight back to the bus route for Nara on R.25 or, if you prefer to return via Horyuji, there is a JNR station there one stop from the JNR Nara station on Sanjodori.

Muroji

If you take the Sakurai railway line from Nara, and get off at Sakurai, you will be close to the Kinki Nippon railway line and the many bus routes radiating from the lumber town of Sakurai.

Interesting excursions from Sakurai include Ryugaiji or Okadera (twenty

Hokkiji

Ricefield irrigation near Hokkiji (*Photo. Author*)

minutes by bus), Gangoji or Hokoji (fifteen minutes by bus), Danzan Shrine (twenty-five), and Hasedera, twenty minutes by bus, or on foot ten minutes northward from Hasedera station east of Sakurai on the Kinki Nippon line.

East of Hasedera, eight km. southeast of Muroguchi-Ono station on the Kinki Nippon line, stands Muroji, near the earlier shrine of Ryuketsu. The story runs that the hermit Shokaku Gyoja lived in a retreat on this site about the year 700. The Hosso priest from Kofukuji in Nara, Kenkei, is believed to have laid out the temple, which as a mountain temple more closely resembles the holy places of Enryakuji in Kyoto than its mother temple in Nara. However, Kenkei died in 793 and we know that the buildings were not finished until the early ninth century. The dragon venerated in this fertile valley as a rain god began to be worshipped here at Muroji too. When the temple fell into the orbit of Shingon esotericism, it was taught that the bridge over the river Muro formed the literal and metaphysical bridge between the ordinary everyday world outside the temple complex, and Muroji formed part of a natural mandala.

Your eye is first caught by the five-storey pagoda dated to about 800, of timber-frame construction with shingle roofs, surrounded by a thick wood of cryptomeria. The purpose of the pagoda is to act as a reliquary, the relic itself being located below the central supporting column. Above the topmost storey there are a number of rings or wheels (sorin) capped generally by a flame and two circles, one the 'precious pearl' and the other the 'dragon's car', but the pinnacle here rises towards a round canopy and a bottle of divine ambrosia.

This pagoda, tiny in comparison with others in Nara and Kyoto, is the only original building to survive intact at Muroji, though part of the Kondo is original, the rest having been burned down during some of the many fires that devastate Japanese wooden structures. The Mirokudo, Hondo and Niomon are of Kamakura date (13th century), sensitively restored, but many of the sculptures are earlier and are worth coming a long way to admire.

The timber-framed Kondo houses a sublime wooden figure of Shaka Nyorai, 2.4 m. high, dated to the middle of the ninth century, the most moving sculpture since the Nara period that I had seen in Japan. The open right hand is raised near shoulder height in the so-called 'abhaya' mudra signifying the banishment of fear. Other mudras (positions of the hands) are – in the recognised Sanskrit forms – dhyana, for meditation, hands folded on the Buddha's lap either open or interlocked; dharmacakra, for turning the wheel, that is teaching the doctrines, hands held up to the chest with thumb and second finger nearly or actually touching; varada, for blessing, the left hand outward; bhumisparsa, for calling the Earth to witness the truth and importance of his mission, the right hand turned down from the knee to touch the ground; and vitarka, for discussion and inducing all creation towards enlightenment, one hand up to the chest, thumb touching second finger. Apart from these mudras, frequently found in Japanese sculpture, Shingon recognised no fewer than 385 others in its esoteric rites.

To Shaka's left are figures representing Yakushi (and protected in front by the twelve divine generals who are however much smaller than Yakushi) and Jizo Bosatsu; to Shaka's right are an Eleven-headed Kannon and Monju Bosatsu.

In the Mirokudo you will find a splendid standing image of the Future Buddha, Maitreya or in Japanese Miroku, with an even more remarkable ninth-century seated Shaka Nyorai, except for knees and hands made from a single block of hinoki or Japanese cypress. It was once completely covered with colour, traces of which remain in the form of white gesso.

The mudra is dharmacakra, and the 'rolling-wave' drapery folds are characteristic of the Jogan period (859–877). Here – as in so many other places – I felt the unity between honne (the real voice) and tatemae (the public face), between inner and outer feelings, that usually in Japan find themselves separated by the kejime, or boundary between what is said and shown on the one hand, and what is unspoken and concealed on the other. The Japanese make a virtue of maintaining this frontier, where in the west we embarrass others by spontaneity even if it is out of place.

If you ascend to the Kanchodo, you will again be astonished by sculptural quality: here the Nyoirin Kannon (Avalokiteshvara with the Wish-Granting Jewel) is seated in the position of regal repose ('rajalila' in the original Sanskrit), with six arms, each wielding a different symbol. There is no sense of awkwardness in the resolution of the artistic problem: how can human form accommodate six arms? The solution existed in Hindu art and has been expertly transposed into Buddhist tradition. If you have time (and time slips like sand through your fingers at Muroji), take a path beyond the pagoda into the wood and up to the temple of Kobo Daishi, with his image inside, called Okunoin Mieido, 'Distant Pavilion of the Honoured Shadow'.

Hasedera

If at Muroji you feel lost in the wilds, as at Enryakuji, then Hasedera will allow you to find your bearings, for though essentially rural it reminds you, if you stand near the middle of the depression, of a Roman amphitheatre, the wooded slopes rising above you all around the bowl, for all the world like steps for an audience of woodland gods. Hase, one of the thirty-three Kannon temples in the region of Kyoto, is stated by the priest with whom I spoke to have been founded in 686, though the original main hall seems not to have been completed before 727. Also known as Chokokuji or Kannondo, Hase Monastery is the headquarters of the Buzan school of Shingon Buddhism. Come in April if you enjoy cherry-blossom, or in May if you prefer the lovely peonies: the court of Nara frequented Hase in the eighth century, since when the tradition of a spring visit has increasingly been maintained.

The central object of artistic and religious interest at Hasedera is a bronze plaque dated 698 and stating that it was made by the priest Domyo and eighty other priests and laymen as a memorial for the spirit of the Emperor Temmu (673–686). The plaque, 84 cm. high, is based on a passage from the Lotus Sutra, showing a three-storey pagoda, the Buddhas Shaka and Taho with attendant divinities in early Tang style. Taho, not particularly common in Japanese sculpture, is the Sanskrit Prabhutaratna, who appeared to Shakyamuni Buddha while the latter was reciting the Lotus Sutra and congratulated him on his exposition.

Hasedera's original pagoda burned down in the nineteenth century, and the five-storey building you see today was built nearby in 1952. The Kannon worshipped here is not the original dated 729, but a new eleven-headed Kannon made in 1538, with a staff in its right-hand like that held by Jizo Bosatsu in his soul-saving quest through the six ways. Kannon also incorporates features of Amida Butsu. Thirty-three images of Kannon are painted on wooden tablets that surround the plinth.

The covered corridor leading up to the Main Hall was built in 1039 with one hundred and nine pillars, the one hundred and eight spaces between them indicating the total number of sins committed by the average pilgrim in the course of a year: by passing through this corridor you hope to expiate those sins.

If you see a greater proportion of women than usual at Hasedera, this is because women have always been welcomed here (as opposed to some other temples), for a woman achieves satori in the Lotus Sutra, which is venerated here.

Danzan Shrine

Take a bus from Sakurai station due south to Mount Tonomine, and in twenty-five minutes you will come to the celebrated Danzan Shrine, founded in 701 by Joe, a priest who was the son of Kamatari Fujiwara (614–66), first of the line, who is buried at the top of the hill. The Shrine was effectively merged with Myorakuji Buddhist temple as a token of Shinto-Buddhist identification, but eventually nothing was left of Danzan-Myorakuji except the thirteen-storey pagoda of 1532. The current restoration, known as the Nikko Shrine of the Kansai district, has a bright exterior and rather empty interior. You can see an eighth-century figure of Kamatari in the Honden, and on the second Sunday in November they hold a ceremonial kemari match, reviving the tradition of graceful court football.

Okadera

West of Danzan lies Okadera, which is amply worth any amount of trouble to reach because of the superb ninth-century lacquered wooden sculpture of the Hosso priest Gien, who died in 728. Technically, the body is made of kanshitsu lacquer, strengthened by a light wooden armature, the drapery modelled in sawdust hardened with lacquer; the head by contrast is almost entirely carved in wood, with only a fine coating of lacquer.

Like Hasedera a monastery of the Buzan school of the Shingon sect, it dates back to the seventh century, when it was converted from a secular palace by Gien. The chief image of veneration is Nyoirin Kannon, an early Heian work in terra cotta measuring 4.5 metres high.

Angoin

Near Okadera stop awhile at the Tendai monastery of Tachibanadera, founded by Crown Prince Shotoku in the early seventh century and now reduced from its former grandeur to a Kondo restored in 1864 and a Kannondo. North of the crossroads between Okadera and Tachibanadera, you can explore the environs of Angoin, the only surviving fragment *in loco* of the enormous Asukadera, also called Hokoji or Gangoji, established here in

596 by Soga Umako. The Soga clan, desirous of introducing Buddhism throughout Japan with the aid of their Korean allies, had overcome their Shintoist enemies Nakatomi and Mononobe in a battle of 587. The first temple they built to celebrate their triumph was the Shitennoji (currently in Osaka), and the second Asukadera, again with Korean craftsmen and artists. We know from excavation that three main halls (east, west and north) surrounded the central pagoda, but the great Shaka Buddha 2.76 metres high cast in bronze by the Korean Tori (606) is the only sculptural relic of the original monastery, and – despite its numerous and often clumsy restorations – it remains the earliest surviving Buddhist sculpture in Japan. Everything is patched up except the face above the mouth.

The monastery was removed to the new capital of Heijo-kyo (now Nara) in 718 and given the new name of Gangoji.

Taimadera

Shimoda, on the Kinki Nippon line, is the station for the monastery of Taimadera; you can take a bus from the station, or walk the two kilometres if the weather is clement.

Taimadera is believed to have been established in 612 by Maroko Taima, founder of the Taima clan which favoured the strengthening of the new Buddhist religion from the Asian continent over the old native Shinto gods. It was greatly expanded later in the seventh century, and in the eighth occurred one of those legendary events which can make a Lourdes or Fatima wealthy overnight. It is said that in 763 Princess Chujo, a daughter of Toyonari Fujiwara, wove a mandala overnight, depicting the Western Paradise. She is also known by her religious name of Honyo, and is commemorated annually on 14–15 May by a popular dramatic performance. The original, in tattered fragments, is too faded to give any real idea of its significance or beauty and is stored in the temple's treasure-hall. The substitute, woven in 1487–9, can be seen nowadays in the Hondo, itself restored on several occasions.

An eighth-century bronze bell is contemporary with five sculptures as intriguing as they are lovely. A central Miroku Bosatsu (the 'Buddha Who Is To Come') is protected by four guardian kings who may have a Korean source. Their long sleeves resemble those of the guardian kings in Horyuji's Kondo; their faces possess a naturalism that we have come to recognise as typical of the mature Nara style.

Toshodaiji

A red electric train of the Kinki Nippon railway will bring you two stops from Yamato-Saidaiji station south to Nishinokyo, sited between Toshodaiji and Yakushiji, ten minutes' walk apart down a perfectly straight road. I was lucky enough to possess a letter of introduction to Mr Morimoto, Chief Abbot of Toshodaiji, and I waited in a little ante-room while my credentials were being examined. I was then welcomed to a mat in the guest quarters, where self-conscious cross-legged visiting businessmen in dapper suits were sipping tea from tiny bowls in a row, facing the reverend abbot. I was brought tea by a young lady traditionally dressed in silk kimono and obi: we bowed in unison, and I drank in silence, absorbing the atmosphere. A charming lady, Seiko Okawa, then introduced herself as my guide round Toshodaiji. I already knew that the area had been granted by the Emperor Shomu to the Chinese priest Chien Chen (in Japanese, Ganjin), who had been invited to bring Buddhist doctrines and train priests to spread the word of Buddha throughout Japan. He made five vain attempts to cross the sea to Japan over twelve years, and became quite blind before he reached his adoptive home. The blind teacher: Homer, Borges, Ganjin. In each civilization he personifies the unseen truth behind the illusion of appearances.

Toshodaiji. Entrance to Chief Abbot's Residence (*Photo. Author*)

24

He was welcomed in Nara at Todaiji, where he attempted to introduce the formal monastic discipline (*vinaya* in Sanskrit) imposed by the Vinaya sect in India, the Lü sect in China, and the Ritsu sect in Japan. But he wished to create a sanctuary at Nara to be known as the 'monastery where the *vinaya* was first propagated'. He was awarded in February 755 land which had belonged to Prince Niitabe. The novelist Yasushi Inoue takes up the story in his novel *Tempyo no iraka*, translated by James T. Araki as *The roof tile of Tempyo*: 'Although construction was suspended when the retired Emperor died, Empress Koken willed the fulfillment of his imperial wish, and in 757 ordered the construction of a hall of worship and other buildings. The monastery was completed in August of 759. Displayed on the main gate was a gift from the Empress, a framed plate on which was inscribed the name Toshodaiji, or 'T'ang Buddhist Monastery'.

Ganjin lived and taught at Toshodaiji between 759 and 763, when he died at the age of seventy-six. His disciples caused a seated image of their master to be carved, and this dry-lacquer sculpture is enshrined in the Mieido, or Founder's Hall, despite its relatively small size dominating the landscapes painted in 1980 by Kai-i Higashiyama on the screens throughout the building.

The Golden Hall (Kondo) faces the smaller Lecture Hall (Kodo). The Kondo dates from Ganjin's time, and reflects the architectural style of the T'ang dynasty, measuring 29 metres by 15, with massive wooden columns. These columns, with the walls, were once adorned with painted Buddhas, but these have long since vanished. We can still admire the sculptures, however, such as the great dry-lacquer Vairocana Buddha, attributed to Ganjin's Chinese disciples T'an Ching and Sze Tou, the largest of its genre. Most of the thousand small Buddha-images on its halo still survive. On its left stands a dry-lacquer Nara-age figure of the Kannon with a Thousand Arms (Senju Kannon) and a standing Yakushi dating from 796. The altar is protected by the Four Heavenly Kings, sculptures attributed to Chun Fa Li.

The Lecture Hall (Kodo) was once the Morning Assembly Hall at the Imperial Palace in Nara, then it was donated to Toshodaiji; it was rebuilt in 759 by Chun Fa Li but has undergone many repairs and is now very little like the original Hall; it is possible that Chun was the artist responsible for the seated wooden Maitreya.

The bell in the belfry between Kondo and Kodo is of Heian date. The Shariden (Relic Hall) also between Kondo and Kodo is the scene every 19 May for the ceremony of scattering fans, or Uchiwamakie, dating back to the Kamakura period, when it began as an act of homage to the holy priest Chuko. Nuns who had benefited from his teachings used to place round fans on Chuko's grave on the anniversary of his death, and then offer these fans to the worshippers. Today the scattering causes a mad and merry scramble, but nothing a

◁ Toshodaiji. Dry lacquer sculpture of the founder, Ganjin (c.763)
(Photo. courtesy Mr Morimoto, Chief Abbot of Toshodaiji)

western football hooligan would consider violent. If you prefer to see Toshodaiji on a more tranquil day, avoid 6 June, the anniversary of the temple's foundation, and 19–26 October, when worshippers come in crowds to celebrate the Shaka Nembutsu ceremony.

You will not be able to see the Shosoin of Todaiji close up, so this is your chance to see even earlier structures in the log-cabin or azekura style: one storehouse for the sutras, or Library, and one for arts and crafts, or Treasury. Toshodaiji has its own museum, open from 9 to 4.30 between 21 March and 19 May and 15 September to 3 November. Do not miss the three-tiered Kaidan or Ordination Platform in the western part of the compound: it was made in imitation of the Kaidan at Todaiji where Ganjin first ordained monks in his Ritsu school.

It happens that we possess a spring haiku by Basho set in Toshodaiji. It refers to the sculpture of the seated patriarch Ganjin dated to the second half of the eighth century.

Wakaba shite	I want to wipe
Onme no shizuku	the tears from your eyes
Nugu wa baya.	with new leaves.

To understand how Japanese works, the first line means 'new leaf' and 'by or with'; the second 'honourable eye', 'of' and 'drops'; and the third 'wipe' and 'I wish'.

Another Nara haiku by Basho written in spring or early summer runs:

Na no hanaya	Yellow rape blossom
Nara ni wa furuki	at old Nara's
Hotoketachi	Buddhas!

The first line means 'yellow rape blossoms'; the second 'at Nara'; *furuki* means 'old', *hotoke* 'the Buddha' and *tachi* is a plural suffix.

So it was at the monument to Basho that I paused finally, before leaving Toshodaiji. I had first read his *Narrow Road to the Deep North* in 1966, two years married in Libya, and I never thought that this day would come: when I should be speaking with him across the centuries, yellow sunlight slanting on grass. I stretched out my fingers (and the toes cavorting unobtrusively in my shoes) and laughed with a kind of drunken realisation that Li Po would have acknowledged. The moment filled like a balloon before it bursts. I wrote 'If the Absence were Presence':

> *He waits to visualise whatever is white*
> *become increasingly white;*
> *he stays to hear air solidify.*
>
> *All around him whatever is*
> *awaits him*
> *(this he seems not to expect)*

Whatever is not
inheres
(this he can scarcely realise)

Defenceless
the heart
of Amitabha Buddha

Grey Youth

On the narrow road to Yakushiji I ran the gauntlet of hundreds of grinning schoolchildren calling 'Harro!' I tried hard, but unsuccessfully, to concentrate on Nagarjuna's precept, 'He whose mind is imbued with compassion for all sentient beings, and only he, is on the path to salvation and divine wisdom'. It depends, I suppose, whether you think of the hordes of Japanese schoolchildren as sentient beings, or robotic chanters, victims of the 'grey youth' which inflicts fifteen years of examination drill on ninety per cent of Japanese children. Professor Kobayashi insists that educational goals must be deflected from nationalism towards internationalism, from rote learning to open-ended learning and the cultivation of creativity, and from conformity to individualism. Teachers and pupils alike are not consulted: it is the parents, and notoriously the 'education mamas' who push their infants into the 'best' kindergarten, then all the way, rung by rung, to the 'best' university, by which they mean the over-populated Tokyo University. To effect this, they send their children to private schools if they can afford it, or to the evening juku or crammer, which has the same explicit intention to turning out freshmen at T.U. The present system has turned out industrial and service workers by the million, and made possible Japan's social and economic renewal after the devastation of World War II. It may even suffice to keep Japan's cultural heritage intact, but will it allow the expansion of thought, art and society to enable Japan to match its undoubted financial strength with vital new forms in which the middle classes can develop from obsessions with past glories to new frontiers? The tea ceremony, sumo, ikebana: these change imperceptibly. What are the innovative expressions of the Japanese spirit? Behind them, the civilizations of China and Korea. Before them, I worried, could it be a kind of U.S.A.? Baseball is already the national sport and American fast-food chains have colonised the smallest town. The Russians have already russified Uzbekistan and Kirghizia, for example: can it be that the Japanese language, so extraordinary in beauty and difficulty, will give way to American English? Will the western furnishings already crowding at least one room in the average city house be permitted to invade the rest?

Yakushiji

I had arrived at Yakushiji, and could take my mind off the giggling, nudging children to concentrate on this, one of the Seven Great Temples of Nara, headquarters of the Hosso sect. The other six are traditionally Todaiji, Horyuji,

Kofukuji, Daianji, Saidaiji and Gangoji, but oddly not Toshodaiji.

The temple was started by Emperor Temmu in 680 to pray for his Empress (on her coronation named Jito) but he died before it could be completed at its original Fujiwara site, and Empress Jito was responsible for its completion and dedication in 697 to Yakushi Nyorai, the Healing Buddha. In 718 Yakushiji was moved to Nara, but none of the buildings except the eighth-century pagoda is earlier than the thirteenth century and the Kondo (Main Hall) was rebuilt in 1600, and again in 1976.

The Kondo's seated bronze Healing Buddha, in Sanskrit Bhaisajyaguru, was blackened by the fire of 1528, like the attendant standing bodhisattva figures of Nikko and Gakko, personifying sun and moon. They may date to 697 but 'new statues were cast' according to the records in 728 and it is likely that these are the new images, though the haloes are definitely later still.

Yakushiji. The Healing Buddha, with attendant bodhisattvas

Yakushi's pedestal is carved with a Hellenistic-like vine-scroll and lower down five panels of 'barbarians' or 'foreign devils' represent the savages (like Yakshas in Hindu sculpture) who may acquire salvation by calling on the Healing Buddha, here seated on a medicine box instead of the usual lotus. Below these are the green dragon of the east in Chinese myth, the white tiger of the west, the red phoenix of the south, and the dark tortoise and serpent of the north. These designs derive from T'ang China, rendering the whole eclectic pedestal a symbol of the Silk Road linking Japan in T'ang times – however tenuously – with the Mediterranean.

Yakushiji is the first Japanese temple which incorporated both a western and eastern pagoda. The supreme eastern pagoda appears to have six stories, whereas in fact it has only three, each floor having a lean-to or mokoshi added to it. It survived the great fire of 1528, and is thus the only architectural relic of the Hakuho period, 673–686. The sorin, or metalwork ornament surmounting the pagoda, incorporates the kurin (nine rings signifying the nine spheres of the Buddhist heaven), and the finial (suien) 190 cm. high showing a flame as a charm against destruction by fire, the only such charm that ever seemed to work in Yakushiji's long and eventful history.

The western pagoda, a victim of the fire of 1528, was rebuilt in 1980: as usual the restoration seems wholly authentic and in keeping with the atmosphere of the temple compound.

Yakushiji. The pond mirroring the western pagoda

Strolling between the two ponds from the Kondo you arrive at the Kodo, with another, lesser Yakushi triad, of the same Hakuho period as the eastern pagoda. The Kodo itself, of mid-nineteenth century date in its present incarnation, presents the sutra-turning ceremony here on the eighth of every month. Returning to the Nandaimon, you can see the Bussokudo on your right and the Toindo to your left. The Bussokudo is a hall displaying a stone carved in 772 with Buddha's foot imprints, bearing the circles of truth called horin. In the history of Buddhist iconography, the feet of Gautama were worshipped before the Hellenistic-Indian full figure was adopted.

The Toindo, rebuilt in 1285 on the site of the original Toindo of 721, displays the Sho Kannon, in Sanskrit Avalokiteshvara, spiritual child of Amitabha Buddha, and in China the Goddess of Mercy, though in Japan 'she' has no defined sex. This standing image (192 cm. tall) is clearly influenced by Indian sculpture of the Gupta period which reached Japan through T'ang China.

Visible only between 1–15 January and 20 October–10 November is a painting on hemp of the Hindu goddess Sri Maha Devi, in Japanese Kichijoten, goddess of wealth and good fortune. Reputedly the earliest independent coloured painting in Japan, it shows a lady in eighth-century court dress who has sometimes been thought to be Empress Komyo. Ceremonial worship of Kichijoten was first recognized in Japan in 767, and the first services known to have been held in her honour were those of Todaiji five years later. Remember to look for the coloured clay image of her, which may be the original object of veneration, in the Sangatsudo of Todaiji.

Before leaving Yakushiji visit the Hachiman Shrine, for the painted wooden figures of Hachiman, Shinto god of war, in the guise of a Buddhist monk; the Empress Jingo (also sometimes transliterated Shinko), wearing court dress of the Chinese style; and Princess Nakatsuhime, in like apparel. These three masterly figures of 890 have long remained in my mind's eye, embodying as they do that remarkable synthesis between native Shinto and imported Buddhism, between the arts of peace and war, styles of costume both Japanese and foreign, woman's grace in submission to man as protector and deity, and man's glad acceptance of these rôles.

Shin Yakushiji

It is only in China or Japan, India or the classical cultures that something 'new' (the meaning of 'shin') could date from 747, but that is the year of this main hall's foundation. 'New' Yakushiji because the original was founded in 680 and moved to its present site in 718, as we have seen.

Shin Yakushiji was established by Empress Komyo to pray for the restored eyesight of her Emperor Shomu, and its chief object of veneration is the seated Healing Buddha who rules over the Eastern Paradise, exquisitely carved in Japanese cypress, and dating from about 793, after the fire of 780 which

Shin Yakushiji. One of the Twelve Heavenly Generals. (c.793)   ▷

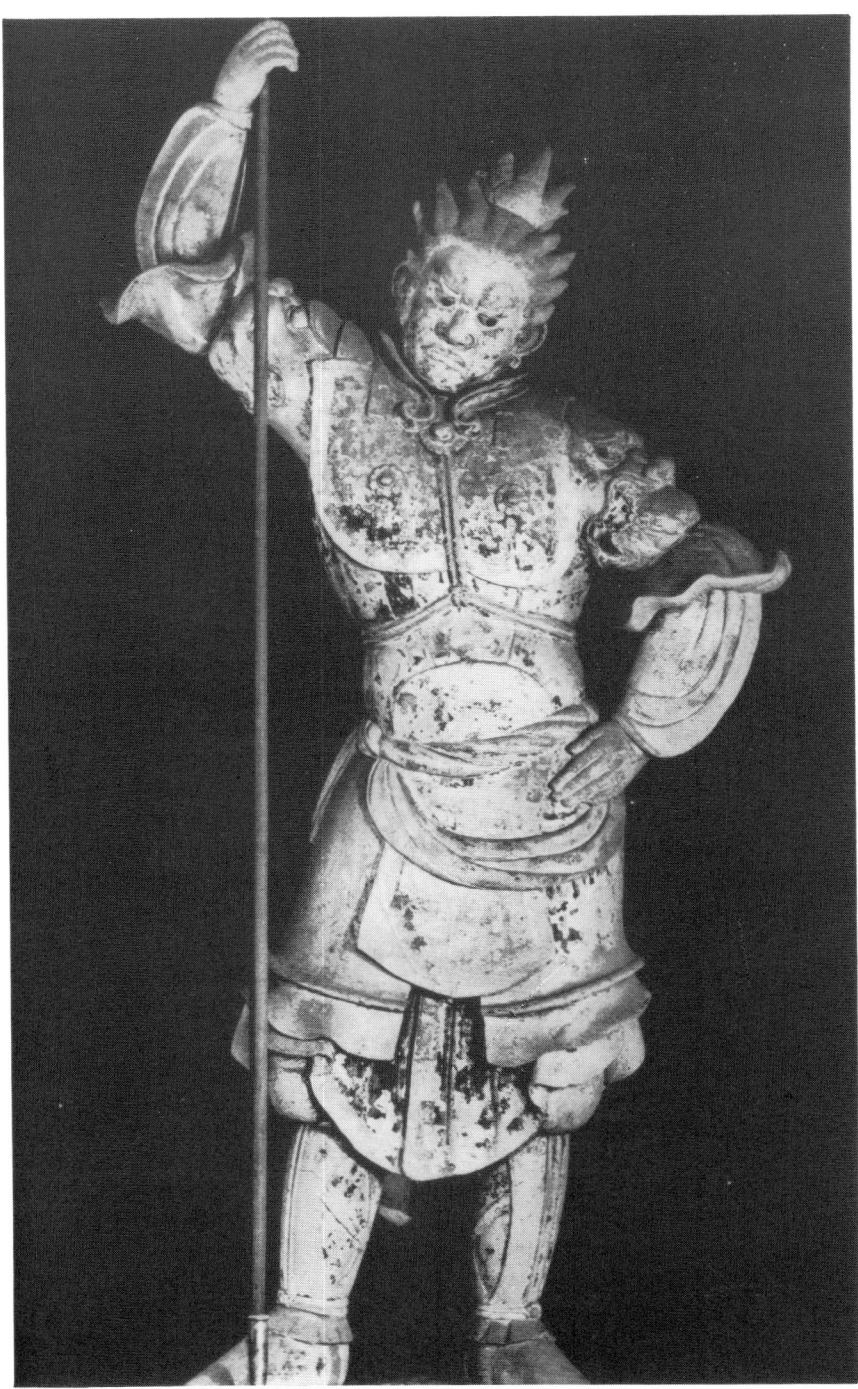

destroyed the original Yakushi of 747. It belongs to the sochizo ('natural-figure') style in which the natural wood remains unpainted except for eyes, lips and occasionally facial hair. All is carved from a single block of wood apart from the arms; the halo with six tiny Buddhas is contemporary with later gilding. Next to it is an Eleven-headed Kannon, and they are encircled on a high circular clay pedestal by the Twelve Divine Generals, themselves of clay, who comprise with the building, Yakushi and Kannon a remarkable eighth-century ensemble, having survived together civil wars, world wars, pillaging and fire.

Their faces, weapons and stances vary: with an axe, spear or staff they threaten and gesticulate, their height ranging from 1.6 to 2.4 metres high. The military garb is Chinese, some attired with helmets, while the hair of others stands on end. Their identification is confused because Shin Yakushiji local tradition differs from the scholarly opinion enshrined in the catalogue of the Japanese Commission on National Treasures. But they are clearly attributable to the Todaiji sculptors who produced the Four Heavenly Guardians at Todaiji's Kaidanin.

Near Shin Yakushiji stands the Zuto, or Head Mound, with carved stones showing Buddha and bodhisattvas in a Nara style of the later eighth century. The hillock is artificial and was probably set with votive tablets in imitation of an Indian stupa.

I lived at Shin Yakushiji, a fifteen-minute walk uphill from the ring-road bus. Even nowadays the village streets nearby have a rural feeling, and I rested tranquil in the atmosphere of the silent temple grounds after the main hall had been shut for the night. I let myself in by the side door, like that into the secret garden at Longleat.

Mrs Toshiko Nakata, the temple-master's wife, made me comfortable, arranging breakfast in the room at eight, and providing the scalding traditional bath between 6 and 7 p.m. First of all I scrubbed myself clean all over with a soap and brush, rinsed thoroughly, then drew in my breath with shock as my first tentative foot sought the protection of the floating wooden board in the thieves' cauldron. As my second foot found wooden comfort from the bottom of the barrel in the scalding water I recalled the swirling lines and taut terror in Kuniyoshi's woodblock print triptych of Miyamoto Musashi's escape from the bath-house in which Genzoemon had planned to boil him alive. My hostess in Shin Yakushiji clearly had no such intention, so I relaxed, and as my skin turned scarlet I relaxed even more. I knelt gingerly, heeding the advice not to touch the iron sides of the bath-barrel with any part of my skin, and keeping rock-still. Even so, I had to exhale from the pit of my stomach as I immersed more than a tentative foot. The bath not only cleanses the impure body (and pollution is a problem in Japan as in any other advanced industrialised society) but calms both body and mind. As you reflect on the extraordinary moments of the day behind you, close your eyes and allow your con

Shin Yakushiji. East Gate ▷

centration to evaporate, cultivating 'the floating world' sensation. Doctors are by no means agreed that such heat is beneficial, but I found the goemonburo calming and soothing, and clearly all Japanese concur. You can dry yourself by rubbing down with a towel even if it is wet, because the friction alone will do the trick.

My six-mat room had a solid wall at one side, facing a partition of four sliding-panels leading to the next room. The back of the room consisted of sliding cupboards with bedlinen and towels, and the front of four sliding panels which, when opened, revealed a bamboo grove with monkeys, and at midnight slivers of a moon slit by bamboo. A coatrack provided a concession to western trousers and jacket, but otherwise the only furniture was a low table and a cushion on which to sit crosslegged. The lighting was by three concentric neon circles in the centre of the ceiling, with four switches: one for off, one for one ring, one for two rings, and one for the small dim night light in the middle. I was brought tea in a flask and a piece of sugar cake, with a mosquito coil and a box of matches to light it. I took the hint, though mosquitoes seem to find me unpalatable even in the jungles of Indonesia where one might have thought white flesh a rare delicacy. While I read Ivan Morris' translation of Sei Shonagon's *Pillow Book*, I listened to the sound of running water, the sky darkened, and large drops of rain splashed near my door. 'Things that give a clean feeling', wrote Sei Shonagon in the closing years of the tenth century, 'are an earthen cup, a new metal bowl, a new wooden chest, and the play of light on water as one pours it into a vessel'.

Todaiji

The Great Eastern Temple, headquarters of the Kegon Buddhist sect, is world-famous for its Great Buddha, one of the largest bronze images in the world.

Imagine that you are in the Oriental equivalent of the Pisan Camposanto, or at Agra's Taj Mahal: the whole focus of a small town. Hundreds of thousands of pilgrims, tourists, travellers, and the simply inquisitive traipse through the vast enclosure, hardly aware of the other riches that Nara has to offer: concerned simply with this enormous wooden Hall of Buddha and its gigantic bronze image of Buddha which threatens to roar down the centuries and down the highways of Japan, if you come too close.

Defeat by the united forces of China and Korean Silla led the amorphous and shaky Japan of 665 to dispatch a peace-seeking mission to China, aiming to discover the secret of Chinese strength and stability. Confucian by statecraft, Buddhist by religion, and hierarchical by temperament, China became a rich source of learning both secular and spiritual.

Having failed to unite his own country against Hirotsugu Fujiwara and his potent family, the Emperor Shomu (exiled in 740 from Nara to Kuni, Shigaraki and Naniwa) decided to cast a giant bronze Buddha which would symbolically unite the warring country in the new religion, as the huge Buddha of Loyang had helped to unite China. Two such attempts failed, but at Nara, on this site

Todaiji. Outside the Great Buddha Hall

just north of Kofukuji, the hundreds of tons of copper and tin brought to the capital were finally cast in 749. It is 16.2 m. high, with a face 4.8 m. long and 3 m. wide. The left hand is in the yoganin position (granting our wishes) and the right in the semuiin (granting peace of mind). The pedestal, 20.7 m. in circumference, comprises fifty-six bronze lotus-petals, each three m. high. The designer of the Great Buddha of Todaiji was the Korean known in Japan as Kimimaro from the adopted village of Kuninaka. The gilded wooden halo behind Buddha's head dates from the end of the seventeenth century, and the Buddha itself was restored in its present form in 1692.

The pedestal was carved by eighth-century artists with the Lotus Treasure World as described in the 'Flower Wreath' sutra. At the top is the Cloud Realm of Manifest Buddhas, above the host of bodhisattvas attending Shaka Nyorai; lower down is the Realm of the 33 Divinities Inhabiting Mount Sumeru, and at the foot is Mount Sumeru itself, heaving up from the great ocean.

Of late 17th-century date are the gilded wooden images of Nyoirin Kannon (answering prayers) and Kokuzo (a bodhisattva granting wishes with the sacred jewel), and works of the late 18th century include two heavenly guardians of Buddha: Tamonten in the right-hand corner behind the Great Buddha, and Komokuten in the left-hand corner, trampling demons under their feet.

If you can emerge from the trampling visitors (most of whom are luckily much smaller and lighter on their feet than the average foreigner), you can survey the Hall of the Great Buddha (Daibutsuden). Look for the model of the original hall, just to the right of Komokuten, which was burnt by the Taira clan in 1180, when they razed Kofukuji. Chogen restored the hall in 1195 until the conflagration of 1567, following which it took until 1709 for the task to be completed. The last major renovation of 1914 took more than a quarter of a million man-days. The hall measures 57 m. long by 50.6 m. deep by 48.8 m. high and, although only two-thirds the size of the original hall, remains the largest single wooden building on earth.

Only now did I consider the fascinating Deva Kings in the Great Gate by which I had entered. It is unpopular to strive against the tide of incoming visitors, but I felt I should come to terms with the gigantic Buddha before returning to the Nandaimon to understand the creative impulse that led Unkei, Kaikei and their assistants to produce, in 1203, this pair of ferocious protectors. The wood is built up of yosegi fragments and hollowed out, though the effect is as monumental as the ferocious, sinewy *Moses* of Michelangelo in S. Pietro in Vincoli. We might relate the swirling effect of the drapery to French or Austrian rococo, but this only exemplifies my Eurocentric upbringing and will be as infuriating to Japanese connoisseurs as any comparison of Rembrandt or Dürer with Japanese counterparts would be to us.

Mark instead the uniqueness of the shibi, or ridge-end ornament on the roof of the Daibutsuden, or the octagonal bronze lantern of the eighth century just in front of the hall.

Now visit the Kaidanin, a small temple complex of which all surviving are the Kuri (priests' living quarters), Senjudo (1603), and Jukaido (rebuilt in 1732). The wooden Taho pagoda possesses small images of Shaka Nyorai (Shakyamuni) and Taho Nyorai (Prabhutaratna), two of the five aspects of Buddhist contemplation, the others being Yakushi, Dainichi and Ashuku. I cast my mind back to the original ordination platform made for Ganjin in 754 in front of the Main Hall, using some of the soil from Mount Wu Tai, and visualised the scene as five hundred young priests were ordained, and the effective missionary work of Buddhism began in these isles. To protect the faith the Four Heavenly Guardians mount watch: these are if possible even more strikingly impressive than the twelve at Shin Yakushiji. Komokuten, guardian of the West, watches patiently, with a frown of concentration, to ensure than no evils pass. Zochoten, guardian of the South, crushes a demon with his feet while gesturing threateningly, left arm akimbo. Their expressions

Todaiji. The bronze Great Buddha (749)

and costumes are realistic; their variety of movement and inner tension can be seen as epitomising the finest art of Nara between 742 and 746.

One of the great bells of Japan can be seen in the belfry east of the Main Hall. Originally cast in 749, it was recast first in 989 and then in 1239.

I ascended (one might, as on Mount Hiei in Kyoto, take the ascent figuratively as well as literally) to the Second Month Temple (Nigatsudo), so called because the ceremony of Shunie was held there every February, but now takes place from 1–14 March, and reaches a climax during the torchlight procession on 12 March. The temple was founded by Roben's disciple Jitchu in 752, but the present building is of 1669. Its splendid panorama, open twenty-four hours a day, invites comparison with Kyoto's Kiyomizudera. Nigatsudo possesses a hibutsu (secret Buddha) representing Eleven-headed Kannon which is permanently concealed from view, and may not even be photographed.

Sangatsudo (Third Month Temple) is so called because of the reading of the Lotus Sutra every March, which is why it is also known as Hokkedo (Lotus Hall). Void of schoolchildren, for no apparent reason, the hall was clearly a place for rest and reflection. It is open, like the rest of Todaiji's fee-charging temples, from 8 to 4.30 November–February, 8 to 5 in March, 7.30 to 5.30 April–September, and 7.30 to 5 in October. All but two of the images are of the eighth century, the exceptions being Jizo and Fudo (in Sanskrit Ksitigarbha and Acala) of the 13th–14th centuries, the only ones made of wood.

The central object of worship is the standing dry-lacquer Fukukensaku Kannon of 747, with small clay attendant figures of Gakko (left) and Nikko (right). The largest lacquer statue surviving from Japanese antiquity, it is exactly contemporary with the other lacquer figures: four heavenly guardians in the corners, the open-mouthed and closed-mouthed thunderbolt-bearers (Kogorikishi) whom you will recognise from the Great South Gate of Todaiji, Bonten (in Sanskrit Brahma) standing to the right of the major Kannon, and Taishakuten (Indra) to the Kannon's left. A particularly cherished work, considered a masterpiece by the abbot Roben, is the Shukongojin (Vajradhara) kept shut away in the sanctuary behind Kannon except for one day in the year, 16 December, the anniversary of Roben's death.

I walked round the perimeter of Daibutsuden towards the compound of Shosoin, and there looked through the fence at the log cabin on stilts (the style known as azekura) which has acted as Todaiji's principal treasure repository since the eighth century. I asked if I might enter, but the courteous reply was that I should require a letter from my embassy in Tokyo, which in my case (to paraphrase Henry Reed's 'The Naming of Parts') I had not got. An excellent consolation for those who never manage to set foot in Shosoin, or anywhere else in Japan, is Ryoichi Hayashi's excellent illustrated history, *The Silk Road and the Shosoin* (Weatherhill, 1975), volume 6 in the 'Heibonsha Survey of Japanese Art'. A selection of the objects from Shosoin is made each year and displayed (with a fresh catalogue) at Nara National Museum from late October to early November, when Shosoin is opened to allow the crisp autumn air to circulate around the precious antiquities. And what antiquities! Imagine a treasure trove that collected in one place the most precious objects from the Silk Road: from Alexandria and Antioch, Baghdad and Isfahan, Samarkand, Kashgar, Tunhuang and Ch'ang-an, the then Chinese capital now called Xian. And not only precious objects traded by merchants but religious books, pictures and images brought by pilgrims and scholars such as the Chinese translator Hsüan-tsang, who travelled to India in search of Buddhist scriptures.

There is no comprehensive inventory of Shosoin treasures: the one published in 1951 lists only 794 items, counting sixty knives as one, and ignoring the 120,000 pieces of cloth and the ten thousand and more ancient manuscripts. There are more than forty folding-screen panels, 170 Gagaku masks,

Todaiji. Sangatsudo. Fukukensaku Kannon (747) with attendant bodhisattvas

565 bamboo flower baskets, thousands of arrows and hundreds of metal plates and trays. The bead collection is huge, and there are more than fifty mirrors, eighteen writing brushes, fifteen sticks of black sumi ink, and household furnishings and table utensils of every possible type. Buddhist regalia might well be expected in abundance, but the range of musical instruments derives from India, Korea and China as well as from Japan. Arms and armour, games, medicines and herbs: there is no end to the variety, from Persian glass decanters and Indian lutes, to Central Asian carpets and Chinese silver. Most of these objects were given to Todaiji by Emperor Shomu's widow after his death in 756, and provide a unique kaleidoscope of the life and art of the Middle and Far East during the eighth century. Nara craftsmen were given easy access to these masterpieces of jewellery and glass, arms and costume, mirrors and boxes, and their free imitations of technique and motif were sooner or later assimilated into the repertory of Japanese decorative art.

Todaiji. Entrance to Shosoin

Kasuga Shrine

The five leading Shinto shrines are Kitano in Kyoto, Ieyasu's at Nikko, the Sun Goddess' at Ise, Hachiman's at Kamakura, and Kasuga at Nara.

Kasuga Taisha, properly translated as Kasuga Grand Shrine, was founded in the mid-18th century, while Nara was still the capital, but became even more prestigious when its founding Fujiwara clan reached dizzy heights of political power during the succeeding Heian period. The actual foundation date is not known, but it was certainly before 768 (the date cited in the official guide to Kasuga), for we have a poem of 751 or 752 in the *Manyoshu* in which the Empress Komyo prays 'at the Kasuga Shrine' for the safe journey of her nephew Kiyokawa Fujiwara as ambassador to China. This embassy, consisting of four ships, left in the fourth year of Tempyo-Shoho, corresponding to 752. Her poem, unremarkable enough it in own right, runs:

> *In the great ship, full-oared,*
> *I speed this man of mine to the Land of Korea;*
> *May the Gods bless him!*

The divinities especially revered at Kasuga Taisha are Amenokoyane no Mikoto and Hime (Daughter of the Sun), both legendary ancestors of the Fujiwara, and two Kanto deities: Takemikazuchi and Futsunushi, who had traditionally brought to heel rebels against Amaterasu, the Sun Goddess. It was then that she presented her grandson Ninigi with the three sacred treasures which became forever identified with Imperial Japan. These are the jewel, sword and mirror.

Shinto has always identified mountains as the abode of nature gods, and the position of Kasuga above the Fujiwara temple of Kofukuji symbolises shelter of the Buddha by kami, or spirits. Deer, which roam freely throughout the shrine at all times of year, and are fed by visitors with 'deer cakes' that you can buy from itinerant vendors for ¥100 a packet, are considered to be the evocation of these mountain gods. The philosophical concept linking Shinto and Buddhism, called honji-suijaku, stands four-square with the early identification of Futsunushi with the Healing Buddha, Takemikazuchi with the Goddess of Mercy, Hime with the Eleven-headed Kannon, and Amenokoyane with the god of children Jizo.

Audacious ingenuity impelled the writer of the hand-scroll *Kasuga gongen reigenki* (1309) to compare Mount Kasuga with the Indian mountain at which Gautama Buddha delivered the Lotus Sutra to the world, so that a pilgrimage to Kasuga can replace a Buddhist's pilgrimage to the holy places of Buddhism in India and Nepal!

If you are lucky enough to be present in Nara during performances of Gagaku (religious dance drama of the Nara period) or its successor Bugaku (a more complex and refined dance drama performed at Manyo, outdoors, on 5 May and 3 November), do not miss an opportunity of seeing these ancient art forms at Kasuga, which is also a centre for Noh, Kyogen, and their ancestors Dengaku and Sarugaku.

My most vivid memories, apart from the delight of caressing gentle, inquisitive deer as they came up to me, were of the myriad stone iron, wood and bronze lanterns offered by dozens of generations of worshippers. The buildings of the sanctuary, faithfully reconstructed in wood painted in the vermilion characteristic of Shinto, may be among the most important Shinto architecture extant, but they are as recent as 1956. The Great Central Gate is much earlier, however, and dates from 1179, like the Great South Gate and Attendants' Gate (Naishimon).

The first mighty torii was set up in 836, while the second, marking the lower limit of the shrine's inner precincts, dates from 1160.

Kasuga's Treasure Hall is open annually between 1 April and 24 June. I describe it here because it is omitted from the Japan National Tourist Organization's official list of 'Museums and Art Galleries'. In a modern, purpose-built structure, it houses numerous famous objects, such as a Bugaku mask signed by Insho and dated 1184, a late Kamakura helmet, a Heian sword with a scabbard inlaid with mother-of-pearl cats and sparrows, a lacquered Heian koto (a Japanese zither), and a pair of silver cranes.

The first festival of the year at Kasuga is the Lantern Festival on 3–4 February, when all the lanterns are lit simultaneously, and shrine maidens

Kasuga Shrine. Deer Park

dance Bugaku by torchlight. The Buddhist temple of Kofukuji, just below, closely associated with Kasuga until ties were officially severed in 1868, holds at the same time a ceremony devoted to exorcising demons and proclaiming the end of the worst of the winter. The Lantern Festival (Mandoro) is repeated at Kasuga on 15 August.

Every 13 March Kasuga's own special festival takes place, re-enacting the ancient ceremony of receiving the Imperial Messenger, with rites such as purification, oblation, offerings and the procession of the sacred horse. The Yamatomai, a stately dance performed by priests, can only be seen at Kasuga now and on 17 December, during the Wakamiya Festival lasting from 15–18 December. Wakamiya is a subsidiary temple within the Kasuga compound, and its festival, On-Matsuri, is the largest in Nara, attracting visitors from all over Japan and from overseas to the procession on 17 December, and the various theatrical performances.

You may be in Kasuga on 15 March, when the shrine maidens celebrate the Rice-Planting Festival, or on 8 April, when a master-chef of court cuisine demonstrates the preparation of food, followed by Bugaku dance drama. Or in October, when stag-antlers are trimmed to protect injury to the thousands of visitors to Nara Park and Kasuga in particular.

I stopped at the kiosk where fortunes were being sold and told. 'FORTUNES IN ENGLISH' read the sign. 'English Fortune. Shake well the yellow box. Remember your number of the stick from the small hole. Tell the number and have your good fortune.' I resisted the temptation, unlike many clamouring Japanese, who seemed to be taking the procedure seriously enough.

Saidaiji

Taking the Nara line of the Kinki Nippon railways from Kintetsu Nara, the second station (the first after Shin Omiya) is Yamato-Saidaiji. Saidaiji (Great Western Temple), counterpart to Todaiji, Great Eastern Temple, is headquarters of the Shingon-Ritsu sect. Having clambered over the railway tracks, I found the walls and trees of the Saidaiji complex already visible – there was no entry fee and no stamp for a souvenir, but I was shown around by Sakai Motomi, a Nagoya-born student living in Mishima City, who wanted to practise his English. Though he knew little of Saidaiji, he was indefatigable in his attempts to secure answers to my questions, and to secure entry even where it seemed difficult to do so. Saidaiji dates from 765; it was built by Empress Koken, daughter of Shomu, who had gathered in her Buddhist fervour as many as five thousand monks in Todaiji. She reigned first from 749–759, was persuaded by Nakamaro and his brother Toyonari Fujiwara to abdicate in favour of Prince Oi (later known as Junnin), who became a puppet in the hands of Nakamaro, The priest Dokyo achieved a similar ascendancy over Koken and, after the bloody battle of 764 between supporters of Dokyo and supporters of Nakamaro, the victorious Dokyo persuaded Koken to regain the throne and exile Oi to the island of Awaji, where he died the following year.

It was in 764 that Koken authorised the casting of bronze images of the Four Heavenly Guardians trampling on demons to symbolise the rule of Buddhist peace over the warring forces of evil and strife. The irony is that the protecting kings were long ago destroyed, and on several occasions restored, so that we cannot be sure that they looked like the images we see today, while the bronze demons proved much more resilient. The toothy demon writhing under the foot of Zochoten is as lively today as when cast in 766–7. Leaving the Shiodo for the Shakado, one admires the impressive four Buddhas which are insecurely named as Ashuku, Hojo, Amida and Shaka, though Takeshi Kobayashi considers that the figures represent Yakushi, Miroku, Amida and Shaka. Made of wood, and dated to the last quarter of the eighth century or first quarter of the ninth, they retain Nara-period characteristics, such as magnanimous facial expressions, half human and half divine, and bold, individual execution. The best of them, Amida, recalls the Roshana of the Todaiji.

The priest Eison, who died in 1290, revived Saidaiji as a Shingon-Ritsu Buddhist temple during the thirteenth century, and every second Sunday in April and October a tea ceremony is held in his honour. This is intriguing because tea is drunk from a cup larger than an average kettle. But after the great fire of 1502 Saidaiji declined, and half-hearted efforts during the Edo period to restore its vitality failed to impart a sense of that awe and mystery still so potent at its eastern counterpart, Todaiji. Its major art treasures are the Shaka sculpture of the thirteenth century ordered by Eison to be copied from the Shaka in Seiryoji, Kyoto; and the twelve hanging scrolls of the Twelve Heavenly Kings (Juniten) dated to the ninth century.

Akashinodera

North of Yamato-Saidaiji station, ask directions to Akashinodera, founded in 780 by the priest Zenshu as the last temple to be inaugurated by the Bureau for the Construction of Todaiji. The whole temple burned down in 1135 except for the Lecture Hall, which was repaired and transformed into the Main Hall, or Hondo, as a memorable surviving example of Nara architecture. Four sculptures demand close attention, though only their lacquer heads are original, the bodies having been supplied by the school of Unkei in the Kamakura period (1185–1336). The lacquer is coarser than is found in works earlier in the Nara period, and the faces of the figures are less refined. But the Gigeiten (protectress of arts and crafts and probably of Shinto origin) is most appealing, while the bodhisattva Gudatsu, Bonten and Taishakuten can also be enjoyed as works of art in their own right as well as instances of late Nara sculpture.

Yamato Bunkakan Museum

Two stations farther out from Nara, alight at Gakuenmae for the Museum Yamato Bunkakan, and take the exit marked to the Museum. At the downhill fork turn off first left then right. The ticket-window can be seen at the end of a wide expanse of gravel, and the gravel avenue up to the museum itself (admis sion ¥400, 10–5 every day except Monday) is flanked by splendid pines. Free iced water welcomes the visitor, with comfortable armchairs on which to enjoy it.

There is no general catalogue: indeed many of the greatest masterpieces are not on show at all, and can be admired only in one or other of the various sectional catalogues, such as the *Paintings and Handwritings*, no. 2, 1974, with reproductions of Japanese, Chinese and Korean masterpieces, the captions being in Japanese and English. The museum itself is open, airy and uncluttered, the very antithesis of the Hermitage in Leningrad or the Louvre. In the centre, a *real* bamboo grove stands open to the sky, as if to mock the artists who spend all their lives recreating in black ink on white paper the 'essence' of bamboo. At the back of the gallery a view opens on to a lawn, with low benches and high trees. The special exhibition during my visit was devoted to the work of Tomioka Tessai (1836–1924), whose wit and sly obliquity to the traditional genres of landscape and nature make him an awkward fit in the jigsaw of early modern Japanese art. Tessai was steeped in the tradition of religious tolerance, and one of his most inspired works is 'The Patriarchs of Religions set sail in a single boat'. A prolific artist who painted almost up to the last day of the last month of his ninetieth year (as the Japanese calculate), he was as proud of his calligraphy as of his ink painting, such as the Zen 'Ten Bullocks' picture, in which he encapsulated the traditional ten stages towards enlightenment in a single hanging scroll, still in his characteristic 'free-and-easy' style. Since 1965, when Kenzo Tange's national indoor stadium raised its sinewy head at Yoyogi in Tokyo, Japanese artists and architects have challenged Western dominance and we have had such magnificent creations as Murano and Mori's Nissei Theatre, Tokyo (1964) and Yukio Otani's Kyoto Conference Hall (1966). Painting and sculpture broke away from the national traditions after World War II (how could it have been otherwise after Hiroshima?) and while Zenzaburo Kojima could produce a recognisably realistic 'Farmhouse awaiting spring' in 1939, by 1958 Tatsuoki Nambata could create a 'Rhythm of lines' and by 1959 Kyu Ei an untitled work which had already begun to assimilate the ideas of Mark Tobey, Kurt Schwitters, and Paul Klee. It is no longer possible to tell whether a 'pop art' canvas or an action painting emerges from Los Angeles, Copenhagen, or Osaka.

At the Yamato Bunkakan, many marvellous masterpieces stand out, among them the unique Matsuura screens dated by Yuzo Yamane to 1624–44 because of the all-gold background and their connection with the garment-screen genre. Commonly known as 'Women's Entertainments', the pair of sixfold screens is not really about what the women are doing, with a *go*-board, cards, mirror, or shamisen, but about what they are wearing. It is a fashion designer's shop-window, with the colours and designs as radiantly brilliant as when the work was first created. We do not recognise the master's hand, and indeed it seems oddly backward in its refusal to attempt the third dimension. But it is unique, and well worth close study. Among so many treasures, it may be invidious to select one more, but I cannot omit Honnami Koetsu's waka

'Shikishi', beautifully written in 1606 on paper decorated with designs of bell-flowers and pampas grasses in gold and silver dust.

Nara Prefectural Museum

Fastidious curators make a practice of not crowding Japanese gallery space with sculpture or walls with paintings, giving each work room to 'breathe'. The result is that many works are perpetually in store, so when you visit a Japanese museum my advice is to examine the albums and catalogues in advance, asking which works are actually on display and ensuring that you can at least judge the residue in print. Nara Prefectural Museum is a perfect case in point: when I was there, a special exhibition relegated many master-pieces to store, and I could only judge the range and quality by the excellent catalogues: do not be put off by the fact that everything is in Japanese, for the illustrations are first-rate and provide a worthy guide to what you may have missed in the way of painted scrolls and screens, fans and combs, costume, ceramics, prints and above all calligraphy. Nara Prefectural Museum, just over halfway to the National Museum from Kintetsu Nara railway station, off the left-hand side of the Noboriojicho Road, is open every day but Mondays from 9 to 4.30, and contains Japanese and foreign modern art.

Neiraku Art Museum

To be seen at the same time as the Isuien Garden, the Neiraku is open every day but Tuesdays (except in April, May, October and November) from 10 to 4.30. It features Korean celadon and bronzes, and fine bronzes from China.

Nara National Museum

The most outstanding museum in Nara is the National Museum, on the bus route to Todaiji, east of Kintetsu Nara railway station. It is open every day but Mondays from 9 to 4.30 and remains indispensable for a panoramic view of the development of early Japanese art, with treasures from many of the temples (like the three illustrated here) and, from late October to early November, also magnificent examples to reveal the wealth of Todaiji's Shosoin repository dating back to the heyday of the Silk Road.

Hokkeji

A good walk north-west from Shin Omiya station, on the line back from Yamato Bunkakan Museum and Saidaiji, Hokkeji is well worth seeing for the standing Eleven-Headed Kannon so typical of the transition from Chinese to Japanese taste inherent in Jogan sculpture between the eighth and tenth cen-turies; for the life-size ninth-century seated wooden figure of Vimalakirti (known as Yuima in Japanese); and for the early eleventh-century hanging scrolls of Amitabha Buddha (Amida Butsu in Japanese) with rather later flank-ing pictures of a standard-bearer (right) and (left) the bodhisattvas Seishi and Kannon on thrones of lotus. Amida himself floats on a lotus, his hands in the raigo mudra.

The Healing Buddha (*Photo. courtesy Nara National Museum*)

Eleven-headed Kannon (*Photo. courtesy Nara National Museum*)

Shaka Nyorai preaching at Mount Ryoju *Photo. courtesy Nara National Museum*)

Gardens

The finest garden in Nara is the Isuien, Suimon-cho, a quarter of an hour's stroll from the main Kintetsu Nara rail station. A fine strolling landscape garden, the Isuien is open daily except Tuesdays from 10 to 4.30 throughout April, May, October and November. Dating from the seventeenth century, it is roughly contemporary with Ninnaji temple garden in Kyoto and the Hama Palace garden in Tokyo, Its omission from the official guide issued by the Japan National Tourist Organization is quite unaccountable.

If you missed Kyoto Botanical Gardens, then try to find time for Nara's Manyo Botanical Gardens, east of Nara National Museum, in the grounds of Kasuga Shrine.

As the train silently glided out of Kintetsu Nara station, I recalled the poem by Tabito Otomo (665–731) preserved in *Manyoshu:*

> *Can the prime of youth come back to me?*
> *I fear that I may die*
> *Without seeing the city of Nara once again!*

But the omen was propitious: though Tabito was sixty-three when he wrote these lines he *did* return to Nara two years later, as Grand State Councillor. I lifted my head to scrutinise the old man opposite, with brightly-polished black shoes and immaculate blue suit, spectacles gleaming intelligently as he gazed at me with a half-smile, half-bow. He too knew the lines of Tabito. He too would return.

Kyoto Tower

Your first stop in Kyoto will be to find accommodation, obtain the free city map (which also covers Nara), a table of admission fees and times for the main temples and shrines, and perhaps an appointment for the Moss Temple, Saihoji, which will be for several days – if not weeks – in advance, due to the popularity of this secluded retreat and the limit placed on numbers of visitors. I then suggest a quick flight in the elevator for a bird's-eye view from the top of Kyoto Tower, which houses the Tourist Information Center on the ground floor (first floor Japanese-style). Kyoto Tower is the third highest in Japan, after the Tokyo Tower and the Nagoya Tower, standing 328 feet above the main building, and its views as far as Osaka give the best possible introduction to the valley site of Kyoto and the surrounding hills: Arashiyama to the north-west, Hiei to the north-east, and Higashiyama to the east. The temple immediately below you to the north is Higashi Honganji, headquarters of the Otani school of the Jodo-Shinshu sect, an offshoot of the original Honganji school whose headquarters can be seen just west ('nishi' means west and 'higashi' east) at the Nishi Honganji temple. Look for the Imperial Palace in the middle distance due north. Just west of this stands Nijo Castle.

Kyoto Tower is a microcosm of Japanese city life. Apart from the guest rooms and restaurants of the Kyoto Tower Hotel itself, you can explore the department store and beauty parlour, banks and travel agencies, while the basement offers a grill, shops, public baths and a barber's salon.

Accommodation

There is no problem about securing accommodation at all price levels in Kyoto providing you have either booked a room in advance or providing you arrive at the Kyoto Tourist Information Center (just opposite the main rail and bus stations) during their opening hours of 9 a.m. to 5 p.m. on weekdays and 9 a.m. to noon on Saturdays (tel. (075) 371–5649, paying ¥10 for three minutes). The characteristic flavour of Japan is best savoured in one of the hundreds of minshuku or guest-houses, and in the many shukubo or temple-lodgings. My suggestion would be to try a minshuku for a few days (say in the south) and then transfer to a shukubo in another part of the city (say in the north) once you have explored the vicinity of your minshuku. Twelve typical

QUICK ITINERARIES IN KYOTO

Nobody should plan to spend less than a week in Kyoto, even richer in monuments than Florence, and second in the world only to Rome. But for those who *must* deprive themselves of sufficient time to appreciate this haven of calm and beauty, I suggest that on a one-day tour from Kyoto station you should start at Nishi Honganji, proceed to the National Museum, Kiyomizudera, Kinkakuji and conclude at Daitokuji, with a snack-lunch near Kiyomizudera.

TWO DAYS
Day 1. Imperial Household Agency to request permits for the Former Imperial Palace (today) and Katsura Imperial Villa (tomorrow). Imperial Palace – Nijo Castle – Nishi Honganji – National Museum – Chishakuin – Sanjusangendo. Evening at a Noh play.
Day 2. Katsura Imperial Villa – Tenryuji – Ryoanji – Kinkakuji – Daitokuji and if time either Kitano Shrine or Kimogamo Shrine.

THREE DAYS
Days 1 and 2. As above.
Day 3. Tofukuji – Fushimi Inari – Uji – Daigoji including Sanboin.

FOUR DAYS
Days 1–3. As above, except on Day 1 request permit to see Shugakuin on Day 4.
Day 4. Shugakuin – Ohara for Jakkoin and Sanzenin – Ginkakuji – Nanzenji – Chionin.

FIVE DAYS
Days 1–5. As above, except on Day 1 ask Tourist Office in Kyoto Tower to phone for permission to see Saihoji on Day 5.
Day 5. Saihoji – Enryakuji – Kiyomizudera. If time, Chishakuin and Sanjusangendo (unless seen on Day 1).

minshuku are listed in the JNTO *Budget travel in Japan* booklet available both in Japan and at JNTO offices abroad as listed in 'Useful Information' at the back of this book.

I stayed in a splendidly convenient minshuku near the rail station and the route of bus 206, a loop from the rail station to Gion, Kitaoji and Shijo. Mrs Yoshida is a charming hostess, overworking herself with great enthusiasm to provide an endless stream of foreigners and Japanese with clean bedlinen, breakfast, and a welcoming Japanese tea and sweetmeat on arriving back in the evening. Some minshuku provide meals, but there are so many restaurants to suit all pockets that there is little point in paying extra for meals in minshuku when you are unlikely to be returning in time for more than a few: the extraordinary spectacle of Japan and the Japanese going about their everyday business is entrancing enough, let alone the special occasions of shrine festivals or garden-visits. Most travellers use lodgings merely for sleep and breakfast.

In a ryokan

My minshuku looked just like any other two-storey wooden house near the banks of the Kamo River, so close to its neighbours that the merest spark would cause a dreaded conflagration: nothing would be left in an hour. The ground floor consisted of two double rooms connected by sliding doors to the dining-room and thence to the corridor and kitchen, with a lockable bathroom next to the dining-room; toilets and wash-basins, a coin-op washing machine, and behind these the Yoshida family rooms. The first floor, with stairs for the guests at the front and for the family at the back, comprised four double rooms separated by two single rooms, with wash-basins at the head of the stairs and behind them two family rooms. Check-in was at 4 p.m. and check-out at 10 a.m. Breakfast started at 8 and an evening meal, for those already returned, was offered from 5 to 6.30. Regulations in English attached to the wall in each room read:

'1. Please check cash, jewelry and other valuables with the front desk.' (There is no front desk: you cough in the hope that Yoshida-san will hear you). 'We are not responsible for loss of valuables left in your room.' (But you need not worry, for keys are provided).

'2. The following items are prohibited: (a) Animals or birds; (b) Items with a strong, offensive odour; (c) Ignitable or inframmable material; (d) Any item prohibited by law.'

My room was named 'Room of the Haiku' and beyond an opaque sliding door, to all appearances, it contained only a low square table with an ash-tray and mosquito coil. A closer inspection of the cupboards however revealed a futon, or mattress, a number of quilts, sheets, and pillows, and a freshly starched yukata, a roomy cotton dressing-gown. A plastic basket contained a bath-towel and hand-towel. Soap was provided at the wash-basins.

I remembered that I was expected to scrub myself clean and rinse properly before entering the scalding o-furo (honourable hot bath), prefixed like o-cha (honourable tea) with inherent intimations of the sacred, for the Japanese practise with zeal that idea of 'cleanliness next to godliness'. The etiquette of footwear is a constant anxiety during one's first few days in Japan, whether at home in a minshuku or visiting temples and gardens. Shoes are worn out of doors, slippers are worn indoors, and special geta (clogs) or slippers used instead of indoor slippers before one enters a toilet. Most temples provide overshoes or slippers at the entrance, with shoe-racks: but do remember *exactly* where you left your shoes!

Imperial Household Agency

Your second stop in Kyoto will most probably be at the office of the Imperial Household Agency, since it is here that you must obtain permission to visit the Gosho (Imperial Palace), Sento Gosho (Former Sento Imperial Palace, nearby), and the imperial villas of Katsura (south-west Kyoto) and Shugakuin (north-east Kyoto). Those in a hurry should time their arrival at the Imperial Household Agency at either 9.30 or 1.30, that is half-an-hour before the official visits start. You *must* have your passport with you, and you will be treated as an honoured guest, for Japanese hoping to visit these palaces are obliged to wait up to six months, such is the interest that these guided tours arouse – with obvious justification. There are no visits on Sundays, Saturday afternoons, public holidays, or between 25 December and 5 January. Do try to avoid the week in early April and early November each year when the Gosho is open to the public, for the huge crowds destroy the aristocratic dignity of the palace; the serenity of the gardens; the tranquillity of the ensemble.

Avoid choosing the same day for your visits to Katsura and Shugakuin, for they are too far apart. Combine if you can Katsura with the Saihoji (Moss Temple), accessible from Kamikatsura, the next station northward on the Arashiyama line of the Hankyu Railway, remembering that advance permission is also required for Saihoji; or with Nishi Honganji (no permit) or Higashi Honganji (permit one day in advance). Combine Shugakuin with Ohara or Enryakuji.

Garden Tours

Three tours of Kyoto gardens are operated daily, all finishing at Kyoto rail station and taking 5½ hours. The 'R' tour starts from the station and visits Shorenin, Tenryuji and Ryoanji, starting at 2 p.m. The other two start from Kyoto Tower (opposite the Station) and are correspondingly more expensive because they include a Japanese-style lunch. The 'F' tour departing at 9.15 and 9.45 comprises Zuihoin, Daitokuji, Daisenin, and duplicates Ryoanji and Tenryuji of the 'R' tour. The 'J' tour departing at 10 a.m. includes Murinan Villa and nearby Nanzenji (with Konchiin), Hakusasonso Villa (which the visitor would normally see with Ginkakuji), Sanboin and Kanjuji. For convenience of transport, the 'J' tour is by far the most useful: it would take two days to cover the same ground in any detail on your own, whereas both the 'F' and 'R' tours are quite easily followed by public bus. However, the experienced traveller will not wish to trail a group at other people's speeds, with an incessant, if cheerful, commentary parroted without change year in and year out. Guided tours are compulsory at Katsura, Shugakuin, Gosho and Sento Gosho; where they are not compulsory my strong advice is to go your own way. The Kyoto street map free from JNTO is bilingual, so if you ask a passer-by with a wordless smile for the location of a given temple or garden, she or he will be able to read the Japanese characters and point you in the right direction. Buses have numbers which match the numbers on the transport diagram on the *back* of the street map.

Museums

Museum-going in Kyoto begins at the National Museum which occupies the block opposite Sanjusangendo on Shichijodori. It is open daily except Mondays from 9 to 4.30, and has its own restaurant. Temporary visiting exhibitions (such as the important 'Ancient sculpture from India', 22 May to 8 July 1984) are held in the Old Exhibition Hall, to which special tickets allow entry.

The New Exhibition Hall (opened to the public in October 1966), contains a permanent display of national treasures on two floors, where you may not take photographs or use ballpoint or fountain pens. Room 1 shows early archaeological discoveries from 3000 B.C. to 600 A.D. Haniwa, the baked clay images of men, animals and artifacts that encircled burial mounds from the third to the seventh centuries, are the subject of an enchanting monograph of the same title by Fumio Miki (1974) and can be seen here, with a superb Yayoi pottery jar. Room 2 exhibits objects from the Nara to Heian periods (eighth to twelfth centuries), such as a funerary urn glazed over three colours.

Room 3 displays Japanese ceramic history from the Nara to Edo periods through a succession of masterpieces of widely-varying styles and aesthetic principles, while Room 5 offers a view of representative Chinese and Korean pots from the Han through to the Ch'ing. I particularly enjoyed a humorous pottery figure of a Han warrior, and exquisite examples of Sung celadon ware.

Sculpture can be found in rooms 5, 6 and 7; close study of these expertly-restored *chefs-d'œuvre* is made possible by easy access and imaginative lighting. Buddhist images predominate, though Shinto images (gods or guardian dogs) do occasionally find a place. Only the captions leave much to be desired, often omitting provenance.

Paintings on the upper floor give the same overall impression of fine connoisseurship, of uncrowded rooms well lit. Room 8 shows Buddhist paintings of the Heian and Kamakura periods (ninth to fourteenth centuries); Room 9 ink paintings (suibokuga) and sliding-panel paintings (fusuma-e) of the Muromachi period (fourteenth to sixteenth centuries); Room 10 scroll paintings (emakimono); Room 11 screen paintings of the sixteenth to eighteenth centuries); Room 12 paintings from China. Especially memorable are 'Three men laughing at Tiger Ravine' by Chuan Shinko (15th century), Keisan's portraits of Han Shan and Shih-te, a black and white painting by Shikan of wild geese flying down to a sandbar, an 18th-century scroll illustrating the *Taiheiki*, Sotatsu's 'Fujin and Raijin' (to be contrasted with their images seen at Sanjusangendo), a 14th-century Lotus hanging scroll from Hompoji, and an extraordinary display of imperial calligraphy, including the will of Emperor GoToba (1180–1239) with his palm-mark in red ink. Among the delectable calligraphy in Room 13 I picked out postcard souvenirs from the *Kokinshu* (11th–12th centuries) and from the Myohorengekyo Sutra (12th century), but there are in fact no second-rate objects in this remarkable museum. Room 14 displays textiles, Room 15 lacquer, and Room 16 metalwork, all of exceptional quality. Astonishingly, among the textiles I found a Gobelin tapestry portrait of Henri le Grand (1553–1610) from the Yasaka Shrine. Nobody knew when it had arrived in Japan, but it looks as odd here as a haniwa house from Okayama would seem in the Tate Gallery.

Just north of the National Museum, in Kaneimachi, Gojozaka (2 minutes' walk from the Umamachi bus stop on Higashijodori) stands the House of

Kawai Kanjiro, now a museum celebrating the life and works of the great potter who died at the age of 76 in 1966. Like the National Museum (and most others) it is closed on Mondays; it also closes between 10 and 20 August, but on other days it remains open from 10 to 5, the admission fee being double in 1984 the ¥250 which you pay to enter the National Museum. If you are staying for some reason in a Western-style hotel, this is a fine opportunity to enjoy the crafts and taste of a traditional Japanese house; in this case you can see the two kilns and studio where Kawai Kanjiro's pottery was produced.

Apart from these museums, and those in temples which are themselves treasure-houses of paintings and sculpture gaining from long association with their environment, there is a wide variety of other museums in Kyoto.

If you get off the number 5 bus at the Bijutsukanmae stop and enter Okazaki Park you will come to the Municipal Museum of Traditional Industries (9–5; closed on Mondays), for lacquer, silk, bamboo and ceramics, a special attraction being a reproduction of a traditional Kyoto house. Next door is the National Museum of Modern Art (10–5; closed on Mondays), which shows contemporary Western art as well as Japanese work. Five minutes' walk to the east is the Municipal Museum of Art (9–5; closed on Mondays), close enough to its national counterpart to be avoided on the same day. The Zoological Gardens are also to be found in Okazaki Park, though the Botanical Gardens lie to the north, just beyond the Kitaoji subway terminus.

Lesser museums abound, but I will list just four, allowing you to find others for yourself. Close to Arashiyama station, the Arashiyama Museum (33–22 Tsukurimichi, Saga Tenryuji, Ukyo-ku; open 9–5.30) has a high admission charge but is well worth a visit for those keen on swords, armour, helmets and weapons generally, together with the cult of the samurai. On the side of Horikawadori opposite from Nishi Honganji and just to the north you can find the Costume Museum (Floor 5, Izutsu Building; open 9–5 except on Mondays), specialising in a range of traditional costume displayed on life-size mannequins. Of the art galleries devoted to single artists I enjoyed most the Ikeno Taiga Museum (57 Matsuomangokucho, Nishikyo-ku; open 9.30–5.30) by the Kokedera bus stop on the road to Saihoji, devoted to calligraphy and black and white paintings (sumi-e) by Ikeno Taiga (1723–1776), also called Mumei, a pupil of Gion Nankai. Between Ryoanji and and Kinkakuji the *aficionado* of modern art might visit the Domoto Insho Museum (26 Kamiyanagicho, Hirano, Kita-ku; open 10–5 except Mondays, 21–28 February, and 21–31 August), which is a showcase for the ceramics, paintings and prints of Domoto Insho (1891–1975).

Sanjusangendo

As I was living close to Shichijo Station, my first exploration of Kyoto was the complex of buildings just to the east: Sanjusangendo, the National Museum, and the temples of Chishakuin and Myohoin.

Sanjusangendo means 'Hall of Thirty-Three (Sanjusan) Bays', and is the

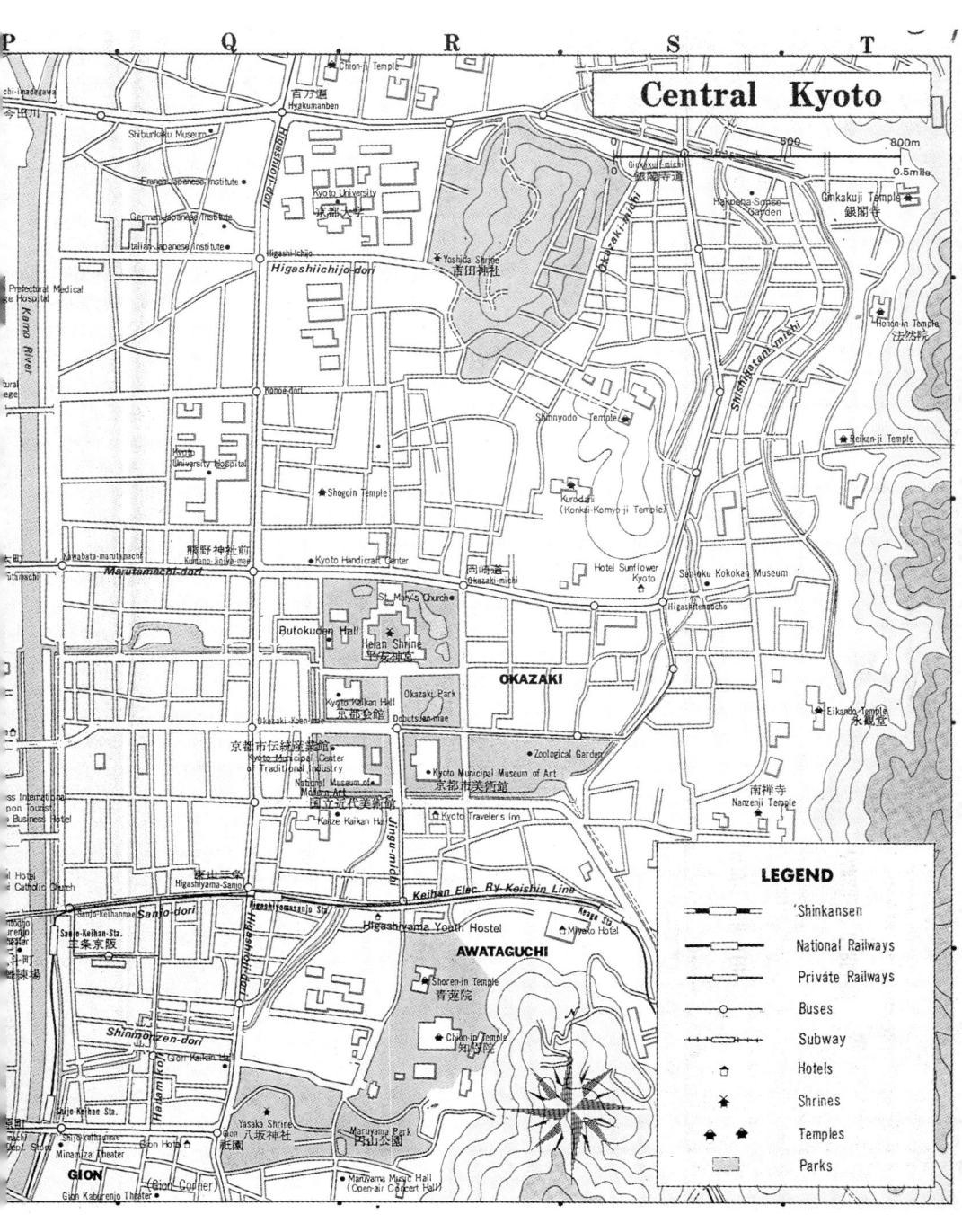

Central Kyoto

P   Q   R   S   T

chi-imadegawa
今出川
今出川

百万遍
Hyakumanben

Chion-ji Temple

Shibunkaku Museum

Ginkaku(michi
銀閣寺道

Hakusha-Sonso
Garden

Ginkakuji Temple
銀閣寺

French-Japanese Institute

Kyoto University
京都大学

German-Japanese Institute

Italian-Japanese Institute

Higashi-Ichijo

Yoshida Shrine
吉田神社

Higashiichijo-dori

Okazaki-michi

Honen-in Temple
法然院

Prefectural Medical
e Hospital

Kamo River
Kamo River

Konoe-dori

Shinnyodo Temple

Shishigatani-michi

tural
ege

Kyoto
University Hospital

Reikan-ji Temple

Shogoin Temple

Kurodani
(Konkai-Komyo-ji Temple)

Kawabata-marutamachi

熊野神社前
Kumano-jinja-mae

Kyoto Handicraft Center

岡崎道
Okazaki-michi

Hotel Sunflower
Kyoto

Saikoku Kokokan Museum

Marutamachi-dori
Marutamachi-dori

tamachi

Higashitennocho

St. Mary's Church

Butokuden Hall

Heian Shrine
平安神宮

OKAZAKI

Eikando Temple
永観堂

Okazaki Park

Okazaki-Koen-mae

Kyoto Kaikan Hall
京都会館

Okazaki Park

Debutsuden-mae

Zoological Garden

京都市伝統産業館
Kyoto Municipal Center
of Traditional Industry

National Museum of
Modern Art
国立近代美術館

Kyoto Municipal Museum of Art
京都市美術館

南禅寺
Nanzenji Temple

ss International
pon Tourist
Business Hotel

Kanze Kaikan Hall

Jingu-michi

Kyoto Travelers Inn

l Hotel
Catholic Church

Higashiyama-Sanjo

Keihan Elec. Ry Keishin Line

Sanjo-Keihanmae

Sanjo-dori

Higashiyamasanjo Sta.

Keage Sta.

Higashiyama Youth Hostel

Miyako Hotel

Sanjo-Keihan Sta.
三条京阪

ō
renjo
eater
a
場

Higashiyama-dori

AWATAGUCHI

Shinmonzen-dori

Shoren-in Temple
青蓮院

Chion-in Temple
知恩院

Gion Kaikan Hall

Shijo-Keihan Sta.

Yasaka Shrine
八坂神社

Maruyama Park
円山公園

nt Store
nza Theater

Gion Hotel
祇園

Minamiza Theater

GION

Gion Corner

Maruyama Music Hall
(Open-air Concert Hall)

Gion Kaburenjo Theater

800

800m

0.5mile

LEGEND

━━━	Shinkansen
━━━	National Railways
━━━	Private Railways
─○─	Buses
━━━	Subway
⌂	Hotels
✶	Shrines
⌂⌂	Temples
▒	Parks

popular modern designation for the Rengeoin which belongs to the Myohoin Temple nearby. The first hall was built at the behest of Emperor GoShirakawa in 1164, but burned down in 1249. The hall we see now is a reconstruction of 1266 ordered by Emperor GoSaga, and is thus in the Heian style that preceded the Kamakura period.

The hall is untypically long and low, with a thousand smaller figures of Kannon Bodhisattva about five feet high glinting dull gold surrounding the beautiful central Kannon, about ten feet high, carved in 1254 by Tankei at the age of 82, working in the hall where his father Unkei had worked before him. Some seventy sculptors took part in the mighty endeavour, working with the technique called yosegi-tsukuri. By this method, a roughly-carved basic body is put together using hollow blocks of wood; the exterior is then perfected with fine carving; the figure is painted or lacquered, and finally covered with gold leaf. The principal image is a work of extreme refinement and serenity, with eleven faces on the head and twenty pairs of arms symbolizing 1,000 arms, for each arm can save twenty-five worlds.

Take equally careful note of the twenty-eight divinities (Nijuhachibushu) subject to Kannon at the back of the hall. These include the graceful Daiben-kudokuten, a maiden with a delicate hand gesture and a gently-flowing robe, the god of music Jinmoten as he plays small cymbals, the Vedic creator of Heaven and Earth Indra known in Japan as Taisyakutenno, the crocodile deity Konpirao, the five-eyed lute-playing Magorao, the praying Mawaranyo, and

Sanjusangendo. Interior

the supreme achievement Basusennin or Vasu, the ascetic who journeys through the wilderness borne down by the sins of millions of men and women whose evil he has chosen to accept.

Behind these brilliantly-defined deities stand the God of Wind Fujin and the God of Thunder Raijin, each with one knee stretched out in front of the other, straining every nerve with physical effort.

Again outside, look along the narrow verandah and you will find yourself transported to the archery contest which dates back as far as 1606, when the tradition of shooting arrows from the south end to the north began. Starting at 6 p.m., the match continued for 24 hours, the archers seeing how many arrows they could let fly to reach the other end. The record of 1686, by Wasa Daihachiro, consisted of sending 8,133 arrows to reach the north end out of 13,053 shot. The competition is no longer held, but every 15 January it is commemorated by a re-enactment of the ancient contest.

Chishakuin

If you have time, you can cross the road past Chishakuin to see the rest of Myohoin, which belongs to the Tendai sect of Buddhism. The great reception hall was the Japanese Apricot Chamber (Umenoma) used by the Dowager Empress Tofukumonin, and is brilliantly painted with works by Shoei Kano (1520–93) and Eitoku Kano (1543–90).

Chishakuin is notable primarily for its garden laid out by the tea-master Sen no Rikyu (1522–1591) but dating in its present form to the Late Edo period (1750–1867). A secluded haven after the pandemonium of Sanjusangendo (where hundreds of primary-school children scamper and thud seemingly as quickly as possible along the endless wooden floorboards), Chishakuin is a 'landscape garden for viewing from within a building', and makes a pleasant transition, while you sit and contemplate in any season, before the walking tour of the Kyoto National Museum.

Insects called water-boatmen careered across the still surface of the pond like ice-skaters on a snowy February lake in Siberia.

The waterboatmen cannot hear pines grow
for the tumbling of a waterfall.

The temple is the headquarters of the Chisan school within Kukai's Shingon sect, with about three thousand affiliated temples throughout the land. To celebrate the 1200th anniversary of the founder's birth, a new Great Hall (Daikondo) was completed in June 1973, the 48th year of the Showa era. Chishakuin is your local temple if you choose to stay at the Kyoto Park Hotel.

Avoid Mondays and the noon hour, and you will also be able to see (between 9 and 4.30) the Momoyama-period paintings on walls and screens. A special new airconditioned gallery (unusual in Japanese temples) with a glass barrier to protect the works from being touched have together preserved these glorious paintings attributed to Hasegawa Tohaku and his son Kyuzo. They were created for the living apartments of the Shounji, a temple erected at the command of Toyotomi Hideyoshi in memory of his son who died while only three years old, in 1591. In 1605, after the fall of Osaka Castle and the Toyotomi family, Shogun Ieyasu gave the temple to the Chishakuin, where the paintings suffered from fire and theft, so that only half survive today. Of these, the outstanding masterpieces are the group known as 'Cherry and Maple Trees', though the 'Pines and Flowering Plants', and 'Pine and Plum Trees', and 'Pines, Hibiscus and Chrysanthemums' also dazzle the visitor by their elegant composition and extravagant colouring, emulating the garden outside which is in turn inspired by Lu Shan in China. The garden was laid out by the seventh abbot, Unsho, in 1674, and incorporates a pond extending under the shoin to give the appearance that the building is a lake pavilion (tsuridono).

Former Imperial Palace

The former Imperial Palace (Gosho) is best reached by bus 204 (stop Karasuma-Marutamachi) or Underground (station Imadegawa), allowing ten minutes' walk from either. The official guided tour in Japanese takes an hour, allowing plenty of time for questions, and to observe the immaculate reconstruction of a monument of the first importance.

You first pass through the Okuruma-yose (Carriage-Porch) to the three rooms collectively known as Shodaibunoma (Dignitaries' Rooms), where noblemen awaited an audience with the Emperor. These are the Tiger, Crane and Cherry Tree Rooms.

Now follow a passage called Wataro to the Seiryoden (Pure Cool Chamber), which the Emperor used as a secluded private residence until the middle Heian period, when it was transformed into a court ceremony hall. Again one is struck by the intimate scale of the imperial style in Kyoto: there is no ostentatious display of wealth, and no obsessive siege system of mottes and baileys, but a simplicity of materials (polished cypress floors and columns within; symmetrical grey tiles, plain stone platforms and gravel without) which displays sensibility and modesty even in the greatest. The equivalent perhaps of speaking softly in architectural terms. Before entering the Seiryoden, the visitor's steps are betrayed by a board called the naruita, which squeaks to alert the emperor's bodyguard that a stranger is at hand. Like many of the buildings in Kyoto, Gosho is a careful reproduction of earlier architecture destroyed a number of times by fire. It dominates the Imperial Park stretching away from the busy north–south highway Karasumadori in the west to the smaller Teramachi on the east: an area of over 840,000 square metres. Despite its present name, the former Imperial Palace was not inhabited by the Emperor Kammu, who settled his capital at Heian-kyo in 794. The Emperor built his Daidairi (Imperial Enclave) between the Katsura River and the Kamo, at the northern edge of the urban rectangle, itself modelled on the Chinese capital of the T'ang dynasty, Ch'angan – as were Nara and Nagaoka before it. Indeed, some of Nagaoka's new buildings (the city had been capital for less than a full decade) were simply dismantled, carried to Heian-kyo, and there reassembled in much the same position relative to the rest of the new capital.

Imagine the Great State Hall (Daigokuden) of the Daidairi as it was in early times, 'standing on a stone platform, surrounded by red-lacquer balustrades. It consisted of a single vast hall, 170 feet long and 50 feet wide, under a roof supported by fifty-two pillars, the whole painted vermilion, and the roof tiled emerald blue. The Imperial throne stood in the centre of the Hall, on a dais under a canopy surmounted by phoenixes painted gold'.

Gosho, by contrast, was originally the home of noblemen, such as Tsuchimikado in the Fujiwara period; only in 1308 was it designated a place where emperors might stay for any length of time. It became the official imperial residence in 1331. Though most of Kyoto was burnt to the ground during the Onin Wars of 1467–77, Gosho survived. The old palace was destroyed by fire in 1788 and its successor completed in 1790. This too was burnt down, in 1854, and the present buildings date from 1855–6.

In the main, central hall of the Seiryoden stands the michodai, or imperial throne. One corner of the hall is not floored, to enable the emperor to stand on the earth itself when worshipping the imperial ancestors. The paintings on the fusuma (sliding screens) are of the Tosa school established in the 13th century by Fujiwara Tsunetaka, whose title was Tosa Gonnokami. The Tosa school broke away from the pervasive Chinese themes and styles, choosing subjects from Japanese myth and history. A charming ripple of water can be heard by the sharp-eared on even dry days, for a stream has been diverted from Lake Biwa to course below the Seiryoden.

Now you enter the Shishinden (Ceremonial Chamber), housing the imperial throne, the takamikura, decorated with golden phoenixes, behind which is a copy of the eight-panel painting by Kose no Kanaoka, dating to the late 9th century, portraying thirty-two Chinese scholars. The original painting was destroyed by fire, and the present reconstruction is by Sukenobu Kano. Functions held in the Shishinden included the imperial coronation and the important New Year's ceremonies.

The Shunkoden (Sanctuary) was erected for the enthronement of Emperor Taisho in 1915. At one time the Sacred Mirror (part of the imperial regalia) was guarded there, but it is now to be found in the Imperial Palace in Tokyo.

Kogosho (The Smaller Palace) was intended as a ceremonial hall for the Crown Prince, and has three eighteen-mat audience chambers giving on to a lovely garden. It dates from 1958, its predecessor having burned down four years earlier. Seen from Oikeniwa, the Lake Garden, Kogosho seems almost apologetically drab, the only colours beyond grey-brown and white being the blue sky above and a strip of carefully-tended green lawn below. Once inside, however, the exquisite proportions take one's breath away, the play of horizontals and verticals reverberating from long mats to complex ceiling panels.

North of Kogosho you can see the courtyard where Japanese football or kemari was traditionally played by courtiers.

The football court differed from our football pitches as far as the elegance of the game differed from our competitive spirit today. One of the most amusing passages in the *Confessions* of Lady Nijo (translated by Karen Brazell, 1983) tells how the retired Emperors Kameyama and GoFukakusa planned an archery competition, the loser to show his court ladies to the winner. GoFukakusa, who lost, asked for an original device to reveal the charms of his ladies and the lay priest Sukesue suggested: 'Let's select eight court ladies from each of the top three ranks and dress them in the attire of the three classes of kickball players. Then we can set out the traditional trees in the corners (willow in the south-east, maple in the south-west, cherry in the north-east and pine in the north-west) and the ladies can act out a kickball game. That would certainly be a rare sight'. The ladies protested, but they surrendered gracefully and played.

Now you come to the Ogakumonjo, a six-roomed building devoted to literature. Readings, lectures, discussions and monthly poetry parties were held here. Three of the rooms with transom windows and coffered ceilings face east, and the upper room, Jodannoma, is distinguished by a tatami dais for the Emperor and a delicate tokonoma (alcove for a hanging scroll). The other rooms take names from their décor: Kiku (Chrysanthemum), Yamabuki (Yellow Rose), and Kari (Wild Geese).

Everywhere you will see the Emperor's crest: the sixteen-petalled chrysanthemum, the Empress's crest being the leaves and blossoms of the paulownia imperialis, or kirinoki.

North again to the Omima ('Three Rooms'), which served as chambers for informal audiences, and to the Tsunegoten (Informal Palace), more pleasant to live in than the formal buildings we have so far seen, and dating from the 16th century. Enjoy if you have the chance the refined Chinese paintings on cedar doors in the southwest side of the Tsunegoten and ask to see the Inner Garden (Gonaitei) to the east, with its charming pavilion known as Jishinden (Earthquake Hall) because it was constructed as a refuge for the Emperor in times of exceptionally violent seismic disturbance. The radiant colours in trees and shrubs of the Inner Garden are offset by the circular window in the pavilion cut by three symmetrical vertical lines.

The Osuzumisho (Pure Cool Hall) is a low structure in dark brown, lightened by rectangular white windows, where the Emperor spent hot summer evenings, with the tea pavilion called Chosetsu just to the north, connected by a narrow corridor open to the leafy garden on both sides. One of the cupboard panels of Chosetsu is decorated by a parrot on a perch. Next stands the Ohanagoten, or Crown Prince's Palace, where Emperor Meiji lived until his coronation in 1867. Farther north again, but generally not shown, is the Empress's Palace, the Kogogoten.

Kitano Shrine

After visiting the former Imperial Palace, you may choose to see a Shinto shrine (Hirano or Kitano) to the west, or a Rinzai Zen Buddhist temple (Shokokuji) much closer to the north, just past the leading Christian university, Doshisha, founded in 1873.

Hirano was transferred from Nagaoka, the capital transitional between Nara and Kyoto, in the late eighth century, but the four shrines you see nowadays date from the seventeenth. More than eighty varieties of cherry blossom have made this sanctuary, devoted to the protection of Kyoto, a true spring glory of the Heian capital.

Nearby Kitano Tenjin is a shrine devoted to 'Tenjin', the god of thunder subsequently identified with the spirit of Michizane Sugawara (845–903), an adviser to the successive Emperors Uda and Uda's son Daigo. Disgraced by calumnies at court, he was exiled to Kyushu in 901 and died shortly thereafter. His passing away was attended by such ferocious floods, epidemics, storms and earthquakes that it was decided to appease his spirit by erecting in 947 a shrine in his honour, planted with his favourite Japanese apricot trees.

The present shrine, like the Osaki-Hachiman Shrine in Sendai, was built in 1607, with the Main Hall, Hall of Worship, and connecting gallery in the new Momoyama architectural style adopted during the time of Hideyori Toyotomi. To enjoy annual festivals at this impressive shrine, come on 25 February for Baikasai or on 26 November for Ochatsubo Hokensai. The shrine is particularly revered by sake brewers.

Shokokuji

The three main phases of this site started with the construction of a Tendai temple called Izumoji; continued with the building of the Rinzai Zen temple Shokokuji by Yoshimitsu Ashikaga (1358–1408) in the decade following the completion of the Shogun's official residence nearby; and culminated in the restoration of parts of the fire-ravaged temple, destroyed in the 15th century, by Hideyori and subsequently by Ieyasu. Following more fires, all that remains of former glories is the Lecture Hall, with a lovely image of Shakyamuni Buddha and the great pines, melancholy in even the slightest zephyr, towering above the tombs of Yoshimasa Ashikaga (1435–90) and the scholar Seika Fujiwara. Yoshimitsu himself, like so many predecessors, became a priest after an active life, and retired to Kinkakuji. His successor, Yoshimochi (1386–1428), was an accomplished ink painter and student of Zen. Under his enlightened patronage, and that of the abbot Zekkai Chushin (1336–1405), Josetsu began the tradition of ink painting that resulted in the naming of a 'Shokokuji School', including Shubun of whom you can learn more in Takaaki Matsushita's *Ink Painting* (1974).

Zekkai, Gyokuen Bompo, and other leaders of the gozan literary movement not only studied Zen texts but also classical Chinese literature and painting, Taoism and Confucianism. (Indeed my own strong conviction is that Confucianism has played a powerful part in Japanese life right up to the present day). Gozan writers created an amusing legend that Michizane Sugawara had actually visited China (the hallowed immediate origin of great learning as well as of all schools of Japanese Buddhism), studied Zen under Wu-chun Shih-fan on Ching Shan, and there achieved satori. Tokusei made a delightful portrait of Michizane as a Confucian (with a Zen stole) and a sprig of plum blossom, which is now in the Tokiwayama Collection in Kamakura. The full humour of this arises from the fact that Michizane had little feeling, if any, for Zen, and refused to visit China when asked to do so in 894 on the grounds that T'ang culture in decline was no longer worth such a hazardous sea voyage. This momentous resolution might be viewed in retrospect as a cardinal moment in the evolution of Japan's self-confidence.

Myoshinji

From Kitano Shrine, walk westward to Kitano-Hakubaicho, terminus of the Kitano Line on the Keifuku railway, and alight at the second stop for Myoshinji, or the third stop (Omuro) for Ninnaji.

There are many visitors to Japan so entranced with Zen paradox that they equate the Kyoto experience with the Zen experience. We have seen that such a view is grossly unfair, but confronted with the marvels of Myoshinji (near the Yamagoe terminus on no. 26 bus from Kyoto station), it is very difficult to refute. Like Ryoanji and Nanzenji, Myoshinji belongs to the Rinzai school of Zen and offers both art treasures and gardens of great natural beauty and artifice. Myoshinji takes up the space previously occupied by the villa of former Emperor Hanazono, who ruled from 1308–18, and spent three decades (between his abdication in favour of GoDaigo and his death) at Myoshinji, which became almost a small town of temples, halls and living-quarters, many created and patronised by powerful samurai families.

Tanyu Kano, whose work we shall admire at Nanzenji, also painted the dragon ceiling in the Myoshinji Lecture Hall and caricatures on fusuma in the subordinate temple of Kaifukuin. Sanraku Kano (1559–1635) is represented by important paintings in the Tenkyuan, and by 'The Four Sages of Mount Shang' in Taizoin, which boasts the great 'Mastering a Catfish with a Gourd' by the Zen monk Josetsu (1394–1427). Shogun Yoshimochi (1386–1428) commissioned Josetsu to create an ink painting (suiboku) on the koan-like theme of how to overcome a catfish with a gourd. He then summoned some thirty Zen masters from the major Kyoto monasteries and asked each to 'interpret' the problem in verse. He then mounted the painting on one side of a small standing screen, and the verses on the other, though the modern mounting has the verses above the painting. The first monk invited to contribute a verse was Taigaku Shusu, who died about 1423. 'Birds can be downed with slings, fish can be trapped in nets, but how can one capture a squirming catfish in the slime of a wide puddle equipped only with a smooth, rounded, empty gourd? I wrote as follows:

Poised! With a gourd
he tries to take that slippery fish.
Oil poured on the gourd
Would add zest to the hunt!'

Like all Zen poems, it is not intended to be taken literally, but is supposed to indicate that human problems are man-made and that, by exploring and recognising the unities of all things, one can overcome the distinction between catfish and gourd, mind and no-mind, yes and no.

The meeting of poem and painting was intended to produce a unity, and indeed calligraphy in Japan is always more pictorial than in the West, where we are inhibited by the impersonal dullness and predictability of an alphabet, whether Greek, Latin or Cyrillic. A single theme can be brilliantly observed by a style of writing conforming sensitively to the style of the painting, and the linearity of the draughtsmanship can – and frequently is – inspired by calligraphic elements in a previous or contemporary work.

'Motonobu' Temple is a popular name for the sub-temple Reiunin, within the Myoshinji temple compound. 'Reiun' is the Japanese form of the Chinese name Ling-yün, and Motonobu Kano (1476–1559) is one of the most distinguished members of the Kano school. Take for example the fusuma painting 'Landscape with birds and flowers' dated 1543. His earliest known work (1509) is the 'Zen Master Achieving Enlightenment' painted on fusuma in the Hojo of Daisenin, a subtemple of Daitokuji, now found as a hanging scroll in the National Museum in Tokyo. It shows the Zen master Hsiang-yen Chih-hsien (in Japanese Kyogen Shikan) at the moment of satori as a broom with which he sweeps the ground dislodges a stone which hits a length of bamboo. The work belongs to the didactic genre known as zenkizu, and in its rather pedantic, precise realism owes much to Ma Yüan. His later works become softer, and more eloquently Japanese in mood, with daringly dramatic emphases of decoration offset by subtle colours. In his late sixties he manages to combine the poetic eloquence of exactly-defined Japanese lake shores with the ethereal enchantment of understated and even barely suggested mythic landscapes which are no longer inspired by Chinese models, or Japanese memories, but belong to a new world of the imagination. If one is tempted to compare this effort of the exploring mind, it might be with the European Romantics. 'The artist's feeling is his law', said Caspar David Friedrich. Claude Lorrain's ideal landscapes are perhaps even closer in feeling to Motonobu, as they are closer in time. Towards the end of his life, however, Motonobu painted vividly-coloured bird and flower studies on a gold ground appealing to the taste of the new generation of samurai, and this style dominated Momoyama art (1568–1603).

The garden of Reiunin may not seem to be linked to its art treasures, but it was in fact designed by the Zen painter Shiken (belonging to Shokokuji, like Josetsu and Shubun) and in its unexpectedly tiny form it manages to be as tactile as a sculpture, as colourful as a painting, and yet breathe like a man, the foliage changing relationships as it grows in symbiosis with stones, wall, tiles and gravel.

The Taizoin garden is of the dry landscape style; although the temple was built by the nobleman Hatano Izumo-no-Kami for the Zen priest Muin in 1404, it was razed during the Onin Wars of 1467–77. The garden we see now was designed by the painter Motonobu Kano, and it is easy to see how, with the skilful introduction of sand to represent water and rocks as islands, Motonobu created a complex landscape showing a fresh view at every step. Rock formations artificially placed symbolise the mythical islands of Horai believed by the ancient Chinese to lie in the Eastern Sea. It was to Horai that the Chinese emperor sent in 221 B.C. a physician (called Jofuku in Japanese): he arrived in Japan, and transmitted the name Shin to his descendants. As in so much else, the reality of Japan has been suffused with the unreality of Horai-san, and it is at Taizoin garden that one may absorb the magical micro-cosm of such neat confusion. Is the 'dry' waterfall a metamorphosis of falls near Nikko, themselves viewed by Chinese explorers as genii-infested phan-toms of falls near Lu Shan? See how the sherds of shale are grouped like boul-ders below towering mountains; how the natural rocks, placed just so by the hand of a landscape-painter, have weathered over the centuries just as he had once predicted.

Zakkein has a garden of the early Edo period in karesansui style, with six-teen stones alleged to represent as many Buddhist saints (Juroku Rakan) in an arrangement inspired by Zen. The designer, Gyokushin, was a priest of the Nichiren School, but learned much from Kobori Enshu and Shosho Horin, both Zen priests.

All the other principal gardens in Myoshinji date to the middle or late Edo (1720–1867). Keishunin (open 8–6 in summer and 9–5 in winter) combines karesansui, tea garden, and a landscape garden for strolling, and will thus appeal to the broadest spectrum of visitors.

The most fastidious connoisseur will take exceptional pleasure in the flat garden of Gyokuhoin (next to the 16th-century Bishoan and the 17th-century Gyokuho-Zengu), and the European will recall the cool geometric whites of Mondriaan's canvases in these subtle patterns of flagstones and raked gravel, with a single slender tree-trunk to add the spice of asymmetry.

Tokaian's main garden, with three man-made hillocks to represent moun-tains, was designed by Toboku, a priest of Kaizoji temple, in 1814. Two other stone-and-gravel gardens can be found at Tokaian: a pure, bare arena in front of the Hojo, and an artfully-laid string of rocks on a gravel ocean in the garden surrounded by Shoin and Hojo.

Ninnaji

Visit Ninnaji Temple, for its 17th-century garden for strolling and viewing-within-a-building, and the lovely tea-pavilion known as Ryokakutei. Origi-nally known as Omuro Palace, it was begun by Emperor Koko in 886 and com pleted after Koko's death by Emperor Uda, who reigned until 897, when he became the temple's superior until he died in 931. He was not only the first emperor to become a Buddhist priest, thus making Ninnaji the first monzeki temple, but also the first emperor to have a tomb made for him on a hill behind nearby Ryoanji. The Kondo (Main Hall) built for Uda's principal residence in 901 has not survived: in its place stands a late 16th-century building from the former Imperial Palace. The five-storey pagoda of 1637 is roughly contemporary with the other remaining buildings. Ancient cherry-trees in the grounds are particularly well-loved by the people of Kyoto, who throng Ninnaji every April.

The charming tea-pavilion, plain and unobtrusive, has four main rooms: the main entrance (tomomachi), the front main room (hiroma) and back office (mizuya), and the room for the tea-ceremony itself. The built-in cabinet or tana (shelf-arrangement), has gilt sliding-doors, the only concession to luxury in the spacious pavilion built to the open-plan sukiya-tsukuri style.

Wandering in Ninnaji, I recollected anecdotes of disreputable priests there which Yoshida no Kaneyoshi called 'Kenko' delighted to recount. A farewell party was being offered for an acolyte about to become a priest at Ninnaji and the guests had become more than a little inebriated. The story has been translated by Donald Keene from the 14th-century *Tsurezuregusa*. 'One of the priests, drunk and carried away by high spirits, picked up a three-legged cauldron nearby, and clamped it over his head. It caught on his nose, but he flattened it down, pulled the pot over his face, and danced out among the others, to the great amusement of everyone.

After the priest had been dancing for a while he tried to pull the pot off, but it refused to be budged. A pall fell over the gathering, and people wondered blankly what to do. They tried one thing and another, only succeeding in bruising the skin around his neck. The blood streamed down, and the priest's neck became so swollen that he had trouble breathing. The others tried to split the pot, but it was not easily broken and the reverberations inside were unbearable.'

If you want to find out what happened, you must find a copy of *Essays in Idleness* (Columbia University Press, 1967). But the point is that, if you thought the Japanese inscrutable and their sense of humour uncrossably removed from occidental fun, you need only turn to Pirandello's (much longer) novelette *La Giara* to find an identical situation treated in much the same way.

Ryoanji

It is an intriguing fact that what Leonardo's 'Gioconda' is to the Louvre, what Frans Hals' 'Laughing Cavalier' is to the Wallace Collection, Ryoanji is to Kyoto: the one feature inexorably identified with the spirit of the city. And yet it is quite wrong to see Ryoanji as a distillation of Kyoto's spirit, for its celebrated Zen garden is as untypical as is the congested hall of Buddha images in Sanjusangendo or the sacred palanquins for Gion Matsuri in Yasaka Shrine.

Kyoto is a kaleidoscope of a myriad visions over all four seasons.

Ryoanji was founded in 1473 by Katsumoto Hosokawa, a leader in the Onin Wars, on the ruins of a temple built by a retired emperor, and belongs to the Rinzai sect of Zen Buddhism. Its fame dates to 1500 or thereabouts, when the rock garden was constructed, supposedly by Soami (1472–1523), in a near rectangle of about 50 feet deep by 102 feet long, except that there is a cut into the east side. But the famous, classic view now accepted as original by the countless visitors is quite different from the plan of the designer, since the wall at the back of the view is recent, replacing an open view down to a pond below. The present varied treescape was originally a 'borrowed landscape', in a familiar Japanese mode.

Fourteen of the fifteen stones so harmoniously set in a fine gravel ground are from Kyoto; the fifteenth, long and low near the far wall, comes from Shikoku. The western wall is the oldest, and its carefully-constructed perspective (seven inches higher near the Hojo than in the far corner) gives a strange impression of distance. The eastern section of the wall, by contrast, is very recent.

A notice at the entrance to the garden compares it with nothingness and eternity, or a tigress swimming across water with her cubs. The Abbot, Genryu Kinoshita, has written: 'We can view the garden as a group of mountainous islands in a great ocean, or as mountain tops rising above a sea of clouds. We can see it as a picture framed by the ancient mud wall, now in itself regarded as a national treasure, or we can forget the frame as we sense the

Ryoanji. The Zen garden

truth of this sea stretching out boundlessly'. These are only explanations for those who cannot bear the thought of Void, No-Mind, of Emptiness. Yet Zen does not accept the consciously rational; analysis of life and its phenomena kills the free flow of what is living. In Eugen Herrigel's *Zen in the art of archery* and Hirohide Ogawa's *Enlightenment through the art of basketball* the entire emphasis is placed on action without commentary or explanation. If you begin to think about how difficult it is to ride a bicycle, you will fall off. Zen has been called 'the sound of one hand clapping'; one facet of its paradoxical essence ('teaching' is too strong a term, when many masters disclaim all authority) can be summed up in the following story from a work by Daiju Yekai (in Chinese, Tai-chu Hui-hai).

A Buddhist, Doko, asked a Zen master: 'In what frame of mind should one discipline oneself in the truth?' The master answered: 'There is no mind to frame and no truth in which to be disciplined'.

Rejoined Doko, 'If there is no mind to frame and no truth in which to be disciplined, why do you have a daily gathering of monks studying Zen and disciplining themselves in the truth?'

The master said, 'I have not a single square inch to spare, so where could the monks foregather? I have no tongue, so how could I advise others in the truth?'

Doko angrily replied, 'How can you say such lies to my face?'

The master retorted, 'As I have no tongue to advise others, how can I tell you a lie?'

Said Doko, shrugging his shoulders, 'I cannot understand your line of reasoning.'

The Zen master concluded, 'Neither can I'.

*   *   *

No primary-school children are allowed to enter Ryoanji in case they desecrate the tranquillity of the temple, but sadly there is no tranquillity left to desecrate. Unless you vault over the Muromachi wall to experience the garden before the floods of Japanese and foreign visitors troop in, there will be no peace; a Japanese lady screeching again and again 'there is no serenity to equal that of Ryoanji' over the public-address system can only just be heard above the excited chatter of secondary-school children and the click of a thousand cameras. Monks seeking satori left Ryoanji many years ago, and indeed it would be agreed by any Zen Buddhist that enlightenment can be found as easily in the scrutiny of his staff or garden-rake as in the contemplation of fifteen stones living in gravel.

> *My cat will not consider Ryoanji;*
> *in the fire's semi-circle*
> *she wakes, washes,*
> *wakes and sleeps.*

But even if you have seen through the rock-garden to the earth below, where the spirits of Shinto are still laughing, you will want to wander in the grounds which cover 120 acres of Ryoanji: the tombs of the Hosokawa family, and the pond, as well as the abbot's quarters or Hojo, its adjacent moss garden, and the altar with, from left to right, a statue of Katsumoto Hosokawa; the family tablet of the first abbot, Giten; an image of Monju; an image of Shaka behind three prayer tablets; an image of Fugen; and statues of the abbots Giten and Chuko. The paintings on the fusuma (sliding-panels) of the Hojo were painted by Kakuo Satsuki in the 1950s.

Opening hours of Ryoanji are 8–5 (the bus-stop is Ryoanji-michi, served by the 59 bus to Yamagoe in north-west Kyoto which also serves Kinkakuji (bus-stop Kinkakujimae) and Imadegawadori, turning south along Kawaramachidori to Sanjo-Keihan. Kinkakuji is open 9–5.30 (except 9–5 from October to March).

Kinkakuji

'The Temple of the Golden Pavilion' is the English form of Kinkakuji, and the translated title of the powerful novel by Yukio Mishima which first appeared in English in 1959, nine years after a psychotic Zen acolyte had burned down the pavilion, which dated back to the end of the fourteenth century.

Kinkakuji, also called Rokuonji, was a temple affiliated to the Rinzai sect of Zen Buddhism. The grounds belonged to the aristocrat Saionji Kintsune, a descendant of the Fujiwara, who built his temple Saionji and his villa Kitayama here about the year 1220, but both fell into disrepair. In 1378, the Shogun Ashikaga no Yoshimitsu (1358–1408) started building the Shokoku Temple, and completed it in 1388; in 1394 he abdicated in favour of his son Yoshimochi and began the Kitayama palace complex, including the Golden Pavilion, which seems to hang – situated as it is on the edge of a pond – between Heaven and Earth. The pavilion itself was not at first used as a temple but as a stage for Noh plays, for garden viewing and other pastimes such as the incense game, and for diplomatic intrigue, isolated from the gossip of central Kyoto. It was only on Yoshimitsu's death that the phoenix-capped pavilion was transformed into a Zen temple, and renamed Rokuonji by the priest Muso Kokushi.

The ground floor, Hosuiin, is Heian in style; the first floor, Choondo, is the true temple hall; the second floor, Kukkyocho, is like a Zen cell. The whole, rebuilt in 1955 carefully to reflect its predecessor, is surmounted by a phoenix, the lowest storey painted white and the other two in gold.

The garden, of the strolling kind, covers 92,000 square metres, the centre-piece being the pond Kyokochi, with its islands and rocks. At one time the pavilion was entirely surrounded by water, access being by a curved bridge; another important feature of the viewing is the teahouse called Sekkatei, on a hill above the pavilion and pond. You can also explore Ryumontaki waterfall and Gankasui pond, because (as at Ryoanji) there is no guided tour to follow.

Kinkakuji. The Golden Pavilion

This is a favourite haunt for school parties of hundreds of giggling uniformed schoolchildren led by patient teachers with flags for identification as if on some mysterious military exercise. Everyone will have different memories of Kinkakuji in addition to the colourful impression of pavilion and pond immortalised in 1830 in a woodblock print by Hiroshige. Mine are of the elegant verticals of the bamboo grove, as if a camera had caught a torrential sheet of green rain; the Fudodo (small temple hall dedicated to Fudomyoo) with its delicate moss garden, and the verdure on and behind the island of Ashihara so dense that the eye constantly dances from foreground to background to discover where the island ends, and invariably fails.

I thought back to that epic conflagration and wrote 'Kinkakuji, 1950':

> *Fire has eaten the pavilion. Calm.*
> *Moss, rain, time have eroded*
> *the Buddha to a speck of dust*
> *on the ground.*
> *Glory.*

Kamigamo Shrine

The great greensward expanse before the entrance to the Kamigamo (Upper Kamo) Shinto Shrine culminates in cherry trees and the dwarfed red torii, or open gateway. On a fine summer day you might imagine cricket on this village green in England; on a snowswept winter day you might envisage a Hendrik Avercamp ice-scape in Holland. I was shown around Kimogamo by a lady, Rikako Nakago, who gladly answered my questions, preferring to waste her time with a total stranger rather than going home with a full shopping bag. Outside the shrine a warnings board showed which ages were considered dangerous in this, the 59th year of the Showa era: women at risk were those aged 7, 13, 19, 32, 33 (very dangerous!), 34, 37 and 49. Men liable to disaster were those aged 7, 13, 25, 41, 42 (very dangerous!), 43, 55 and 61. A much larger wooden structure carried long wooden tablets inscribed with the names of donors to the shrine. The first line consisted of donors who had presented one million yen, the second line 500,000 yen, and the third 300,000 yen.

The chief deity worshipped at Kamigamo, mainly by farmers, is Wakeikazuchi, god of rain and consequently of fertility. Peaceful shaded grounds are watered by streams, encountered here and there. Equally surprising is a small cascade. For some reason I noticed moss nagging on the temple roofs. A red-robed priest was reading the daily paper, with little business to distract him. I bought a wooden votive tablet, not of a pair of mice (it was the Year of the Mouse) but of a colourful samurai, who might have emerged from a Tokugawa period film, made on Kyoto's Uzumasa movie sets. One writes a wish, for the health of one's family, success in examinations, or prosperity in business, on the blank obverse of the wooden tablet, and hangs it up amid clusters of similar little boards that clap and clatter in a high wind as if to applaud the shrine and its patrons.

Try to visit Kamigamo Shrine on 5 May, for the horse-riding festival (Hashiriuma) intended to secure a good harvest and calm in the realm; or on 15 May for the far more elaborate Hollyhock Festival (Aoi Matsuri). The latter began in the sixth century, when a deity spoke thus from an oracle still preserved in the shrine: 'If you wish to see me, make a sacred pole (are) with a branch of a sakaki tree brought from deep within the mountains, decorating it with ribbons of many colours. Also contrive a head-dress of hollyhock and sprigs of cercidiphyllum (katsura), and adorn that too with beauty'. The Kamigamo Shrine prepares each year two igeta (squares with projecting sides) with eight sprigs of hollyhock, and a katsura sprig in the middle.

The imperial messenger arrives to perform sacred rites, to pacify the local deity and protect the people of Kyoto from natural calamities during the forthcoming year. Dancers in the retinue of the Imperial Messenger dedicate their archaic sacred dance azuma-asobi to the god Wakeikazuchi while the singers recite the song called surugauta. The dancers on the Bridge Corridor wear gorgeous ceremonial red robes, swords, and girdles of linked jade plaques.

The hashidono or Bridge Corridor is also the scene of the Imperial Messenger's address, read aloud to the god. The messenger, dressed in dark robes and shaded from the sun's glare by the corridor's roof, intones the address written on red paper. (The address to the Shrine of Ise is inscribed on blue paper, and those to other shrines on yellow paper).

As in so many quiet gardens, I picked up a fallen leaf as a souvenir of this remarkable shrine and slipped it into a small envelope. Not a botanical specimen, but evidence in colour, shape and touch of a moment that by definition can never return, for no moment ever does.

For those – like me – who cannot read Japanese, shop-signs and hoardings form a calligraphic art gallery of every street. The shock is in finding romaji or Roman letters as the Japanese call them. On the way from Kamigamo to the Kitaoji-Horikawa bus stop to pick up a number nine bus, I was puzzled by the sign PIPI – ENJOY FASCINATING LIFE, and a restaurant called MESSY HOUSE advertising a dish named SPECIAL MESSY.

Entsuji

Bus number 4 from the Shimogamo (Lower Kamo) Shrine, on Shimogamo-hondori, the northern extension of Kawaramachidori, will take you to Midorogaike, from which it is a pleasant walk, again northward, to Entsuji. This started life as a mansion for the retired Emperor GoMinoo, where he could enjoy views of Mount Hiei far from court intrigue and ritual. Its karesansui garden, attributed to the Emperor himself, is open daily between 10 and 4. It has been extensively redesigned, notably in the 17th century, still taking full advantage of the backdrop provided by Mount Hiei, with its own microcosm of the earth as sea (moss) and islands (rocks) below the mighty mountain, a *Zauberberg* more symbolic and mysterious than anything devised by Thomas Mann.

Toji

In the general enthusiasm for Zen, students of Japanese Buddhism tend to minimise the importance of other aspects of Buddhism, many much longer and more deeply entrenched, such as the six sects of Nara Buddhism, the Tendai brought to Japan from China by Saicho (767–822), and the Shingon brought to Japan from China by Kukai (774–835). Zen precepts had been introduced in earlier times, but found no firm support until the times of Eisai (1141–1215) and Dogen (1200–1253).

So, after having prepared by reading the *Major Works* (1972) of Kukai in the translation by Yoshito S. Hakeda, I visited the Toji temple just southwest of Kyoto Central Station. Kukai's esoteric principles were practised unopposed on Mount Koya (south of Osaka) but he also felt the need, in pluralistic Heian Kyoto, to establish his own temple headquarters in the capital. This temple, started by Kammu in 796, was given by his successor Saga to Kukai in 823. Here, Kobo Daishi ('Great teacher who spreads widely Buddhist teachings', his honorific title awarded posthumously by the Heian court) propagated Shingon teachings, including the revolutionary new concept that mankind can attain Buddhahood in present existence by faith and practice, instead of having to wait through aeons of time for ultimate rebirth as a Buddha at the end of the karmic cycle.

Kobo Daishi taught that Buddhahood was accessible to all, male or female, rich or poor, nobles or commoners, and in the framework of this democratic world-view he opened a school for all classes with free meals, and compiled the first known Japanese dictionary to help pupils come to grips with their own written language.

Toji (East Temple) is so called – despite its formal name, Kyoogokokuji – because it stood as a ceremonial guard, with the Saiji (West Temple) to protect the city of Heian-kyo from the influence of evil spirits. Such an arrangement derived from Nara, defended from malign influence by the Todaiji (Great East Temple) and the Saidaiji (Great West Temple). Kyoto's Saiji (the only other temple allowed by Kammu) was almost totally devastated by fire in 990; its pagoda burned down in 1233, and was never rebuilt.

Toji itself fell a victim to the civil wars of the 15th century, and the buildings you see today date largely from the 17th century. The five-storey pagoda of 1644, built by the third Tokugawa shogun, Iemitsu, is claimed to be the tallest pagoda in Japan (56 metres from the top of its base). Also officially-designated National Treasures are the Rengemon Gate of 1191, the founder's hall rebuilt in 1380, and the main hall, one of the largest Momoyama-period edifices still standing, rebuilt by Hideyori in 1603. The founder's hall, with a statue of Kobo Daishi dated 1233, stands on the site of the founder's living quarters.

The Lecture Hall exemplifies through sculpture the teachings of the sutras particularly close to Kukai's heart: the Shugokokukaikyo and the Nihokyo. Buddha Dainichi, in the middle, is encircled by four Buddhas of the Diamond

World. On one side of this group is Fudo and other gods of anger who save the most recalcitrant of non-believers from their ignorance; on the other is Kongo Haramitta and other worshippers of Buddha Dainichi who renounced buddhahood to save mankind by intervening in the endless cycle of karma. At the four corners are the Four Kings of Heaven, or Shitenno, who guard the many worlds of Buddhism from the forces of evil. Fourteen of the 21 images date from Kukai's commissioning.

Do not miss the unconnected Chinese figure of Bishamon, protector of the north, usually shown with a pagoda in one hand and a spear in the other. Now in the Shokudo or refectory, it came from the Rashomon (the southern gate of Kyoto) which no longer exists but gave its name to the wonderful story by Akutagawa Ryunosuke (1892–1927) published in 1915 and transformed into a classic film (with *Yabu no Naka*) in 1915 by Akira Kurosawa.

Jonangu Shrine

If you take the Kinki Nippon Railway from Kyoto Eki, the first station is Toji (for Toji temple) and the fourth is Takeda, where you alight for Jonangu Shrine, walking westward, in what was once the Palace of Toba. Emperor Toba was born in 1103, became a puppet child-ruler in 1107 and abdicated in 1123. The four gardens at Jonangu provide a miniature history of the Japanese garden, dating from the Heian, Muromachi, Momoyama and Showa periods, the last being contemporary. They can be seen between 9 and 4.30. Toba (whose name derives from this area) was the port of Heian-kyo, since it lies near the confluence of the Kamo, Uji and Katsura.

Anrakuji

Emperor Toba is buried at Anrakuji, which lies south of Ginkakuji, between Honenin and Reikanji: all three are well worth visiting after Ginkakuji, passing along the eastern side of the old canal, parallel with the so-called Philosopher's Path. At the other end you come to Eikando, Nanzenji, Konchiin and Shirakawadori.

Honen, propagator of the worship of the name of Buddha which later became accepted as the central doctrine of the Jodo sect, lived between 1133 and 1212 and is buried in Kyoto at Chionin. His teachings were fiercely opposed by the Tendai monks of Enryakuji and the six sects of Nara, to the extent that Jodo or Pure Land Buddhism was not formally acknowledged in Kyoto until the seventeenth century. Its popularity widened with the passing years, however, for it demanded little in the way of scholarship, relying on faith in the efficacy of the name of Buddha alone. Anraku was a martyr to his master Honen's faith, being executed for having literally or metaphorically seduced one of the Emperor GoToba's concubines away from his court and its religious tendencies towards the Jodo sect. Asked to recant, Anraku refused, and was executed (possibly not merely for his teachings). His master Honen was banished for teaching the Nembutsu, but proselytized in the countryside, winning ever more disciples to his easily intelligible way. Eventually Honen was recalled to the capital by GoToba, and died there, reconciled in triumph. He built the small country temple of Anrakuji, and the larger Honenin. Anrakuji was erected in the 13th century, but the present Hondo dates from the 1580s. Anrakuji contains images of Honen, his pupils Anraku and Juren, with the two ladies of the imperial court who created the scandal of becoming nuns on hearing the preachings of Anraku and Juren. Ask to see the figures of Amida, Kannon, Seishi and Jizo protected by a screen.

In the grounds, camellias make a charming picture, separating at least in death the two monks from the nuns Suzumushi and Matsumushi, whose tombs are discreetly kept far apart.

Honenin

Honenin would be worth the visit for paintings of trees, flowers and birds by Mitsunobu Kano (1561–1608), but of course we come to remember Honen here just as we journey to Assisi for the church and milieu of S. Francis. Originally, Honenin consisted of nothing but an open-air image of Amida in paradise ascribed to Eshin. This is now set in the mid-17th century Hondo at the heart of the present temple, surrounded first by edifices saved from the earlier Hideyoshi castle at Fushimi, and later by others. You will enjoy a small karesansui garden, divided into two and raked by priests every few days, when you have passed cedars and camellias. The main buildings apart from the Hondo are the apartments which once formed the single audience chamber of Hideyoshi. They look out on to an azalea garden fragrant and intimate against a rural setting of woods alive with birds.

Takao

You can step back in time, to the years before Kukai was given Toji in trust, by taking the maple-viewing trail to Takao, northwest of Kyoto, when autumn colours emerge.

Kukai lived as a priest at Jingoji, founded in 781 and reconstructed from its forlorn ruins in the tenth and – following more fires – again in the twelfth century. You can get to Jingoji by taking the bus for five km. from the Takaoguchi station on the Kitano line of the Keifuku railway, and then crossing the river by the red bridge of 1299. As well as enjoying the maples, and the atmosphere redolent of Kobo Daishi, you should see the famous bell of 875 inscribed by the calligrapher Toshiyuki Fujiwara. Ask to see the charming hanging scroll portraying the priest Mongaku and dated to the 13th century. Not far from Jingoji is the Saimyoji at Makinoo, rebuilt in 1699. Farther on is the famous Kosanji temple at Toganoo, whose treasures were displayed in a special exhibition at Kyoto National Museum held in 1981 to mark the 750th anniversary of the death of the priest Myoe. Ask to see the contemporary hanging scroll of Myoe meditating in the fork of a tree, the Chinese portrait of the priest Pu-k'ung dated to the Southern Sung (1127–1279) in the form of a hanging scroll, and a wooden sculpture depicting the meditation of Myoe, again dating to the 13th century. Myoe, also known as Koben, rejected the notion that calling on Amida Butsu was all that is necessary for salvation, and sought to reaffirm the reformed Kegon teachings propagated from Nara. He planted tea given by Eisai, who was responsible for introducing Zen, and until recently tea from these plants was still called the 'true tea'. Compare this with the famous green tea of Uji. My own favourite treasures are the four caricature scrolls. The first of the four Kosanji animal caricature scrolls (Choju-giga), ascribed to Kakuyu (1053–1140), is believed to be allegorical and satirical, in broad terms poking fun at the declining aristocracy during the rise of the samurai. The second, also probably by Kakuyu, has no apparent satirical content, showing animals real and imaginary in more realistic ink drawings. The first part of the third scroll shows clerics and lay persons and the second part animals parodying human doings; like the fourth scroll, this is undoubtedly later than the first two. The fourth is less elegant, with wilder strokes in a different key.

Chionin

Honen (1133–1212), whose teachings led to the establishment of the Jodo ('Pure Land') sect, was an older contemporary of Myoe. His father was fatally wounded while Honen was still a boy but, on being urged to enter a monastery instead of seeking vengeance, the young Honen spent some time meditating on Mount Hiei, then roamed Japan as a hermit before living in a hut in Kyoto where Komyoji temple is now situated (in Ao suburb, west of Nagaoka, south-west of Kyoto) and where his remains were finally brought after rival Mount Hiei priests had desecrated his grave and thrown surviving bones into the Kamo River.

Honen taught where the Chionin temple now stands, and one of his many disciples was the priest Shinran. Honen's teaching – in the line of Ennin (794–864) and Eshin Sozu (942–1017) – was that salvation could be achieved by the heartfelt calling 'Namu, Amida Butsu'. Eshin had permitted the call as sufficient unto salvation within the tenets of the Tendai sect, but Honen placed his entire message on the call. Shinran (1173–1262) was to carry the notion further, after meeting Honen here at Chionin in the year 1201, and his supporters founded the True Pure Land (Jodo Shin) sect, departing from the Jodo in its doctrine that Amida Buddha's vow to save all human beings was in itself sufficient, and no esoteric or exoteric rites were needed. The headquarters of Jodo Shin – now the most populous sect in Japan, ahead of Jodo – are the Nishi and Higashi Honganji temples.

In 1204, the Tendai priests dominant on Mount Hiei proscribed the use of Nembutsu as an exclusive road to salvation, and by intrigue Honen was banished from Heian-kyo in 1207, at the venerable age of 75. Four years later he returned to the capital, and fasted until he died in 1212 in what is now the Seishido, on a hill to the north-east of the Kyozo (Sutra Library) built in 1616.

Chionin. Blossoms at the Gate

At Chionin also look at the great two-storey Sanmon, one of the most awe-inspiring gates in Japan; the Hondo (Main Hall), with its effigy of Honen in a shrine behind the hall; and the 'Hall of a Thousand Mats', with 360 mats. The corridor between the Hondo and the Superior's Quarters has a floor, ascribed to the sculptor Hidari Jingoro, which when touched at every step produces a sound like the song of the Japanese nightingale, the uguisu.

The main features of the Superior's Quarters are the fusuma adorned with paintings of the Kano school. The massive bell weighs 74 tons, and is said to be the largest in Japan.

Shorenin

Close to Chionin stands Awata Palace, also known as Shorenin, with a famous strolling garden attributed to Soami and Enshu. The palace was the official residence of the chief abbot of the Tendai Buddhist sect, who held the rank of imperial prince before the Meiji Restoration. Remarkable paintings on the sliding screens of the Hondo are ascribed to Motonobu Kano and others of that school.

Murinan

A short walk from Shorenin (near the Bijutsukan or Nanzenji bus stops) you will find the villa Murinan, built in 1895 in the so-called 'natural' style by Jihei Ogawa, to instructions by the owner Aritomo Yamagata. A V-shaped opening in the broad meadow, evoking European gardens more than other Japanese views, allows the trees mantling Higashiyama to emerge in all their glory.

Even if it is not festival time at Yasaka Shrine (16–17 July), you can see there in store the sacred palanquins which are trundled out to such impressive effect in mid-summer. Also called Gion Shrine for its location, Yasaka was patronised by the guild of cotton merchants, just as each other shrine was supported by one of the other guilds. Yasaka is sacred to the Shinto family of deities headed by Susanoo no Mikoto. The present shrine, crowded at most times by chattering schoolchildren and adults throwing coins into a slotted wooden box and clapping twice to attract the attention of Susano, his consort and their sons, was built in 1654. The central shrine is of a single storey, with half-hip and half-gable roof covered with keyaki (zelkova) wooden shingles. Look for the brace of carved mythical animals called koma inu (literally 'horse-dogs') carved by Unkei in the early 13th century.

Kenninji

The only original building in the Kenninji complex (named for the period of construction) is the Imperial Messenger's Gate. The rest of the foundation by Eisai under Shogun Yoriie Minamoto in 1202 has been destroyed by fire.

Eisai had just returned from his second visit to China with Zen teachings and the tea plant, first used in China to prevent sleepiness while meditating and adopted by the shrewd Eisai to restore Shogun Sanetomo Minamoto after a drinking party. Kenninji claims primacy for the tea cult, and a ceremony is held there annually on 20 April in memory of Eisai. Eisai taught that Zen would protect the State during the age of Mappo, which in Christian terms might be termed the Apocalypse or Armageddon.

The Abbot's quarters of the early 14th century were originally those of the Ankokuji in Hiroshima Prefecture made for Takauji Ashikaga. The Main Hall dates from 1763. Among the temple's treasures are scroll paintings by Yusho Kaihoku (1533–1613), including a 'Landscape with Figures' showing scholars at chess, calligraphy, painting and music.

Evening Entertainment

Near Yasaka and Kenninji, at Yasaka Kaikan Hall, many visitors take advantage of the 'potted Japan' experience offered at 'Gion Corner' twice each evening from March through November. In an hour, one can glimpse part of a tea ceremony, flower arrangement, a Bunraku puppet play, music of the court called Gagaku, and a Kyoto dance (kyomai) by young girls called maiko.

What else could you do in the evenings? Kyoto offers so much, from quiet meals in a great range of different restaurants, to Noh plays at the Oe Noh Stage, Kongo Noh Stage, and Kanzen Kaikan, all between central Kyoto and the Heian Shrine. I spent one exhilarating evening at the Kyoto Kaikan (as well as 'hall' or 'auditorium', Kaikan can also mean 'orgasm' or 'a suspicious fellow' so be careful how you ask!). Western and Japanese symphonies and concerti were expertly played by the Kyoto Symphony Orchestra and a fine soloist. In the summer free open-air concerts are held at the Open-Air Theatre in Maruyama Park (ask for Maruyama Ongakudo, and walk for 15 minutes from Gion stop on bus route 206, starting time about 7 p.m.). But sauntering along the streets of Kyoto will always provide the best entertainment of all, whether you choose the alleys around Higashiyama leading to Kiyomizudera, the fashionable shopping areas around Kawaramachidori and Karasumadori, or the philosopher's path following the ancient canal between Nanzenji and Ginkakuji parallel with Shirakawadori.

You are safer walking the streets of Kyoto at night than the streets of any European town during daylight, and even ladies alone need feel no anxiety.

Gion Corner. Bunraku

Katsura Imperial Villa

If I were to encapsulate the Kyoto experience, or were compelled to select one moment from a thousand as that ecstatic instant when I felt as much at home in Japan as I have felt transported while reading Kamo no Chomei's *Account of my hut* in my Cambridge armchair, then that moment would be a glimpse of Katsura garden from the second room of the Tea Pavilion or Gepparo.

Having obtained a visitor's permit and an appointment for the 10 a.m. or 2 p.m. tours, give yourself plenty of time for the journey westward. You can take the Hankyu Dentetsu train to Katsura Station (Katsura Eki), where the ticket collector will show you complex and slightly misleading instructions in English on how to walk to the Villa (Katsura Rikyu), but my advice is to take bus 60 from Kyoto Station (Kyoto Eki) and get off at Katsura Rikyumae. Taxis are normally available at Katsura Station if you are late, but this is risky, because you cannot join a tour once it has started, and the 'fifteen minutes' officially quoted for the walk from the rail station must be intended for top athletes. The tour is in Japanese only, so take good care to purchase the excellent bilingual official guidebook at the kiosk before you start.

Katsura Villa was built in the early seventeenth century for Prince Toshihito (1579–1629), brother to Emperor GoYozei (1571–1617), who succeeded his grandfather at the age of sixteen. The story runs that Enshu Kobori, the celebrated landscape gardener, was persuaded to take on the task of creating the garden only after he had been satisfied on three counts: no limit on time taken; no limit on expenditure; and no inspection to be permitted before the job was done. These onerous conditions being met, the job started in 1620 and ended in 1624, but it is a matter of record that the garden was laid out by Enshu's brothers, almost certainly under the supervision of Prince Toshihito and his son Prince Toshitada, who started an extension in 1642 which harmonises so perfectly with the original that the whole seems to be coetaneous. More than that: wherever one stands seems to be the centre of the villa, looking out on the most intriguing view of the garden. A European art historian has well observed that the 'avant-garde principles of the Bauhaus' were anticipated at Katsura by three full centuries. The villa is a marvel of grace, simplicity, and economy of means. The garden, hills and all, is entirely man-made, over former rice-fields. The pond has been planned with five irregularly-sized islets and cleverly-calculated views of 'mountains', 'beaches' and 'inlets' so that the country's landscape emerges in miniature as one strolls from one vantage point to the next. Remember too the range of tactile sensations as you tread on moss, gravel, paving-stones, cobbles, sand, and a dozen other surfaces. Verticals and horizontals interplay throughout, beginning with the polished bamboo of the front gate. Colours vary with the passing seasons; long perspectives give sudden way to intimate surroundings on a domestic scale.

The next gate, Miyukimon, has oak pillars and beams; Miyuki Lane, surfaced with blue-black cobblestones leads to the third gate, Chumon, before which you have a choice of branching off to a promontory on the pond planted with a carefully-pruned pine. From Chumon the Rigid Stepping Stones (flat paving on deep moss) leads to a stone lantern designed by the tea-master Furuta Oribe; the image of the Virgin Mary carved on the base is explained by the fact that Furuta converted to Roman Catholicism.

Katsura Imperial Palace

The imperial villa itself consists of three dwellings connected in such a form as to resemble wild geese in flight. The oldest, Ko-Shoin, was set on raised ground to avoid flooding by the Katsura River.

The moon-viewing verandah floored with bamboo stems overlooks the pond, and a charming curved perspective enchants the eye from the right down to the island with dwarf trees, and down to the water, in which the changing moon is reflected. The spear room has a spear-rack hanging from the ceiling, with room for five spears and two swords. Next door is a room named for the hearth in the middle, the ceiling just above the hearth taking the form of a smoke vent.

Chu-Shoin (Middle Mansion) was Prince Toshihito's living quarters, whose simplicity contrasts intriguingly with the contemporary style of Nijo Castle constructed by the warrior clans of the period. The first room is called 'Mountains and Rivers' after the landscapes by Tanyu Kano (1602–74), who restored the Kano school's fortunes which had declined after the death of Motonobu in 1559. The second room is called 'Seven Sages in a Bamboo Wood', after the amusing paintings by Naonobu Kano (1607–50). The third has 'Pheasants in Snow' by Yasunobu Kano (1616–85). The three-mat musical instrument room housed Toshihito's koto, the Japanese form of the Chinese lyre with 13 strings perfected in the early seventeenth century by Yatsuhashi Kengyo. Enjoy the superb grains of the wood in the recess of the music room from which the prince would watch archery or football played on the lawn.

Shin-Shoin (New Mansion) was intended as the living quarters of Prince Toshitada, but was restyled for the stay by the former Emperor GoMinoo. He reigned from 1612 to 1629 and then abdicated in favour of his seven-year-old son, who then became the puppet of Hidetada, third son and successor to the Tokugawa shogun Ieyasu. Hidetada stopped commercial relations with all foreigners except a handful of Dutch, Chinese and Koreans, persecuted Christians, and prohibited Japanese to go abroad.

Paintings by Tanyu Kano adorn the door; within, the first room possesses an elegance that western rooms (cluttered with furniture, disfigured by paint or wallpaper) could never hope to possess. The three-mat raised corner is distinguished by a coffered ceiling and elegant built-in furniture, leaving the whole of the centre of the room a spacious environment, again achieving a stunning fusion of taste and elegance by gracious understatement, as for example in the sober uniform brown of the zelkova timber framing.

We now come to the Gepparo, or tea pavilion, so situated as to permit ideal conditions for moon-viewing. Look for the twenty-three lanterns, each unique; for the boat at the pier, symbolising a beach on the ocean-shore. In the Gepparo, dedicated to autumn tints and feelings, note the fine calligraphy above the sliding panels of the second room. Your garden stroll is cunningly devised as a sequence of visual and tactile *coups de théâtre*, and it is as well if you have your aesthetic senses honed for Katsura, so if you are feeling ill or tired do not waste this precious hour by coming to Katsura.

One path flanked by maples takes the form of stepping stones to Cycas Hill, with a rustic roofed bench used as a prologue to the tea ceremony at Shokintei. Another path is cobbled straight to the pond's edge.

Look for the elaborate sea-shore environment emulating the promontory and beach of Amano Hashidate, near Miyazu in the province of Tango north-west of Kyoto. Amano Hashidate is one of the so-called 'Three Landscapes of Japan', the other two being Matsushima near Sendai in northern Honshu, and Miyajima, just west of Hiroshima in western Honshu. Like all such traditional claims, it contains a grain of truth, but the grain irritates in the eye already bewitched by a thousand other lovely views.

On your way to Shokintei, ask politely to see Manjitei, which is not always shown, but defer gracefully of course if permission is withheld.

Katsura. Shokintei

'Shokin' means 'pine-harp' and 'tei' can mean an arbour, pavilion, or mansion. Before entering, look at the stones placed deliberately near the stolid stone bridge; these are stepping stones so that guests of the tea ceremony may wash their hands in the water, which reflects intertwined branches. All sides but the south face of Shokintei permit a view of the pond. The low, deep roof gives protection from the snow in winter (the pavilion's principal season) and from the sun in summer. The tea-room itself has four mats, one of them slightly smaller than the normal size. The first room is of eleven mats, with a stone hearth facing west.

A path now leads to Shokatei, a smaller and rustic pavilion on an island, from which one can view the mansions of Katsura in the foreground. 'Shoka' means 'shop' as well as 'early summer' and the curtains in front of the quaint kiosk evoke a rural general store that one might gratefully encounter while on a hike in the mountains. I entered the empty pavilion, incongruously plebeian in the precincts of an imperial villa. It could have been a cabin by-passed by Basho on his first great travels in 1684, which he records in *Nozarashi kiko*. On the last day of the year, he was still travelling and wrote:

> *With a hat on my head*
> *And straw sandals on my feet,*
> *I met on the road*
> *The end of the year.*

Still dazed by the glories of Katsura, I sauntered back through the grounds, trailing behind the rest of the group with their clicking cameras and social chatter. The sky darkened for the first time in many days, and I took out my pocket umbrella. Lightning and thunder crackled over the imperial villa and its unsurpassed gardens. I became lost on the way to Katsura rail station and eventually found an airconditioned coffee shop. Every table except one was fitted with space-invader games so that you can play before, during and after a meal. I ordered yakisoba (fried noodles), which arrived beautifully presented on a polished wooden tray. A man and woman eating oyako-don (chicken and egg) next to me were relaxed, charming and extravert. Japanese abroad are either nervously excited or numbly overawed; in Japan they are quietly polite, laugh easily and unaffectedly, and are modest and restrained in their relationships with others. (This of course does not apply to the city bars and nightclubs where expense accounts are swollen by the kind of over-charging familiar in European city centres from Hamburg and Copenhagen to Paris and London).

The Japanese Miracle

The Japanese do not stare like the Chinese or beg like the Indians. Their middle class comprises ninety per cent of the nation, and their self-confidence shows it. An intellectual or an administrator is a misfit in Burma or Vietnam: in Japan he is simply taken for granted. His knowledge of English is likely to be adequate for all likely purposes, and is almost certainly better than the European tourist's Japanese, which cannot be said for the average Thai or Afghani.

The inescapable conclusion which the visitor will reach after a few days is that, for all the seeming inconsistencies and puzzles, Japan is a country much more like Canada or Switzerland than it is like China or Pakistan. It is oriental in its geographical location and in its cultural background, but four decades of americanisation have brought a degree of modernisation from the ruins of World War II that only the most fanciful could have predicted. The Japanese have proved incomparably resourceful, patriotic, hard-working, good-humoured and stable in their economic, political, social and cultural life. While China was suffering civil wars, communist revolution, and even more bitter scission through the miscalled 'Cultural Revolution', the Japanese were creating a new society mingling the traditional values of respect and hard work with the newly-acquired skills of technology, commerce, business and management. A country roughly the same size as Great Britain has managed – by a complex network of factors – to catch up economically and commercially from a position close to zero (with the bombing of Hiroshima, with the razing of Tokyo) to a ranking far ahead. Efficiency, speed and courtesy are ubiquitous features of buses, trains, all stores from the little corner shop to the huge department store, hotels and restaurants. Vital decisions are taken by consensus, the all-important nemawashi system. There are many political parties (including the Communists), and the wide spectrum of views for which a Japanese may vote is a fine advertisement for democracy. Trades unions have virtually no power to disrupt the nation's industrial life. While Shinto and Buddhism, like Islam and Christianity, have complete freedom, Japanese society is almost entirely atheist: a recent census at Tokyo's Jesuit-sponsored Sophia University showed that, despite an obvious bias which might have been expected, 98% of freshmen professed no religious belief at all.

When it comes to the freedom of the press and mass literacy, only Sweden has a higher percentage of regular newspapers than Japan, which has 93%. Japanese book publishing is so internationally-minded that most significant foreign books will find a Japanese publisher, though even the most significant of Japanese authors (Sawako Ariyoshi, the woman novelist, is an obvious example) will find it difficult to attain publication in Western languages. Bookshops in Kyoto and Tokyo have a huge range of titles in Japanese, with smaller English departments, and second-hand bookshops thrive in recognised districts much as they do in Paris or London.

These reasons will perhaps serve to show why I, and any middle-class white-collar person like me, feel more at home in Japan than it would be reasonable to expect at first glance. Trim uniformed schoolgirls on the platform of Kamikatsura station could (face apart) have stepped on to the platform at Norwich or Reading. I turned away from them towards the exit, handed my ticket to the inspector, and asked directions to Saihoji.

Saihoji

Conditions may change, but in 1984 a visitor was required to give five days' notice before he could visit Saihoji, such was the demand for admission. Numbers are limited because of the rare and delicate mosses, more than fifty varieties in all, which are damaged by constant wear. Called also Kokedera ('Moss Temple'), Saihoji is thought by some authorities to stand on the site of a temple founded by the great advocate of Buddhism Prince Shotoku (572–621); others credit the foundation to the priest Gyoki in 731. In either case, it was rebuilt in 1339 by the Zen master Muso Kokushi (1275–1351), who was responsible for the strolling garden here, as well as for the great Tenryuji garden to the north, in Arashiyama. The Zen garden, created with an artful simplicity, aims to convey the idea that the pond is directly connected with the mountains behind it. Imagine the buildings demolished during the Onin Wars

Saihoji

(1467–77): in the centre was the exquisite two-storied Shariden ('Reliquary Hall') which we can visualise from the present-day Kinkaku and Ginkaku pavilions overlooking a pond, since they were inspired by Kokedera's Shariden. We can gain a clear idea of Christian Paradise from Dante and Milton, while the Persian Paradise (*pairidaeza*) referred to a walled garden as long ago as the times of Cyrus the Great. In the Buddhist Paradise splendid pavilions stand on the brink of lotus-filled ponds, so close to the Persian ideal that they must have a common origin.

Tenryuji

Bewitched by Muso's garden, you will now make for his even more extraordinary landscape garden for strolling and viewing-within-a-building at Tenryuji, open from 8.30 to 5.30. From Saihoji you can walk back to the Hankyu electric railway, boarding at Kamikatsura and alighting two stations northward, at the Arashiyama terminus. This will enable you to visit Horinji Temple if you have time. Its annual festival is on 13 April, but it is worth visiting at any time for its extreme antiquity (dating back to 713) and its sculpture of Kokuzo, one of the gods of wisdom.

The turbulent reign of GoDaigo, expelled from Kyoto in 1336, ended in exile at Yoshino two years later. Muso Kokushi, Zen master and landscape gardener, advised the Shogun Takauji Ashikaga (1305–58) to build a temple in memory of GoDaigo, whose spirit he had seen emerging as a heavenly dragon from the Oi River. Thus the temple was called Tenryuji ('Heavenly Dragon Temple') and devoted to Zen, despite objections by the Tendai sect, taking five years to build from 1339. The site is that of the Kameyama Palace.

The temple buildings have been repeatedly destroyed by fire over the centuries, and those you see now are careful reconstructions dated 1900 and later. You can see an image of GoDaigo in Tahoden, a hall emulating the simple mansion that the Emperor had inhabited while exiled in Yoshino and, since that is a spectacular site for cherry-viewing, a cherry tree is planted near Tahoden in remembrance.

The pond with rocks and islands was formed like the Chinese character hsin (mind, or heart), in Japanese pronounced and transliterated kokoro. A brushstroke down and swiftly right at the foot, then one drop leftward down at the left, and two successive rightward down drops at the right like splashes of blood. Since the essence of Zen is not Mind at all, but No-Mind (mushin) or No-Thought (munen), it might seem paradoxical that a garden and temple dedicated to No-Mind should have at its heart the character for Mind. Such a conclusion would of course be wrong, for Zen's heart is the paradox, whether of one hand clapping, or of the ejaculation 'Katsu!' Rinzai Gigen (the Japanese form of Lin-chi I-hsüan) distinguished four kinds of 'Katsu!' cries: one like the sacred sword of Vajraraja, which instantly cleaves anything dualistic in its way; another like the crouching lion ready to spring; another like the pole sounded by a burglar to tell whether a house is empty; and yet another serving no purpose whatsoever. Rinzai may have omitted a fifth 'Katsu!': can you imagine what it is?

From the waterfall of Tenryuji the stone bridge and stones seem to be floating on the surface of the water. Stones arranged below the waterfall give an appearance of a huge mountain-range in microcosm.

A young Japanese sitting beside me took equal pleasure in the view from pavilion to waterfall. 'But you should come here in the depths of winter,' he said, 'when the pond is frozen and snow covers the millions of leaves. Just as we have hanami or blossom-viewing in the spring, and tsukimi or moon-viewing in the autumn, so we have yukimi or snow-viewing in the winter. Nowhere is there a hill like this Saga.'

He offered to show me Seiryoji and Daikakuji to the north. We were unable

Tenryuji

to see the celebrated sandalwood sculpture of Shakyamuni at Seiryoji's Shakado, because it is shown only on 8 and 19 April. Daikakuji (open 9–4) was created a temple in 876 by Emperor Junna (824–33) on the grounds of GoSaga's imperial villa, but it still looks more like a villa than a temple, with a maze of fascinating passages connecting the various buildings. The sculptures of greatest interest are those representing the Five *Vidyarajas* ascribed to the ninth-century Shingon priest Kukai. Abundant paintings are worth close study, especially those by the Kano masters Motonobu (1476–1559), Eitoku (1543–90) and Sanraku (1559–1635).

Hozu Rapids

The Hozu Rapids excursion lies in this same direction, but takes a good half-day, so it is a good idea to spend the morning near Kyoto Station (perhaps at the Nishi Honganji, Higashi Honganji with the Kikokutei, or the National Museum), then take a bus or train on the Sanin Line from Kyoto Eki to Kameoka. You should aim to arrive at Kameoka by 2 or 2.30 p.m. for the ninety-minute rapids excursion. The flat-bottomed boats are quite safe, though the trip is exhilaratingly exciting, and is best in September or October (when the season closes till April) while the maple-leaves are turning colour. Cherry blossom is marvellous in spring. Wild azaleas are the attraction in early summer. You get off at Arashiyama, where there are restaurants and ample means of returning to central Kyoto.

Your trip seems disappointing as far as Miyanoshita, where the river suddenly narrows and the rapids begin. Here you appreciate the skill of the boatmakers in choosing pliant planks for these apparently fragile craft thirty feet long and six feet wide, with three thwarts. On your left you can make out a Shinto shrine, Uketa Myojin. Now you enter the rapids of Fudo-no-taki ('God of Wisdom Fall'), rushing through a narrow channel, then head for Koyu-no-taki ('Hut Fall'), where a precipitous rock face looms about the grey-robed boatmen and the shrieking passengers.

The most dangerous rapids are Takase-no-taki ('High Fall') followed by Shishi-no-kuchi, the aptly-named 'Lion's Mouth'. After Nagase you come to a calm stretch. Gakugase is the site of azaleas, if you take your eyes off the deft poleman at the bow, with an oarsman behind him, concentrating and calculating with speed and resolution.

If you look carefully as your boat skims past these rocks, you can see small holes in the rock just large enough to take the tip of a bamboo pole. These crevices are not natural, or even manually contrived, but have been worn by bamboo-pole tips century after century, indicating the precision (to the nearest inch) needed by boatmen and raftmen as they carried goods and passengers down the Katsuragawa.

And if you can prise your anxious glance from the next stretch of rapids, you can see anglers on the river-bank (and there a kingfisher?), cherry trees, old pines, a rickety bridge that could have been drawn by Hiroshige, maples, and

Hozu Rapids

now the first houses as we descend to Arashiyama, with tea-pavilions gazing down on to calmer waters.

Ohara

A small village on the north-eastern outskirts of Kyoto offers a splendid excursion in the middle of the day. As you emerge from Kyoto rail station to the bus terminal, turn to the far left and queue at Stop 1 for bus numbers 17 or 18 which go as far as Ohara (stress the syllables evenly as always in Japanese, avoiding the implication that the name is Irish). A shiny new single-decker bus drew up at 10.28 and by 10.30 it was filled with passengers and sliding out towards Ohara, which we reached exactly one hour later. I used a hundred-yen locker at Ohara bus station for my heavier gear (the lockers will take rucksacks) and followed the signs, starting downhill, to Jakkoin. Since none of Ohara signs is romanised, the four main signs are shown below in characters to be recognised, with their romanisation, so that you will not be lost.

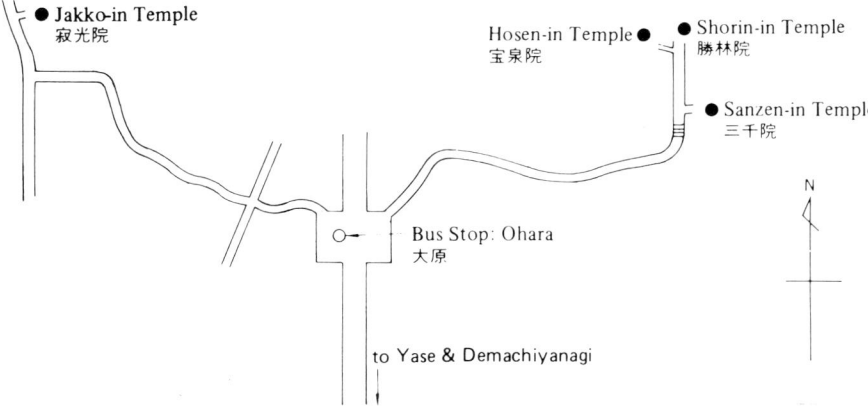

Jakkoin

The stroll to Jakkoin is three hundred metres, mostly on ricefield boundary paths which may be muddy in winter. In summer you will need a sun-hat or parasol.

I paid ¥350 admission to the nunnery, ¥50 for a short booklet in English and ¥300 for a calligraphic souvenir of my visit written (with three red seals to guarantee authenticity) by a scribe. Many temples sell a choice of blank pocket albums, called a stampucho, bound accordion-style, in which a calligrapher can be invited to write, for a fixed fee, which varies from temple to temple. Some temples offer a red or black stamp-pad with ready-cut rubber stamps for you to press down your own record of the visit. The book becomes entirely unique as no two visitors will visit the same temples in the same journey to Japan (unless they happen to be in a group) and if you insert a small piece of paper in each opening to indicate to which temple each stamp refers you can connect this splendidly original calligraphic masterpiece with photographs or postcards when you get home. The stampucho, written on only one side, could thus make a splendid frieze. Some pages might be overcrowded by a zealous artist keen to give value for money, but I prize in particular a distinguished page from Ryoanji. The stamp at Jakkoin is more delicate and nervous, insistently vertical as opposed to the central, square impact of the calligraphy from Ryoanji.

History plays remarkable tricks on people, and the strangest places become historic. Entering the secluded garden of Jakkoin, it strikes even the most casual visitor as incredible that a former Empress, one of a handful of survivors from a great dynasty, the Taira or Heike, should have retreated here. The Heike's titanic struggle with the rival Minamoto dynasty fills thousands of pages in history, legend and romance dealing with the eleventh and twelfth centuries. The climax of the Gempei War (1180–5) came with the Minamoto offensive at Dannoura, where the Taira were crushed in a final sea battle in April 1185.

Tokuko of the Taira, who had become Empress at sixteen, a year after marrying Emperor Takakura, jumped into the sea to drown with the rest of the Taira, but Minamoto men pulled her out from the waves by her hair and sent her back to Kyoto, her husband and son Antoku having been killed. She changed her name to Kenreimonin, after the name of the great southern gate of the Emperor's Palace, a custom of empress-dowagers being to take the name of gates, just as princes of the imperial house were named after palaces and villas. At Kyoto she lived in a poor hut owned by Kyoe, a priest of Nara, without the dignity and wealth which had long been her prerogative. As the epilogue to *Heike Monogatari* says, 'Clusters of vines crept over the rotting roof. Weeds grew tall and thick in the garden. The bamboo curtains crumbled. The bedchamber was exposed to wind and rain . . .'

'At the age of twenty-nine she was still beautiful, as beautiful as peach or apricot blossoms. Her elegant form was like a lotus flower. But what was the use of keeping her raven locks, as lustrous as jade?'

She took the tonsure, the ceremony being performed by a priest living in a cell at Chorakuji, a temple associated with Enryakuji. Then even her wretched hut collapsed during an earthquake and, humiliated by her poverty close to prying eyes in the imperial capital, she sought a secluded retreat. A palanquin was sent by one of her younger sisters, the wife of Councillor Takafusa, and she was carried to the temple of Jakkoin where a hut ten feet (one jo) square was built for her. In one room she slept and in the other she prayed before an image of Buddha. One day she asked an attendant in her anxiety whose were the footsteps outside that had come to trouble her calm. Her lady-in-waiting answered with this poem:

> What visitor dares
> to tread this rocky mountain path
> to see my lady?
> The fallen oak leaves rustle
> under the feet of a young stag.

'Her palace had been all gold and jewels', sighs *Heike Monogatari*. 'Gorgeous brocade had been spread over her bed. Now she lived among thatch and brushwood.'

In 1186 the retired Emperor GoShirakawa set out on a surprise visit to Kenreimonin, who seldom received news from the capital. 'Only the cry of a monkey as it sprang from tree to tree and the sound of a wood-cutter's axe in the mountain could be heard through the dense ivy-covered undergrowth surrounding the hut. "Is anyone there?" called the retired Emperor.' At length an old, haggard nun appeared, explaining that Kenreimonin was picking flowers for the Buddha's shrine. Asked who she was, she broke down and confessed that she had been the Emperor's wet-nurse. He had forgotten her, and she had been reduced to dire poverty, being forced to become a nun. GoShirakawa found images of three Bodhisattvas: Amida, Kannon and Seishi. 'Instead of the fragrance of orchid and musk, which had filled the imperial rooms, the smoke of incense rose before the holy images. He found a poem by Oe no Sadamoto written on a small square of paper and pasted to the wall:

> *The celestial melody of the pan-pipes is heard*
> *from the solitary cloud on high;*
> *the bodhisattvas glide down*
> *to meet me and lead me to Paradise.'*

GoShirakawa then meets again his adopted daughter Kenreimonin, and she tells her story and her hope for salvation in the Paradise of Amida. The final pages of the *Heike Monogatari* are devoted to the death of the former Empress in 1191 (though 1213 is the date accepted nowadays).

These memories, poems and mental images are brought with them by Japanese visitors to Jakkoin, and it is only fitting that the respectful foreigner should be aware of the nunnery's significance, so near in a way to English tales of the Princes in the Tower and yet so far.

Two beautiful Ohara maidens (Oharamae) were visiting the garden with their brother, and charmingly allowed me to take photographs of them in their unique local costume, kimonos dark in colour, sashes narrow, white cotton leggings, and white kerchiefs on their head.

It may be true, as the booklet by Abbess Chiko Komatsu declares, that in 594 Prince Shotoku dedicated Jakkoin to the memory of his father Yomei, the first Emperor to be converted to Buddhism, and himself sculpted the figure of Jizo in the Main Hall. Whatever the facts, Jakkoin has buildings of the 12th century or later (the last major restoration was that by Toyotomi Hideyori in 1603) and it belongs to the Tendai sect, which penetrated Japan only two hundred years after the death of Shotoku. The back of the Hondo dates to the 12th century, and the front to the early 17th. The figure of Kenreimonin is said to date from the 13th century, but R.A.B. Ponsonby-Fane suggests the 17th; the other sculpture is a life-sized bust of Awa-no-Naishi, one of her two loyal ladies-in-waiting.

The Shoin is Kenreimonin's living quarters, restored in the 19th century. The seven-mat northeast room has screens by Hara Zaisen. The six-mat northwest room is adorned with panel paintings of ivy arbours by Tsuji Kako. The three-mat west room has a monkey painted by Miyake Gogyo. The two eight-mat southern rooms have screens painted by Mitsunobu Tosa.

The garden seems even more evocative of the melancholy times suffered by the young Empress Dowager. Coins are thrown into the fountain here just as in Rome. A pond left of the entrance in the kokoro shape (a heart) has been hollowed next to a pine said to be a thousand years old. The recessed waterfall drops in three jumps to a small pond. A tracery of branches above the garden makes it seem dark even in summer. A shiver of inextinguishable loneliness runs down one's spine. And then you realise that everyone else has left. You are alone indeed. You look for the young stag, or for the retired Emperor. But nobody and nothing moves.

Sanzenin

It is time to retrace steps to the centre of Ohara, where one walks 1.3 kms. to the temple of Sanzenin, just before you come to the less celebrated Hosenin and Shorenin.

The story of Sanzenin began in 985, when its Main Hall (Hondo) was first built, as Ojo Gokurakuin (Temple of Rebirth in Salvation), for its builder Eshin

Ohara Village. Sanzenin

(942–1017) taught that all could achieve salvation through sincere belief in the effectual naming of Amida Buddha (Nembutsu). It became a branch of a monzeki, a temple with a royal abbot, in this case Saiun, son of the Emperor Horikawa, when in 1155 it fell under the control of the Kajii monzeki of Sakamoto. In 1698 the monzeki was transferred from Sakamoto to central Kyoto. The abbot lived in the Kajii Palace in Kyoto and performed important ceremonies at Sanzenin. After three years of the disestablishment of monzeki (1868–71), Ohara's Sanzenin became the headquarters of the Kajii.

Eshin's extraordinary Buddha image is unlike all previous figures, which were cut from a single block of wood. Eshin's Amida is made of thin sections of cypress wood covered with layers of cloth in such a way that the edges of the wooden pieces are covered and the surface as smooth as clay. Lacquer covering the cloth is then in turn obliterated by gold-leaf.

As you look at Amida Buddha, on the left is a smaller figure of Seishi, with hands joined in prayer, and on the right a matching figure of Kannon holding a lotus blossom to receive the soul of the departed: both are hollow and seem to be dated by the year 1148 on the black lacquer platform below the image of kneeling Seishi. A woman rubbed her prayer beads together in front of Amida as if trying to polish them clean.

The garden called Yuseien (Pure Presence) is attributed to Kanamori Sowa (1584–1656). Cypresses tower over the moss garden, from which a gardener was assiduously brushing leaves, much as a Zen gardener might rake gravel. But this is a Tendai temple, and the invocation of the name of Buddha is heard everywhere, spoken by priests and lay worshippers alike.

The Shinden in its present form is a 1926 reconstruction of a 16th-century original. The western room contains a sculpture of Fudo Myoo ascribed to Ennin (794–864), the founder of the Tendai sect, known posthumously as Jikaku Daishi. This image of the god who strikes fear into devils appears at one side of the central Amida Buddha; at the other is a Kannon (Goddess of Mercy) dated to the mid-13th century by a letter dated 1246 found when the detachble head was removed. The central room is the venue of the annual Osen Boko ceremony (30 May), designed to ensure the security of the realm and the peace of the world. The central image is that of the god of wisdom Yakushi Nyorai attributed to the priest Saicho (767–822), posthumously known first as Dengyo Hoshi then more familiarly as Dengyo Daishi. The eastern room has a raised floor on which the Emperor sat while reading the sutra during the Osen Boko festival. The air is drugged with incense, yet a powerful surge of outdoor breath is caused by a delicate rainbow rising to the ceiling. A second, fainter rainbow can just be discerned beside the entrance. These subtle screen paintings are by Shimomura Kanzan.

Butterflies hovered and darted as I sauntered to the Reception Chamber (Kyakuden), dating to 1587. Here the temple treasures are displayed. They are particularly rich and numerous because every chief abbot of Sanzenin has belonged to either the royal family itself or to the nobility. All the sliding screens were painted since 1900. The eight-mat living room has a view of dawn at Hakone by Takeuchi Seiho, the eight-mat audience room a view of plovers on the Inland Sea by Kikuchi Hobun, the eight-mat waiting-room a painting of Shaka Nyorai worshipping among pines in a mountain landscape by Suzuki Shonen. Suzuki's pupil Imao Keinen painted the turtles and lotus pond on screens in the southwestern hallway.

If you have time you can explore Hosenin, Shorenin, and the lovely 'Silent Waterfall', so called because the trickle down the 150-foot fall is so gentle that the rushing of water usually associated with such a torrent is almost entirely absent.

Noh Plays

From Ohara I took bus no. 16 en route for Sanjo-Keihan, alighting at the stop for Heian Shrine. For this was the first evening of the two annual performances of Takigi Noh (literally 'Noh Plays by Firelight'), which are vast open-air performances of traditional drama taking place on 1 and 2 June. At other times (usually Sunday mornings and afternoons) you can see Noh plays at the Kanze Kaikan (buses 46 and 206, opposite the National Museum of Modern Art) and at the Kongo Noh Theatre (subway station Shijo), and you can see unique Kyogen farces between 21–28 April at the Mibudera Temple (buses 11, 26, 28 and Shijo Omiya station on the Keifuku line).

But Bonfire Noh presents an unforgettable spectacle. Thousands of spectators pour in, those of us nearest the stage kneeling or crouching, those farther back sitting on chairs, those farthest of all standing almost out of earshot. Many follow the ancient plays with the aid of a written text, while foreigners rely on a useful synopsis printed in the free *Kyoto Monthly Guide*.

The stage was hung around with strips of white paper for good luck as in all Shinto shrines. As we waited for the performance to being at 5.30, ladies greeted each other effusively, bowing and smiling, men were chuckling, schoolchildren giggling in a fever of expectation. This is to Japanese drama what the Open Air Shakespeare Theatre in Regent's Park is to English drama: the study and the classroom give way to the magic of twilight and the dreamy coo of pigeons settling down for the night, having been startled at first by the concourse.

Noh plays themselves are more like Greek tragedy, while Kyogen resemble Greek knockabout which became Plautine comedy, and mediaeval farce culminating in Spanish entremeses like those of Lope de Rueda and Cervantes, the Italian *commedia dell'arte*, the French farce of Feydeau, the farces on the English stage associated with Robertson Hare and later with Brian Rix.

Music and a chorus, with a chanting narrator, are allied to the use of masks and slow, dignified, stylised movement in a hieratic, stately performance which originated in the 14th century with texts credited to Kanami (1333–84) and his son Zeami (1363–1444). A Noh plot is simple, its action often slight. Some works are realistic, but the greatest embody the spirit of yugen, like all the most important concepts indefinable, but a compound of the mysterious, abstruse, haunting, profound, subtle and poetic. Donald Keene's *Twenty plays of the Nō Theatre* (1970) names *Sekidera Komachi* by Zeami as the supreme example of yugen in Noh.

Kanami was a Shinto priest at the Kasuga Shrine in Nara, and an actor. Shogun Toshimitsu was attracted not only by Kanami's acting, but also by his young son Zeami, whose status was transformed from that of a temple hanger-on to court favourite, producer and writer. Or perhaps it would be more accurate to define him as a compiler, for the brief Noh texts are almost invariably taken from existing poetic models (*Manyoshu*) or prose (*Heike Monogatari*). Not only is the language chanted in a particularly mysterious manner, but the hauntingly poetic atmosphere, dehumanised by masques

Heian Shrine. Open-air Noh Festival

and stylised movement, combines with the crackle of burning tinder beside the stage and the rhythmic throaty 'yo–o–o' of the chorus to produce an aesthetic experience which is altogether incomparable.

The first play, *Arashiyama*, shows a courtier on his way to Arashiyama to admire the cherry blossoms, and an old man he meets on the way. Later the old man returns in his true guise as the god who protects cherry trees, and praises the evanescent beauty of the blossoms. The second play, *Tamura*, is also set in Kyoto. A priest visits Kiyomizudera and talks with a child gardener. The priest recites the Lotus Sutra all night, until the 'boy' now seen in his form as Tamura, the founder of the temple, appears and tells of the divine aid he had received from Kannon, the deity of mercy sometimes shown masculine but more often feminine.

After the lighting of the bonfires at seven, the Noh play *Hagoromo* ('Feather-Mantle') is performed. A fisherman finds a celestial dancer's robe, a feather-mantle, hanging on a bough. She asks for its return, but he says he is going to take it home, relenting only when she offers to teach him her heavenly dance and its meaning. The angel, having explained and performed this dance, gradually vanishes like a mountain hidden in mist, an element clearly relating Noh to the purely religious dances which it largely superseded.

Next, as light relief, follows a Kyogen play, *Ka-Zumo*, in which a nobleman asks his servant Taro to find him a sumo-wrestler with whom to compete. Taro brings back a fighter with a face like a mosquito's and the nobleman is vanquished, apparently by a sting. Taro, who is using to comic effect all the mannerisms of a sumo referee, now fans the mosquito wrestler away, and his lord wins the match to uproarious laughter.

According to Toraaki (d. 1662), the priest Gene (1269–1350), who lived in one of the monasteries on Mount Hiei, wrote the first 59 Kyogen plays, cunningly weaving crazy speeches and jokes into matter for spiritual edification and praise of Buddha. But it is now recognised that Toraaki was guilty of inventing spurious ancestry for these interludes, knowing that as he wrote them down for the first time, between 1638 and 1642, they would be read more eagerly if they could be proved ancient.

The last play, *Aoi-no-Ue*, is also the name of the wife of Genji in *Genji Monogatari*, and the theme is jealousy. We are deliberately kept in doubt as to whether the apparition of her rival, Princess Rokujo, and subsequently her demonic form (hannya), are to be considered objective realities or simply figments of Aoi's furious jealousy.

The following night, Bonfire Noh opened with *Yoro*, played by the Kanze Company, founded as its name suggests by the Kanami family which has been performing Noh since the 14th century. An imperial envoy, sent to investigate reports that a miraculous spring gushes forth at a spring called Yoro, encounters an old woodcutter and his son. Hearing that the water is an elixir of youth, the envoy is about to return to the capital when a mountain god appears and dances.

Atsumori (by Zeami, played here by the Kongo family) opens with the words of a priest Rensei: 'Life is a dream and illusion; he only is awake who casts the world aside'. He was once a warrior, who in a famous battle killed the young Atsumori. A party of reapers pass by playing on the flute, and a young reaper stays to talk with Rensei. He then stands revealed as Atsumori himself.

Hajitomi (played by the Kanze family) is another charming dream play. A priest, performing a service for flowers used in Buddhist ceremonies, is presented with moon-flowers (Yugao) by a lady afterwards recognised as a mistress of Lord Genji, Lady Yugao. She dances in recollected joy at the time she spent in this world with Genji. At dawn, her vision recedes and the priest awakes.

Kuchimane (performed by the Okura Troupe) is a Kyogen interlude in which a master tells his servant Taro to invite someone to drink with. Taro brings a

Noh masks shop

rude, quarrelsome neighbour and the master, to avoid Taro's replying offensively to the obnoxious guest, tells Taro to imitate his own way of speaking. This Taro does, mimicking his master mercilessly, to the endless amusement of actors and audience. Akira Shigeyama is the young star of Kyogen, with dazzling verbal and physical technique.

The evening ended with the Noh play *Momiji-Gari*, played by the Kanze family. A court lady and many attendants visit a mountain to view maple trees. Koreshige of the Taira clan comes across them and strikes up an acquaintance, being plied with wine until he passes out. While sleeping he dreams that he receives a divine sword and when he wakes up he finds the 'court lady' in her true guise as an evil demon. He overcomes her with the sword.

Heian Shrine

At other times of the year you can see other great spectacles in the great open-air courtyard and elsewhere in the Heian Shrine: the court dances and music

Gagaku (Court dance drama)

performed in the style known as Gagaku; a confectionery exhibition every November; a flower-arrangement exhibition once a month; a monthly tea ceremony at Choshintei tea pavilion in the Western Garden; the majestic tea ceremony commemorating the enshrinement of the spirit of Emperor Komei on 19 October; and the Jidai Matsuri ('Festival of the Ages'), a glorious procession of historical costume, on 22 October.

Stout vermilion-lacquered pillars and green roof-tiles linger in the memory; it hardly matters, in this vast majesty, that the Shrine is as new as 1895 and its expansion as recent as 1938. The Japanese genius for restoration never impressed more notably than in this Shrine, where four great gardens provide cherry blossoms every spring, irises and water-lilies every summer, bush-clover and maples every autumn, and a tracery and blanket of snow every winter.

Kiyomizudera

So many years ago that I choose to forget how many, a young Englishman marched out of hilly Perugia before dawn, to arrive at the heights of Francis' Assisi on the stroke of noon. The last mile of this ascent was recalled to my

Heian Shrine in winter

mind by the ascent from Kiyomizumichi (the stop on loop bus route 206 from Kyoto Station) to the Monastery of Clear Water (Kiyomizudera).

The way up is steep, but not too precipitous to take one's attention from one's fellow-pilgrims or from the tiny shops crowded on both sides of the road. Mystery rises with the mist up the hillside called Otowa, the Sound of Feathers. What can induce so many, at all hours of the day, from young schoolchildren to aged, bent crones, to climb up 'Teapot Lane' to this huge temple complex?

Legend has it that the Nara priest Enchin, of the Hosso sect, was told in a vision to 'look for the spring of clear water which is the source of the Kizu river'. While searching, he came across a glade in the hillside where a fall gushed fresh water. An old man gave Enchin a log immersed in the spirit of the bodhisattva Kannon, and this log Enchin carved in the image of Kannon and set in a thatched hut in the heart of what is now Kiyomizudera. A famous Noh play (*Tamura*) deals with a variant of the parallel legend in which the samurai Tamura hunted and killed a stag on Mount Otowa for blood which he thought would alleviate his wife's pains in giving birth. He met Enchin, who reprimanded him sternly for taking life and exhorted him to worship Kannon at the site of the clear waters. Tamura and his wife both became devotees of Kannon, and paid for the building of the first sanctuary.

History is – as usual – less romantic. The temple actually dates from 798, its nucleus consisting of the Shishinden of the Imperial Palace from Nagaoka, and thus predating the capital status of Kyoto. Kiyomizudera burned down on many occasions, and most of the present buildings are no older than the restoration by the Shogun Tokugawa Iemitsu in 1633. Though these edifices are of great intrinsic interest, the horde of trudging visitors are on their way up Mount Otowa for the glorious panorama over Kyoto from Kiyomizudera's verandah at the entrance to the Main Hall. A dancing-stage (butai) is flanked by two wings running the whole length of the hall, and here is the view across the city of Kyoto from east to west, with Arashiyama in the far distance. Look down: a leafy valley in the foreground and the patient queue for long wooden spoons to dip in the clear-water basin and drink. Coins are tossed by the pious into the basin while they pray to Fudo, the god who overcomes demons. This is the sixteenth temple of 33 in the Western Japan pilgrimage route devoted to Kannon, the so-called Saikoku Sanjusan Sho. The Kiyomizu-style Kannon in the Main Hall has eleven faces, 'a thousand arms' and 'a thousand eyes'. It is unique in that two of the arms extend above the image's serene head, almost touching each other in a gesture of completeness. A bodhisattva such as Kannon is however theologically incomplete by nature, since she has renounced Buddhahood in the interests of saving others, remaining within the life-and-death cycle.

In total contrast to the timeless majesty of Kiyomizudera's Kannon, scrutinise the votive tablets commissioned from famous painters. The four most significant are all concerned with maritime trade, and were donated

106

around 1634 with the specific mission of ensuring 'a calm sea and a prosperous voyage' for three ships of the Sueyoshi family and one of the Suminokura house. In the last, you can make out negro and European sailors, the focal point being a festival dance on the ship's deck.

No photograph can sum up the extraordinary diversity of this temple, with its roots in the animism of Shinto and its history so closely linked to that of Buddhist Kyoto. While Buddhist roofs are normally tiled, and Shinto roofs are usually shingled, this Buddhist temple has a shingled roof, yet nobody seems surprised. Though all Hosso temples but one are in Nara, this one is in Kyoto – devotees of all sects come here, very often with a view to praying for an easy childbirth in the family.

The three most impressive gates of Kiyomizudera are worth a study in themselves. Niomon (Gate of the Two Kings) has a roof of cypress bark and is surrounded by cherry trees. It is protected by the Japanese ideas of the Hindu Gods Indra and Brahma, four metres high and called 'Diamond Warriors'. It is believed that one image, with its mouth wide open, is saying 'a', the first sound in Sanskrit phonetics, while the other, with its mouth closed, is saying 'om', the last, thus expressing much the same entirety as the Biblical 'I am the alpha and omega'. Niomon is of Muromachi date. Saimon (West Gate) is later – of the Momoyama period – and it too is protected by the two god-kings of Hinduism, adopted into Buddhist belief as protectors of Buddha. Its tall elegance is memorable. Todorokimon (Roaring Gate) is the middle gate, with god-kings protecting east and west, eight gate-pillars and three ridge-poles to support the tiled roof. Look for the washing-basin named for the owl design on the sides, and its splendidly ferocious dragon, spouting water instead of traditional fire. Incidentally, the 'roaring' in the name of the gate refers to the echoing of the teachings of Buddha, and might better be translated 'resounding' or 'trumpeting' in this context.

At all costs spend time in the historic Amida Hall, where Honen, founder of the Jodo or 'Pure Land' sect, on 15 May 1188 for the first time proclaimed the teaching of Nembutsu as a distinct doctrine within the Buddhist family. The charming Shakado (Hall of Shakyamuni Buddha) encloses figures dating to the Kamakura epoch (1185–1382). Behind and between the Amidado and Shakado stands the pathetic Hyakutai Jizoson (Hall of a Hundred Jizo Figures), where about 180 sculptures of Jizo, patron saint of travellers, children and pregnant women, are hungrily inspected by bereaved parents. It is said that they will be sure to find one Jizo figure in the image of their dead child, and, once identified, the double of their child will offer solace and comfort.

Sanjunoto (1633) is the largest three-storey pagoda in Japan, exemplifying the majesty of early Edo architecture. Within stands an image of Dainichi Nyorai (Great Buddha of the Sun). Contemporary is the Kyodo or Sutra Hall,

◁ Votive plaques or *ema*, sold and displayed at Kiyomizudera with the temple scripture library, three Shakyamuni sculptures, and a coiled dragon painted on the ceiling. The graceful Kaisando (Founder's Hall) is an original feature of the temple, dating to Tamura's patronage in the eleventh century, and exhibits figures of the ascetic Gyoei, and the priest Enchin. The Jishinin is a separate temple also known as the Zuigudo from the image of Daizuigi Bosatsu; it is associated with Toyotomi Hideyoshi, who worshipped Daizuigu Kannon, the Goddess of Mercy, flanked here by Bishamon and Juichimon.

Nearby is the separate Shinto shrine of Jishu Gongen, founded about 798 but rebuilt with the rest of Kiyomizudera in 1633. Stone koma-inu (mythical beasts not dissimilar in aspect from lions) provided by worshippers and patrons line the steps up to the Honden (Main Sanctuary) and Haiden

Kiyomizudera. The balcony and view

(Oratory). All kinds of charms are on sale: for love, success in examinations, easy delivery, good health, long life, and wisdom. You can buy amulets for luck in money, luck in marriage, or safety in traffic. I tried my own luck at the 'Fortune-Telling Stones' set ten yards apart. You must start from one, and walk in a straight line to the other with your eyes closed. If you go past it without touching, or veer away, the saying is that you will be unhappy in love. After twenty years of blissfully happy married life I expected to pass the test but, though sober, I found my balance affected in some odd way and missed the target by a foot. An Australian lady cheated blatantly by opening her eyes at every second step.

Nanzenji

Nanzenji and the related Eikando to the north lie within the precincts of the original detached villa built by the former Emperor Kameyama, who ruled from 1260 to 1274. Kameyama's period forms the backdrop to *The Confessions of Lady Nijo*, which also describes events and personalities in the life of his brother GoFukakusa, whom Kameyama succeeded at the age of eleven. Kameyama, a puppet-ruler in the hands of Hojo Tokimune, was succeeded by his own son GoUda and in 1289 received the tonsure and the new name Kongogen. He died in 1304, but not before he had summoned Fumon, a priest from Tofukuji, to exorcise evil spirits from his villa. Fumon was now given part of the precincts, which became the temple of Eikando.

Kameyama now himself carried some earth for the construction of the Nanzenin, in the heart of the detached villa which was transformed into the temple of Nanzenji. It became the headquarters of the Nanzenji school of the Rinzai Zen sect, its unpainted wood and whitewashed plaster exemplifying the Zen precepts of purity and simplicity. I passed the priests' living quarters and a young bamboo grove before seeing the splendid dry garden of raked gravel, reminiscent of Ryoanji except for the intrusive paved stones left and right. This, like the other garden nearby, is reliably ascribed to Enshu Kobori (1579–1647). The Main Hall is of the present century, its predecessor having burned down in 1895. The Hojo (Abbot's Quarters) by contrast was once the Seiryoden of the Imperial Palace brought here in 1611. The smaller suite of rooms were removed here from the Fushimi Castle of Hideyoshi. The striking paintings on the fusuma by the Kano school include a brilliant diptych, 'Tigers in a Bamboo Grove', by Tanyu Kano, the bamboos dominating a tiger on the right screen and a prowling tiger lapping water at the edge of the left screen. Tigers symbolize physical strength and bamboo moral strength.

Now look for the Crane-Tortoise Garden of the Konchiin, still part of this immense temple compound (ask for 'Tsuru-kame-no-niwa'). Looking across the gravel the fanciful claim to discern the shape of a tortoise in the tree and shrub formation on the left, and a crane on the right. This is the other Enshu garden of the sixteenth century. To find a fourteenth-century garden, attributed to Muso Kokushi (1275–1351), ask for the Nanzenin. A leaf descended silently on to my left shoulder, and I recalled wryly Hirohide Ogawa's sardonic criticism of the restless mind: 'He gives up with insufficient cherry blossom on his shoulders'.

Memories I cherish from Nanzenji are pigeons, the fragrance of pines, incense burning in front of the Main Hall, a painting of a poet in a landscape, ten-yen coins stuffed into cracks and fissures in the Main Hall, and the calling of a frog.

> *Hey, frog, can you*
> *remember my friend*
> *Basho?*

How is it possible to have an empty mind, if there is no mind to be empty?

Ginkakuji

You can reach Jishoji, commonly known as Ginkakuji, the Temple of the Silver Pavilion, from Kyoto Station by the no. 5 bus to Iwakura; or on either of the loops: 203 from Hakubaicho or 204 from Kitaoji.

I had spent some minutes enthralled by the din of a pachinko amusement arcade, the garish lights on the pinball machines in such hair-raising contrast to the contemplative mood induced by temple-visiting that one seems to be not merely in a different city but on another planet. There are over ten thousand such arcades in Japan, and whatever hour of the day or night you enter them, there seems to be hardly a vacant seat, as though the Japanese played all day, played all night, working, eating and sleeping at hours that I have never come across. Generally speaking, pachinko is played by the less successful, or by younger men (far fewer girls are in evidence); the more sophisticated tend to play mah-jong after work, usually in restaurants.

My 203 bus passed a sign off left to the British Council, and the public-address tape soon announced 'Ginkaku-ji-michi'. I alighted, saying thank you (*arigato gozaimashita*) to the impassive driver, who bowed his head.

On the way you can admire the little temple called Jodoin (all that is left of the huge Tendai Jodoji complex after the eighth-century conflagration) or the strolling-garden at Hakusasonso Villa designed by the painter Hashimoto Kansetsu in 1915, open 10–5, admission price ¥400.

The Silver Pavilion itself often proves a disappointment at first glance, especially if the visitor has not yet realised that the silver coating of the pavilion once planned was never actually executed.

If you have enjoyed the Golden Pavilion of the Ashikaga Shogun Yoshimitsu, you will want to explore the buildings and gardens created in emulation by his grandson Yoshimasa (1435–90), when he retired from government in 1482. Originally a country villa, taking up part of the grounds of Jodoji, it was transformed into a Zen temple on the retired Shogun's death. The city of Kyoto was virtually razed to the ground by the internecine struggles of the Onin Wars, yet Yoshimasa took as little heed as Louis XIV did of the starving Parisians when building the great palace and gardens of Versailles.

The reputation of the Ashikaga clan has been rightly likened to that of the twelve Caesars so accurately and virulently characterised by the gossipy Suetonius. Yoshimasa turned his buildings to face the peaceful eastern mountain, Higashiyama, away from wartorn Kyoto. But most of them were razed in decades of continuing conflict: the tea-ceremony pavilion, and wooden kiosks for incense connoisseurship, moon-viewing, and for the composition of poems. The only two structures remaining in the 17th century were the 'Silver' Pavilion itself and the Togudo. Then Toyomori Miyagi and his family helped to restore Jishoji: in 1615 it was complete in much the state that we see it today, though it has benefited from constant renewal of decaying wood over the centuries.

Ginkakuji. The Silver Pavilion

Essentially an aesthete's country palace, Jishoji combines the simplicity of Zen with the trappings of wealth and power in a manner that we can only define as thoroughly Japanese. So closely is this Higashiyama culture bound up with Zen in the art of the tea ceremony that Dojinsai, at Togudo, became the model for all future tea pavilions.

The main gate is reached along an avenue of pines and oaks. Once inside, you might be in a carefully-manicured western garden except for bamboo fences above stone walls and below neatly-trimmed pines and camellias.

Many visitors are enchanted by the karesansui garden distinguished by two sand shapes. Ginshadan ('Silver Sand Beach') imitates the West Lake (Seiko in Japanese) near Hangchow in China. Kogetsudai, on the other hand, is a tall sand formation intended to give the impression of a mountain glittering silver under the visiting moon. The garden is greatly influenced by that of Saihoji, and Soami the Zen priest is said to have contributed to its design as well as to that of Ryoanji – remember to look for his fusuma landscape paintings in the Hojo of Daisenin at Daitokuji.

The 'Silver' Pavilion itself consists of two storeys: the lower for living in, now with an image of the god of children Jizo, and the upper ecclesiastical in tone, containing a gilt figure of Kannon carved by Unkei in the 13th century.

As at the Kinkakuji, the building is surmounted by a phoenix, the bird which protected Buddha while he was meditating. The play of white, brown and green of encircling trees is reflected in the still pond. In winter the double roof of the pavilion glints solid white against the brilliant tracery of leaves and branches; in summer moonlight the sand gardens seem like snow illuminated; in summer daylight a sudden radiance of the sun can mimic a transfiguring snowstorm. The mind dances easily among the seasons as birds dart effortlessly from branch to path and back again.

The Japanese anthropomorphic view of landscape is that water resembles blood, trees flesh and rock bone, but at the top of the hill, where we look down on the phoenix, soil has been washed down from bare trees, exposing roots which are more like bone than are the very rocks.

The Hondo and its gate date from the Kanei period (1624–44). The Hondo is said to be reconstructed very closely on the model of the original main hall. Of its four rooms, the western has fusuma with delightful bird paintings by Yosa Buson (1716–83), while the middle and eastern have paintings of celebrated sages by Buson's friend Ike-no-Taiga (1723–76). The fourth room's small altar is dedicated to Shakyamuni Buddha.

The Togudo has two rooms. The first once held three Buddha images, but these have since been replaced by a lifesize figure of Yoshimasa as a priest. Behind it you will find the prototypical tea-room, the Dojinsai ('Friendly Abstinence'), where Shuko and Soami passed the tradition of tea to the next generation. The alcove (tokonoma, literally 'room for a bed') has fusuma rather than the solid wall which later became the norm.

If you want to see what a pavilion for incense parties looked like, examine the Roseitei, a two-room kiosk just to the north of Togudo.

In the second garden, look for the turtles on White Crane Island, set in Brocade Mirror Pond. This ensemble forms a fine contrast to the dry landscape garden nearer the Hondo.

Shisendo

Five minutes walk from the Ichijoji-Sagarimatsu bus stop you can find the temple of Shisendo (Poets' Hall), so called from the portraits of thirty-six immortal Chinese poets (a theme known as 'Sanjuroku Kasen') by Tanyu Kano. The list of poets was compiled in the early 11th century by Fujiwara Kinto and the theme was well-known by the 13th century. This version by

Shisendo

Tanyu combines decorative costumes, calligraphy with a high literary value, and painterly skill. They are no more true portraits than are the crude wood-cuts in Koberger's Nuremberg Chronicle, but what a gulf of sensibility separates the two modes of stylization! The idealized figures are set asymmetrically in a field of space, where the calligraphy does not intrude as much as inhabit, breathing gently in curved characters or nervously in angular strokes.

Tanyu himself, to quote Ernest Fenollosa, 'the great genius of the sixth generation of the Kano family, leaped into rapid prominence soon after 1630 by absorbing, consolidating and extending the new method of work outlined by his teacher, Koi. He made Koi's blurry passages more blurry, and at the same time less muddy.' Again, 'Here was a man, fecund as Sesshu and Motonobu, whose impressionism recalled, without scholarship or deep belief, the refinement of the Ashikagas, an antidote for Yeitoku's vulgarity, a sort of marvellous idealism, whose merit lay chiefly in its aesthetic charm.'

The temple itself, created in 1631 by the poet-recluse Jozan Ishikawa (1583–1672), lies north of Ginkakuji and possesses a charming white sand garden here illustrated. In spring you will be enchanted by azaleas, and in autumn by maples. The garden is of the yarimizu type, that is to say a strolling-garden with running water, and is the more enjoyable in that it is never visited by regular garden tours.

Manshuin

Neither is the 17th-century dry garden of Manshuin, roughly equidistant between Shisendo and Shugakuin. You can reach it from the Shugakuin rail station on the Keifuku line or by bus (allow 15 minutes' walk from the stop at Ichijoji-Shimizucho).

Manshuin has fusuma by Tanyu Kano, whose versatility you will have come to appreciate, in the three-room Koshoin (Little Study). Kobori Masakazu (1579–1647), also called Enshu, founded the Enshu-ryu school of tea and under the patronage of Prince Yoshihisa created the karesansui garden of the Daishoin (Great Study) and the eight-window teahouse. Originally sited close to Kinkakuji, the Tendai temple was transferred here by Yoshihisa in 1656 and, though it fell into ruins after the Meiji Restoration, it has been brilliantly restored since World War II. The garden has two 'islands' and two 'waterfalls' and is particularly beautiful in spring and autumn.

Shugakuin Imperial Villa

Shugakuin Imperial Villa may only be visited with prior permission (free of charge) from the Imperial Household Agency, which is situated inside the compound of the former Imperial Palace in Central Kyoto. You can request a guided tour (in Japanese only) starting at 9, 10 or 11 a.m. or 1.30 or 3 p.m. Unless you are staying very close to the Villa, you should really not aim for the 9 a.m. tour, for there is a fifteen-minute walk either from the Shugakuin

Rikyumichi bus stop (route 5 between Kyoto Eki and Iwakura) or Shugakuin rail station (Keifuku line).

Emperor GoMinoo ruled between 1612–29. He was compelled by Tokugawa Hidetada to marry the latter's daughter and, when their child was seven, GoMinoo abdicated in the girl's favour and built a simple palace in 1630, which you can now explore for it was transformed into the temple Entsuji, accessible by walking from the no. 4 bus terminus at Midorogaike.

This small palace eventually became inadequate and when, in 1655, he visited his daughter Ume, a nun at Enshoji in the foothills of Mount Hiei, he fell in love with the landscape and petitioned the Edo Government to transfer Enshoji to Nara and to finance a new, larger palace.

The complex created between 1656 and 1659 comprised the Lower Villa and Upper Villa, in Japanese respectively Shimonochaya and Kaminochaya. Then, in 1688, a palace was built in the vast grounds for Princess Akenomiya, eleventh daughter of ex-Emperor GoMinoo; when she chose to become a nun, the place was converted into a temple and known as Rinkyuji. With the Middle Garden (Nakanochaya), and the Onari Gate, Rinkyuji and Kyakuden form the Middle Villa. Kyakuden ('Reception Hall') was transferred here from the palace of GoMinoo's consort Tofukumonin after her death in 1678.

The three villas are entirely separate in situation and character, and their gardens reflect this diversity, as you climb forty metres up, stage by stage, from the foot of the slope.

You enter the Lower Villa through Omotesomon, a simple gate of polished bamboo, then through Chumon. Try to visualise the stately aspect of the Wankyokukaku, a two-storey building which originally overlooked the paddy-fields (still being worked today) in the south-east corner of the Lower Villa, an area now overgrown. You now come to Jugetsukan, past two stone lanterns: 'Sleeve' or 'Crocodile Mouth' on the island, and 'The Korean' where the ramp starts. Jugetsukan is a careful reconstruction dated about 1820 of the original imperial apartments. Note the tablet with calligraphy attributed to GoMinoo himself below the eaves of the first of four rooms. Three of the fifteen mats are raised as the emperor's dais. The fusuma have an ink painting of 'Three Laughing Sages at Kokei' attributed to Kishi Ku, also known as Ganku (c.1749–1838), but as he was the founder of a school this may be by a pupil.

The twelve-mat second room is attractively simple in décor and proportion, bearing no resemblance to any royal palace that we know in the west, with wooden ceiling, paper windows, and mat floor in sober shades of white and brown. On one side you find a 4½-mat ante-room and a 10½-mat entrance-room. A five-mat room is believed to have been used by the Emperor's consort.

Emerging from the back gate of the Lower Villa, intimate rather than imperial, we are faced with the contrast of tree-covered mountains, and a pine-flanked path. The guided tour bears right to the Middle Villa, and we pass through two distinctive gates into Rakushiken (Abode of Bliss), named on a nageshi-board above the sliding-doors of the six-mat first room, which boasts a lovely painting by Tanshin Kano (1653–1718), son of Tanyu, depicting cherry blossoms on Mount Yoshino. The second room has a splendid wall-painting of autumn on the banks of the Tatsuta river, again the work of Tanshin. The Kyakuden (Reception Hall) is distinguished by a number of outstanding works of art. The ten-mat second room, for instance, shows lake landscapes in all four seasons. The delicately-proportioned ornamental recess and 'Shelf of Mist' bears poems describing the eight most beautiful views of Shugakuin as chosen in 1658. Hirozumi Sumiyoshi (called Gukei, 1631–1705) is credited with the amusing Gion Festival floats painted on four wooden panels, as well as the marvellous carp on two others. The story goes that the carp were painted so vividly that they escaped from the room every night to swim in the pond outside, until in the eighteenth century Okyo Maruyama added nets to enmesh them, since when they have been trapped.

In the temple of Rinkyu, a polychrome statue of the nun-founder gazes impassively at the passer-by.

We wended our way uphill, past old women in wide straw hats who were bent double hedging and ditching. Other women have cleared up by their manual labour all the débris of the floating world: paths are swept tidy; hedges are clipped straight as rail-tracks; they even seem to startle away stray birds that would disturb the symmetry of padi-fields.

The Upper Villa, you expect, will have the finest views and the finest garden: your expectation is fulfilled. Its pond was created by damming mountain streams and a tributary of the river Otowa, which has been transformed into a waterfall. Silt has formed a ridge which has been cut at intervals to form artificial islands. The pond's perimeter has been decked with pavilions like the reconstructed Rinuntei, 'Next to the Clouds', 150 metres above sea-level, with a view that would be hard to surpass at any season, especially in autumn. Kyusuitei may have been repaired in 1824, but in all essentials it is indistinguishable from the original, created in the late 1650s to celebrate the cult of tea. Of the two waterfalls, the Male is found descending from Rinuntei, and the Female at the southeastern corner of the pond. The art of 'borrowing a landscape' (itself borrowed from China as the name *chieh ching* shows) was widely practised by successive emperors, but most examples have not survived the centuries, and Shugakuin has now the finest 'borrowed landscape' to be seen in 'these horned islands'.

> *By Miho Isle, I step on springy moss,*
> *touch gnarled pine-bark,*
> *and hear behind my back*
> *carp rising at a ripple's edge.*

Enryakuji

The visit to the Tendai stronghold of Enryakuji takes half a day, and is best combined as an afternoon following a morning at Shugakuin, whence you return to the rail station of the same name on the Keifuku line, to the terminus at Yaseyuen. Transfer to the cable railway to Hiei, then to another from Hiei to Eizan-Sancho, a short walk bringing you to the Shimeigadake observation platform with a marvellous view southwestward over Kyoto and eastward over Lake Biwa.

Since nature spirits (kami in Japanese) were thought to be especially powerful in deep forests, wide lakes and high mountains (Hiei, at 850 metres, is the second highest mountain in Japan), it was logical that Mount Hiei would become a centre for Shinto worship, and even now you can find Hie Shrine and Toshogu Shrine near Sakamoto, on the eastern side of Mount Hiei.

Buddhism, as always, adapted what it could from superstitions, such as the devil's particularly potent influence, from the northeast, so Mount Hiei had to be fortified with religious buildings to protect the capital. The priest Saicho (767–822) was born between Hiei and Lake Biwa and, becoming disillusioned with the teachings of Gyohyo at Omi and Nara Buddhism (after being ordained there at Todaiji), he returned to Hiei and built a grass hut for meditation. He sang:

> *Oh Buddhas*
> *of unsurpassed enlightenment,*
> *bestow your invisible aid*
> *on this my poor hut*
> *on the mountain peak.*

At this time (the year is 788), what is now Kyoto was undrained marshland, and it has been speculated that the Emperor Kammu's suspicion of the moral decline and secular ambitions of the Nara Buddhist communities headed by Todaiji was reinforced by Saicho's reformist zeal in the creation of the new Heian-kyo. Certainly Kammu realised that he needed Buddhist support, and equally surely he was determined to reduce the power of Nara. What he could not have envisaged was that communities of warrior monks formed and trained on Mount Hiei would prove an even greater threat to imperial power and stability between the eleventh and sixteenth centuries.

Since China was at least indirectly the spiritual fatherland of Japanese Buddhism, Kammu sent Saicho to China in 804 to master the doctrines of the T'ien-t'ai sect, the school which corresponded roughly to the Mahayana stream of Buddhism. The Nara sects (if we except Kegon) had drawn their teachings from secondary sources such as the commentaries while Saicho's Tendai teachings followed the Buddha's own words as recorded in such key works as the Lotus Sutra. Quite simply, Hosso and other Nara sects taught hierarchical and aristocratic Buddhism, in the sense that some people are denied Buddhist perfection by their innate faults, whereas Tendai claims that each of us can attain the four stages of enlightenment.

In 805 Saicho returned from Japan, bearing documents to legitimise his monastery, called Ichijo Shikanin from its foundation in 788 until 823, when the main hall was renamed Enryakuji, after the name of the period during which the temple had been built. Despite a time of Shingon ascendancy shortly after Saicho's death, Tendai Buddhism gradually became stronger and kept a standing pseudo-priestly army to maintain its position of authority on Mount Hiei and over Heian-kyo. The Emperor GoShirakawa was heard to say: 'There are three things I cannot control: the waters of the Kamo river, a throw of dice, and the bonzes on the Mountain.' Finally, in 1571, General Oda Nobunaga took his troops to annihilate the warrior-priests, burn their three thousand temples, and destroy all evidence of their existence. When visiting Enryakuji, therefore, it should be remembered that all the buildings post-date this carnage of 1571. Reconstruction of a hundred and twenty temples or so took place under Toyotomi Hideyoshi (1536–98) and his successors.

But the secluded calm, idyllic birdsong, and quiet temples lying among fern and cypress in the mountain forests must be met in the knowledge of sedition, murder, and revenge against heresy that make Emmanuel Le Roy Ladurie's *Montaillou* (three decades of hatred between Cathars and Catholics in a French village) seem positively trivial. As you stand in a quiet corner of the Shakado, do not forget how Tendai monks burned the printing blocks of the works of Honen (founder of the Jodo sect) as quickly as they could be carved, over three centuries. While you are pleasantly entranced by incense wafting from the altar of Amidado, recall how Tendai warriors slaughtered more than four thousand Nichiren priests in 1536 and destroyed all their twenty-one temples in Kyoto. Fearsome indeed were these apostles of the Compassionate One! At Jodoin, site of Saicho's tomb, I discoursed with his shade, his phantom, whether he would gladly have given up his teachings if foresight had shown him the carnage his followers would wreak on their fellow-creatures. Thus I thought in Bethlehem, and in Umar ibn al-Khattab's mosque in Dumat al-Jandal. Thus too at that church door in Wittenberg where Luther's theses had once been nailed.

Tendai metaphysics will seem strangely modern to Western physicists coming to grips with the seeming non-entity of the smallest particles. Tendai recognises a mirror, for instance, as 'chu', or 'what is in the middle', the 'thing-in-itself, the Sanskrit *dharmakaya*; it recognises the brightness characteristic of the mirror as 'ku', the Void, 'nothingness'; and whatever is reflected in the mirror as 'ka', appearances. But each of the three characteristics of the mirror is dependent for existence on the existence of the other two. Nothing else can exist apart from whatever touches it or is affected by it. That is why a Tendai teacher would argue that Buddha's existence and properties could be deduced from a grain of sand, and the Universe could be deduced from any single aspect of its nature, however infinitesimal.

If approaching from the west side of the mountain, you will come first to Sannoin, a seventeenth-century reconstruction of the temple devoted to Sanno, or Hie or Hiyoshi, all Buddhist names for the Shinto ruler and god Onamuji. The temple therefore clearly assumes the rights and duties of a

Shinto shrine. Onamuji was a governor of the sixteen southwestern provinces of Honshu.

Next, after a steep walk downhill, you will find Jodoin, originally built by Saicho to accommodate his own figure of Amida now in the Hondo, and it is here that Saicho is buried, in a building north of the Hondo. The present Jodoin is, however, recent. Most notable is the practice of 'sweeping'. Priests staying at Jodoin are required after early morning prayer to sweep the grounds and the buildings for at least six hours, inducing a trance-like fatigue. The aim is to offer menial service for the Buddha and for one's fellow-men in a literal and metaphorical way. The ritual cleanliness demanded in Shinto is subsumed in this duty, carried out in silence.

You are now heading along forest paths to the Western Precinct, which has its own discreet car- and coach-park. Do not be astonished by the irruption of a hundred identically-uniformed schoolchildren with scrubbed faces, picnic satchels, and high-pitched voices. They are not calling you a hero: it is just that 'Hero!' is the nearest a Japanese child can get to 'Hello!'

Enryakuji's western precinct is dominated physically and spiritually by Shakado, 'Shaka' being in Japanese the historical Buddha whose image, by Saicho, is never revealed; you may see instead a copy standing in front of it. This building is older than the others, for it did not suffer the wrath of Nobunaga. At the time of Nobunaga's revenge it was the Hondo of the temple of Onjoji, south of Hiei. When Hideyoshi authorised the rebuilding of Enryakuji, he caused Onjoji's thirteenth-century Hondo to be dismantled and carried up the mountainside where it became the historic nucleus of the new monastery.

Shakado has a large, impressive interior. I sat down at a polite distance from a group of worshippers on the raised wooden floor, gazing towards the sunken stone floor used by the priests in the centre of which is a raised altar with images of Buddha and the four guardian kings. Three lanterns in front of the altar, like three crests on the pole near the entrance, bear the imperial chrysanthemum with sixteen petals, an emblem believed to have been taken from the monastery. The lanterns, lit by Saicho, are said never to have been extinguished, but it is hard to imagine their sputtering and flickering through the devastation of 1571.

Flanking the path down to Shakado are Jogyodo on the left and Hokkedo on the right, joined by a covered passage. It is said that the twelfth-century warrior monk Benkei, faithful follower of Yoshitsune Minamoto (1159–89), lifted both temples by raising the passage between them and that they have since been known as Ninaido (Burdens Hall)!

Priests read the Lotus Sutra in Hokkedo while walking ('Hokke' being Japanese for 'Lotus') and meditate while sitting. Room for constant walking is provided by the bareness of the temple, with only Buddha's attendant Fugen, patron of those who practise the ecstatic contemplation called hokke-zammai. He sits on an elephant, which symbolises steadfast self-possession and transcendence. Jogyodo, likewise devoted to walking while chanting, is empty except for a gold-haloed Amida Butsu.

If you have time, explore the distant northern precinct, Yokawa, with its Chudo (Middle Hall) and Shikikodo (Lecture Hall of Four Seasons), but architecturally this is the least significant sector of Enryakuji.

Approaching the eastern precinct, you first see the high, isolated Amidado, dating from 1937, with its mortuary tablets behind the sculpture of Amida Butsu. It reminds us that Buddhism looks towards death and extinction as remorselessly as Shinto engages us in birth and marriage. 'Die that ye may live', urges the Christian. 'Achieve glorious martyrdom in *jihad*', says the Muslim. Buddhism finds its necessary balance in Japanese life with the respect for ancestors and the past embodied in Shinto and with the stress on moral and social values in Confucianism, where education and the passing of successive examinations laid the foundations not only for the great Chinese empire, and the derivative British empire, but for the concern for formal and informal education at all levels in contemporary Japanese life. It is Confucianism, coupled with Western technological development, that has made Japan the most effective and stable wealth-generating society in the world today, as well as the most polite and self-effacing.

On the little hill opposite Amidado stands Kaidanin, the first ordination hall in Japan outside Nara. The first Kaidanin was erected in 827; the present one dates from 1604. Much larger, the Daikodo (Great Lecture Hall) is the former Sambutsudo of 1634 from Sakamoto and brought here to replace the previous edifice destroyed by fire in 1956. The image of the Buddha as Patron of Scholarship, Dainichi Nyorai, is of the 17th century and comes from Mudojidani, on the Sakamoto flank of Hiei. The tiny Zentoin commemorates the place where the priest Ennin (Jikaku Daishi) lived. A pupil of Saicho, he spent nine years as a scribe and copyist in China, publishing twenty-nine different works on his return, and became chief abbot of the Tendai sect in 854.

The climax of your visit to Enryakuji comes with Komponchudo (Main Central Hall). The prototype of this great hall was the tiny building designed by Saicho to house his image of Yakushi Nyorai, the Healing Buddha, and finished in 794. In 884 it was vastly enlarged to cope with the advance of Tendai in popularity, but burned down in 935. The modern building, four times the area of Saicho's hall, dates from 1642, and is a culmination of Momoyama magnificence, tacitly repudiating the simplicity inculcated by Saicho. The darkness characteristic of Shakado deepens here, mystery accentuated by the unearthly grandeur of the religious iconography. Saicho's carving is hidden, but is represented by a copy, flanked by Nikko, Sun God, and Gekko, Moon God, the whole guarded by the four heavenly guardian kings of the four directions.

If you leave the Enryakuji complex by the gate south of Amidado, you will be able to catch a bus back to Kyoto, either to the Central Station or to Sanjo-Keihan.

Sento Palace

Even at the risk of slight inconvenience, it is advisable to visit the gardens of the former Sento Gosho (Sento Palace) on a day when you are visiting no other palace or villa. Apply with your passport in advance to the Imperial Household Agency nearby, and choose either the 11 a.m. or the 1.30 p.m. guided tour, which will be in Japanese. An illustrated album and free map help you to find your way around, but you must keep with the group. If coming by taxi, you still have a long walk from the entrance where your credentials are checked (permit and passport), so allow twenty minutes at least to find your way across the gravel beside the seemingly endless wall. By subway, alight at either Kawaramachi-Marutamachi or Karasuma-Ichijo and allow twenty-five minutes from there to your appointment, for naturally latecomers will be disappointed.

Do not imagine that you will be seeing either an ancient palace or ancient gardens. Despite the assurance in the Japan National Tourist Association leaflet that the 'stroll garden (was) designed by Kobori Enshu', who lived from 1579 to 1647, the gardens you see today date from 1747. There is a palace there, but it is not the Sento Palace built in 1630 during the reign of Emperor GoMinoo and last destroyed by fire in 1854: it is the Omiya Palace constructed in 1867 for Dowager-Empress Eisho, northwest of the Sento Palace. She left for Tokyo in 1872, and Omiya is now used only for imperial visits to Kyoto or for state guests. The latter's site is now a pine grove, though two exquisite teahouses (Yushintei and Seikatei) remain from that age to remind us of what is lost.

You do not enter Omiya Palace, so the visit is confined to the great gardens, extending over more than 90,000 square metres. Highlights include the ever-changing scenes by the North Pond, especially fine in autumn and snow-clad winter; the Pool of Akose with the bridge formed by six cut stones; a bridge laid with earth to Heron Island, and another comprising thick stones paved zigzag to force the stroller to stop and look around him at that moment; and Maple Bridge, over the channel connecting North Pond with South Pond.

South Pond is even more elaborately beautiful: it was intended as a vista for ex-Emperors living in the palace which is now a mere memory. The male waterfall is overhung with trees, contrasting in its swift fall with the indolent ripple of the female waterfall of North Pond. Islands in South Pond once bore delicate pavilions for parties, whether for moon-viewing or waterfall-viewing, but all have vanished. Seikatei, a harmonious tea pavilion at the southern end of the garden, contrasts white and brown with the predominant green beyond its walls. A rectangular pit near here served as an ice-pit in summer. The tea pavilion called Yushintei was brought here from the home of the Duke Konoe in Kyoto in 1884.

Nijo Castle

From the Sento Gosho it is a brisk twenty-minute walk, or five minutes by taxi to Nijo Castle, the entrance to which is opposite the International Hotel on Horikawadori.

Because they are so close, Shinsenen Garden and Nijo Jinya should be visited before or after Nijo Castle, whose nearest bus-stop is Nijojomae on routes 9 or 52 from Kyoto Eki or 12 from Sanjo-Keihan. At ¥450, Nijo Castle and Gardens ask the highest admission fee in Kyoto; still first-rate value. Visiting hours are 8.45 to 4, and since there is no compulsory guided tour to fix your appointment, my advice is to arrive at opening-time, before hundreds of organized coach tours descend. The Honmaru Palace is closed to visitors, so your route will be through Ninomaru palace and the gardens situated south-west of the Grand Audience Chamber (Ohiroma). *Prohibited Admittance*, proclaims a notice in Japanese and English: *Drunkards, pets and dangerous articles*. Ducks ride and watch on the moat waters, gathering noisily when a child scatters crumbs from the bridge in front of the Great East Gate. Voracious carp glitter orange, white, golden, black and greenish below the surface of the water. In the gardens we hear the querulous shriek of peacocks, kept with two peahens in a cage. Sparrows are as busy looting the ground for crumbs as in any London square. Yet we are at Nijo not for these, but for architecture, paintings, and gardens.

The imperial palaces and villas of Kyoto seem vulnerable: almost inviting intrusion. Nijo Castle, the successor to Hideyoshi's Fushimi Castle as a stronghold of the land's effective power, the Shogun Ieyasu, stands protected by turreted stone walls and moats. The imperial family, mere pawns in the power-struggles of successive centuries, survived as best they could in elegant wooden palaces as safe as tinder near paraffin and matches.

Ieyasu himself lived in Edo, appointing a local governor to be his eyes and ears. His Nijo Castle, started in 1603 as a stronghold of shogunate authority, was completed by the third Tokugawa shogun, Iemitsu, and consequently represents the essence of Momoyama military might. It was the official residence of shoguns when they visited Kyoto, and it was only with the Meiji Restoration and the end of the weakened (fifteenth) shogunate in 1867 that the castle was transferred first to Kyoto Prefecture and then to the Imperial Family. In 1939 it was made over the city of Kyoto and has since been open to the public.

At Shugakuin the sense of openness, freedom and freshness invigorates; at Nijo Castle the feeling of withdrawn suspicion and nervous tension induces claustrophobia. At Katsura, the strolling garden relaxes in intimate quiet; at Nijo the strolling garden seems hemmed in by walls that threaten and overpower. And these are not merely subjective emotions, for each of the five buildings, which ascend like steps one after the other, conceals secret cupboards, closets, doors and passages to harbour bodyguards or provide instant

Nijojo

refuge for a threatened noble. Progress was one-way: those seeking to pass from a lower room to a higher needed to secure the unlocking of a screen. Swords were prohibited in the castle for fear of treachery. Floors in the corridors squeaked and mewed (their designation 'nightingale' floors hardly flatters the songbird) to stiffen sentries' awareness, and passages were closed off by mounted wooden screens to trap intruders.

Fear of assassination is astonishingly absent in the Kano-school paintings in each of the five main buildings, luxuriating like western Byzantine art against backgrounds of gold leaf. The first ante-rooms are called Willow and Young Pine from their paintings; they were used for the identification of visitors, who were predominantly feudal lords. Next come three Retainers' Rooms (Tozamurainoma), with fantastic leopards and tigers attributed to Sanraku Kano and his studio. A pair of red tassels on a door signifies the presence of bodyguards. Ladies at desks switch on a Japanese-language descriptive commentary whenever a party of visitors passes through. Attendants ensure that nobody encroaches beyond the rope-barrier and that we keep to the prescribed route.

The second of the five buildings, the forty-five mat Shikidainoma (Reception Room), served to welcome feudal lords and to accept their presents on behalf of the shogun. The giant pine tree was painted by Tanyu Kano at the age of twenty-five. Again we contrast the Japanese taste for nature – animals, birds, trees and landscapes – with the Western obsession with the human figure, whether in earlier Italian and Flemish religious painting by Masaccio or Van Eyck, or in later secular European works, such as those of Vermeer and Goya. Occidental tradition in art stems from the need to convey religious teachings to the illiterate; Oriental art sees the divine in everything, from stones by a lake shore to the giant pines of Tanyu. Buddhist iconography is made not for literal worship, but for contemplation, as if it were a kind of garden, and Zen does away with the need even for symbolic representation.

Nijo's third building is Ohiroma, the Grand Audience Chamber. Lifesize feudal lords in contemporary costume, yellow, brown, orange, grey, bow before the shogun on his raised platform. The glorious coffered ceiling and splendid panels reach the apogee of Momoyama-period shoin tsukuri style (the warrior's 'shoin' room), with the same sober, uniform mats that would dignify any habitation, but magnificent paintings of pine trees, green on gold, that transform a darkened chamber into an ideal garden. Like the peacocks, these pines are painted by Tanyu. If you look carefully, you can make out bodyguard-room doors in the east wall of the upper room. Draw a breath and imagine the scene here in this room in 1868, when Emperor Meiji pronounced the abolition of the shogunate, drawing a veil in a few words over the history of six hundred and seventy-eight years, during which no 'power' of the reigning imperial family could effectively curb the *eminences grises* despite appearances. One recalls that even at the height of excesses by dictators, imperial Rome remained nevertheless nominally a republic, and that 'the dictatorship

Nijojo. Paintings of 1626 by Kano Tanyu and his school in Ohiroma (the Great Hall)

of the proletariat' covered a multitude of sins by Stalin and Mao Tse-tung.

The fourth building is Kuro-shoin ('Black Room'), an inner chamber where the shogun granted audience to hereditary nobles. The charming paintings by Naonobu Kano include a hen pheasant on a bodyguard panel, cherry blossoms, and pines, all characteristically asymmetrical.

Lastly we come to Shiro-shoin ('White Room'), even more delicately decorated by Koi Kano (1569–1636), for some time master of Tanyu and Naonobu. Sparrows in bamboo and plums; a landscape painting in which a solitary boatman is overwhelmed in counter-perspective by an ancient bony tree; hydrangeas painted directly on to the grainy wood: these are treasures which have to be appreciated *in situ*, like Giotto's frescoes at Padova or Mantegna's at Mantova.

Your route back will take you past the other flank of Kuro-shoin, Ohiroma (with a wonderful painting of a pine and beady-eyed hawk by Tanyu) and Tozamurai, where in the imperial messenger's room called Chokushinoma maples by Sanraku glitter like diamonds in the golden background which absorbs whatever sunlight enters and reflects off the tawny golden-yellow mats.

Ninomaru garden was originally created without trees, because the shogun did not choose to be reminded of life's brevity by seeing falling leaves. The recent planting of trees must consequently be wished away by anyone envisaging the nature of the garden made in 1626 by Kobori Enshu. The stones are original, as is the Horai-san type of island landscape, with tortoise and crane islands again insisting on longevity. The waterfall is strikingly 'strong' in its arrangement of large standing stones on both sides of the fall. The garden is best observed from the Ohiroma and the Kuro-shoin. I photographed a gardener so immersed in pruning trees that he seemed oblivious of passers-by, hours, weather, seasons.

> *Listening to the breath of pines –*
> *in – out – held – out –*
> *he tells the time of year*
> *by the patina on stone.*

Ninomaru garden offers camellias in January and February, apricots in February and March, in April hill cherry, weeping peach and giant dogwood, in May Kurume azalea and chisha, in June Nanakamado azalea and Cape Jasmine, Indian lilac in July and August, bush clover in September and October, Japanese maple in November, and narrow-leafed firethorn in December.

At the exit a Japanese asked me courteously if I wanted to hire a bicycle from Taki, and for anyone keen on riding one in central Kyoto, which is flat enough for the experience to be wholly pleasurable, Taki's address is 312 Hayao-cho, Kaminokuchi-agaru, Ninomiyachodori, very near Ryokan Hiraiwa.

Shinsenen

I was on my way south from Nijo Castle to Shinsenen, a single fragment remaining today from the great pleasure gardens which extended over thirty-three acres between Nijo and Sanjo (Second Avenue and Third Avenue) from the end of the eighth century until 1177, when the palace burnt down, and the emperor moved first to Fukuhara (Kobe) and then to the former Imperial Palace in Kyoto.

Pavilions once provided hospitality to moon-viewing parties, incense connoisseurs, and pleasure-seekers fishing, watching wrestling matches or dancing, and taking part in poetry competitions, picnics or banquets. Shinsenen provided the scene for the Rain-Prayer ceremonies; its atmosphere in the ninth century is evoked by these lines roughly translated from Shigeno no Sadanushi's Chinese poem in the *Keikoshu*: 'The path of Shinsenen is swept clean, except for the shadows of willows across it. A white beach trails round the lakeside, and all is serene. A pure spring bubbles off and enters a narrow stream. When we climb the hillock we find wood-doves, who fly off startled and afraid. The dragon pond reflects in turn sun, moon, and stars'. The buildings were covered with the same red lacquer characteristic of Shinto shrines today. In the seventeenth century the grounds were presented to the Shingon temple Toji, whose abbot discovered that buildings and even whole streets had eliminated most of the Divine Spring Garden on three sides, and Nijo Castle had taken up much of the fourth.

Unlike the major gardens of Kyoto, which were created later, Shinsenen is a tiny haven of peace in a busy city. It has a high-quality restaurant, small Shinto shrines, and a high curved bridge of Chinese type. Gardeners punt a rowing boat to reach the two islands; wherever they are absent, crows descend and crark defiant liberty at wage-slaves but the silent gardeners pretend deafness. The trees here are pruned and stunted for aesthetic effect like great bonsai. A slight drizzle made me shiver: an hour had gone by in inactivity, and I sauntered away to eat. At a small restaurant I ordered miso udon (noodles with fish stock) and a bar-girl brought a hot towel wrapped in a plastic bag, and a glass of ice-cold water.

Nijo Jinya

Eventually I found Nijo Jinya, a jinya being defined as a domestic fortress, which could be used as a home in peacetime and in wartime an impregnable castle. To get there, take the first paved road south-east from Shinsenen, and at fifty yards you will find it on the right. This jinya acted for part of its existence as a commercial inn, designed and constructed by Hiraemon Ogawa three hundred years ago, and still inhabited today by the Ogawa family, who agree to show the jinya by appointment, for a current fee of ¥600, if you understand Japanese or agree to bring an interpreter. I was shown round by Yasuhiro Ogawa, with whom I conversed in German, our only common tongue.

Nijo jinya is a revelation, with a false first step down in darkness to rival the nightmare plunge in R.L. Stevenson's *Kidnapped*. Hiraemon Ogawa dealt in rice and pharmaceuticals and decided to satisfy the needs of travelling noblemen who feared for their safety on the road as well as in their own strongholds. The lounge has a clerestory window apparently for light but actually for harbouring a bodyguard who can leap down and disarm an assassin. A miniature garden appears to afford no special security, until you notice that the wall's half-timbers are so spaced as to allow someone in the know to climb up to the ceiling in a trice. From the outside, the jinya seems to have only one storey, but inside one is shown four, including a hidden mezzanine available only to close confidants. The corner tearoom has a cupboard attached, with a back door leading to a hallway, where a secret hook releases part of the 'ceiling' which is in fact a staircase that can be pulled up behind a fugitive like an invisible drawbridge. If a resourceful tracker manages to get upstairs, in the dark he will trip in one of the holes in the floor and twist his ankle. A room like a ship's cabin on the first floor creaks loudly to warn a resident of danger whenever it is touched.

Yet the most remarkable feature of the jinya is its security against fire. When the Temmei fire of March 1788 over three days of hell destroyed the whole of central Kyoto, Nijo jinya survived despite its proximity to its neighbours. Ogawa had fitted clay doors and sliding screens, an ingenious water system, removable shingles and a sheathed roof. The jinya indicates how precariously a nobleman lived in the environs of a jealous shogun. Not for him languid days at the imperial court as recorded in the *Tale of Genji*; nor the security of the shogun's moated castle. A lesser nobleman, forced to leave his family as hostages in Edo while he returned to the provinces, felt threatened on all sides. If he displayed too much wealth, he could be overtaxed and ruined; if he hired too many bodyguards, he could be accused of sedition and executed; if he lived too simply, he and his many dependents would starve.

I felt nearer to the daily perils of a samurai in seventeenth-century Japan here in Nijo jinya than in movies by Akira Kurosawa such as *Yojinbo* ('The Bodyguard', 1961) or his widely influential *Shichinin no Samurai* ('The Seven Samurai', 1954).

Toei Movieland

If you want to see the sets against which current samurai films are being made, you can visit Toei Movieland in Uzumasa, five minutes' walk from Uzumasa Station on the Arashiyama line of Keifuku railways. Here are authentic reproductions of the Yoshiwara red-light district of Edo, a court of justice, a Meiji police box, the Nihombashi (Edo Bridge), a castle watchtower, an upper-class residential area and many more aspects of a period long vanished except for celluloid illusions.

Daitokuji

One day in Venice I set out early to spend a morning in San Marco. One day in Peking I visited the Forbidden City. One day in Kyoto I set out early on a third adventure of like proportions: taking the number nine bus from Nishi Honganji to Kitaoji-Horikawa, and walking westward one block to the monastery complex of Daitokuji. As in the Vatican, or the Potala Palace in Lhasa, it is not permissible to intrude everywhere in Daitokuji: in fact you walk alongside the main buildings, not through them. In addition to the Honbo (Main Temple), there are twenty-four sub-temples, of which six are occasionally or permanently open to visitors.

The principal temple of art–historical importance is Daisenin (open 9–5): you can usually also enter Hoshinin (9–4), Ryogenin (9–5), Zuihoin (8–5), Kotoin (9–4.30), and from time to time Sangenin can be seen, with its screens painted by Zaichu Hara, but I was never lucky enough to find it open during my stay. The 17th-century dry landscape garden beside Daitokuji's Hojo, attributed to Kobori Enshu but probably by the priest Tenyu (about 1636), can be seen only by those taking the 'F' garden tour daily from Kyoto Tower at 9.15 or 9.45 a.m.

Daitokuji, headquarters of a branch of the Rinzai Zen sect, was founded in 1319 on the grounds of an imperial villa by Norimura and Norisuke Akamatsu for the priest Daito-kokushi. Destroyed by fire in 1453 and again in 1468 during the Onin Wars, it was reconstructed by Ikkyu-osho (1394–1481), son of a concubine of the Emperor GoKomatsu and 47th superior of Daitokuji, where he practised painting and poetry. His pupil, the tea master Juko, designed the garden of Daitokuji's sub-temple Shinjuan, which consisted of buildings formerly belonging to the imperial palace, as did the imperial messenger's gate, Chokushimon, transferred to Daitokuji in 1640 by a gift of Empress Meisho. The two-storey main gate, Sanmon, was built by the tea master Sen no Rikyu in 1589, and has Korean sculptures of the disciples of Buddha and a figure of Rikyu carved by himself. The ceiling of the lower storey has a dragon painted by Tohaku Hasegawa (1539–1610). Immediately behind these two gates stands the Butsuden, or Hall of Buddha, rebuilt in 1664 with images not only of Buddha and disciples but also of Daito-kokushi, the founding abbot. The Hatto (Lecture Hall) of 1636 is in the Chinese style. The Honbo (or Hojo) is the administrative centre of the Daitokuji branch of the Rinzai sect.

I retraced my steps towards Kitaoji Street and gazed through the closed gate of Obaiin, a temple originally designed as a tea-pavilion by the Zen monk Soshuku in 1563, then twenty years later rebuilt as a temple by Hideyoshi. Major renovations were in progress, but I could still make out a mossy, sandy garden with dwarf maples.

Daitokuji. Ryogintei. Founder's Temple

Ryogenin

Next to it stands Ryogenin, founded in 1520 by the priest Tokei Soboku, with no fewer than five gardens, as if to emphasise the idenfication of Zen with garden contemplation. Kodatei, also known as A-un ('Inhale/Exhale') is a rock garden, as is Isshidan, whose principal tree died in 1980 when over seven centuries old, an event which caused the present priest Katsudo to reconstruct the garden. The tiny gravel and rock garden Totekiko, was explained to me by a priest as embodying the duality of male/female, heaven/earth, and positive/negative. The sand 'ripples' correspond to the strength with which the stone was 'hurled' into the garden. The moss garden of Keisokusan (front garden of the founder's temple) may not be visited, because of fears for its fragile moss cover, but you can buy a postcard-pack including a view of it. Finally, the ancient moss garden called Ryogintei is a walled universe of grey rock and green hillocks overlooked by Jokan (where the most previous material belongings of a monk are kept: robes and bowl).

Ryogenin's artistic treasures include a pair of monkeys painted by Tohaku Hasegawa, fusuma paintings of a dragon and waves in the Hojo not normally shown, a gold-lacquer go board said to have been used by the shogun Ieyasu, a glorious Buddha image of 1250, and a witty painting of an old fox as pilgrim by Shonen Suzuki of the Meiji era.

Zuihoin

Zuihoin has a beautiful dry landscape garden of moss and gravel created in 1961 by Mirei Shigemori. Bamboo groves and palms fringe the entrance, and with a start of surprise you come across a cobbled garden, with stepping stones at the back. A six-mat room has a charming ink painting of a waterfall. I stayed too long, but then Zuihoin is not on any beaten track and before the revelation of Daisenin I felt the need to collect my thoughts, or at least to pick up one of two of them.

> Moss never trodden,
> rock never guilty of a transitory act,
> yet in the interior of Zuihoin
> stands a wasting clock.

Hoshuin stands out for its pavilion, Donkokaku, by a pond in a charming garden. Shojuin, with flowering plum trees, was closed, but there is a memorable view up the path towards the temple. Shinjuan (founded by the idiosyncratic Ikkyu in 1429 and rebuilt in 1636) has three gardens, of which the most famous – 'Seven-Five-Three' – is named for its stone-arrangement. Kohoan was destroyed by fire in 1793, but the modern buildings were exquisitely achieved by Kobori Enshu's pupil Matsudaira Fumai, and the garden facing the Bosen tea-ceremony room is considered the height of elegance.

Daisenin

But we have come for Daisenin, exemplifying the Zen arts of architecture, gardening, contemplation, tea, and paradox. Everyone will take away their own extraordinary pictures of Daisenin. Mine are as numerous as anyone else's, beginning with the inscription in Japanese over badgers: 'Do not take the monk for granted, for underneath the robe there may be a badger in sheepskin'. The badger – properly 'nycterentes procyonides' (raccoon-faced dog with bushy tail) – stands in Japanese folklore for a crafty deceiver, much like the fox in Western Europe or in the 'Uncle Remus' stories.

A poster reads 'Daisenin accepts offers of wood-chopping, weeding, sweeping and scrubbing'. Green tea is served with a biscuit. In a corner a Japanese sits, silent except for his strident T-shirt proclaiming 'Australian Soccer Federation'. An old pine is supported by bamboo, like a venerable priest on the arm of an acolyte.

The Hondo's central room has copies of twenty fusuma landscapes in ink by Soami depicting the four seasons, whose originals are in Kyoto National Museum. The west room (reception room) is decorated with copies of eight paintings of flowers and birds typical of the four seasons by Motonobu Kano (originals in Kyoto National Museum), also of the 16th century. Paintings by Yukinobu Kano on fusuma in the rest room depict agricultural pursuits during the four seasons. (Again these are copies, the originals being in Kyoto National Museum.) How poignantly they contrast with the 15th-century *Très riches heures du Duc de Berry* created in miniature by Pol de Limbourg and Jean Colombe. Instead of the French precision, brilliant colour and detail, Yukinobu hints vaguely with a minimum of colour and a maximum of poetic suggestion.

The great garden was created by the Zen founder-priest of Daisenin, Kogaku Zenji (posthumously entitled Daisho Kokushi) in 1509 in the karesansui (dry landscape) style to imitate ink-painting – much as ink-painting imitates karesansui. Thirty of the stones are named, and can be identified from the diagram found in the English-language guide to the temple. Fudoseki, the immovable stone, stands between a conformation resembling a turtle and Kannonishi, the Goddess of Mercy's Stone, both nestling below Mount Horai, while beyond a dam floats in sand Takarabune, the treasure ship. A lesser garden, of fine raked white gravel, is interrupted only by a single sarasoju tree – the tree below which Gautama Buddha passed from earthly existence into the state of Nirvana. As the treasure ship passes from the turbulent seas of our present life, with its perilous rocks and islands, it will voyage into the empty, untroubled sea which finally reaches the tree of oblivion.

Zen arrived in Japan in the 12th century, long after the establishment of Tendai and Shingon, with their more or less elaborate ritual. Zen taught that truth is simple: virtue consists as much of menial toil, such as raking gravel or scrubbing floors, as of reciting sutras or practising esoteric rites. Zen brought humble domestic tasks into religious practice, and forest or coastal walks into the garden. Zen also changed domestic architecture radically, repudiating the huge temple-structures characteristic of Nara for buildings more suited to everyday life.

Each room was a separate building, connected with each other by covered corridors. In the Muromachi period (1333–1573), to which Daisenin belongs, one large rectangular building replaced the smaller rooms and was typically divided once longways and twice broadways, to provide six units separated by sliding doors and translucent shoji-paper door-windows. Folding shutters against rain made rooms dark when they were used, and translucent paper windows now avoided the necessity for lighting lanterns during stormy days, and the wooden doors to prevent rain coming in were fitted with sliding tracks.

During the Muromachi period, too, tatami mats became thinner, and were spread evenly over the whole floor, replacing the thick cushion-like tatami which were folded up (which is what tatami means) and put away when not in use. The first tokonoma (alcove) in Japan was created for practical use as a cupboard in Muromachi times, here in Daisenin. Only later did the tokonoma evolve into the decorative element for the display of paintings, calligraphy or flower-arrangement which we know today. The first genkan-ro (entrance porch and corridor) was also introduced at Daisenin, welcoming the visitor so that he possessed entry to the home as an honoured guest instead of having to wait outside like a suppliant until summoned within.

While reading *Genji Monogatari* by Lady Murasaki, or Sei Shonagon's *Makura no soshi*, or *Sarashina Nikki*, we must constantly bear in mind that these Heian works were written at a time before the Muromachi innovations: before systematised Zen study, before hanging scrolls and prints were made, before the tea ceremony and ikebana were formalised, before Noh and Kabuki plays, before the evolution of the samurai, samisen music, geisha girls, haiku, the ethic of *giri* and *on* (duty and obligation): even before the institution of the hot bath.

Daisenin marks no less of a watershed than does Todaiji in Nara or the destruction of Hiroshima. As I strolled past the first Zen Institute of America in Japan, also in the Daitokuji compound, I tried to make the mental leap from harmony-through-simplicity to the manic acquisitiveness of Texas and California. I guiltily realised that I had voyaged closer to the ink painter Sesshu than to Winslow Homer; closer to the writer Nagai Kafu than to Hawthorne or Malcolm Lowry; closer to Daitokuji than to the Mormon Tabernacle. Temperamentally liable to fits of liberty, I chuckle at the figures of 86.2 million Buddhists and 84.5 million Shinto believers cited in official statistics for a population of 120 million (with a further 0.8 million Christians and 11 million worshippers of 'miscellaneous religions'). The Ministry of Foreign Affairs explains this discrepancy by 'the fact that the same person is often counted as a member by the Shinto shrine of his neighbourhood and again by the Buddhist temple with which his ancestors were affiliated. The membership of Christian churches, in principle, excludes that of other religious groups.' Precisely.

Koetsuji

Anyone staying at the Kitayama Youth Hostel in northwest Kyoto will come to delight in the closest temple, named for the connoisseur, painter, potter, calligrapher, tea-master, and lacquer-artist Honnami Koetsu (1558–1637). Shogun Ieyasu granted him a tract of land so ample that Koetsu was enabled to found an artists' village, the Montmartre of its day. Together with the painter Nonomura Sotatsu (1576–1643), Koetsu created a new style based on the old Yamato-e school, as opposed to the Kano or Momoyama. The village, during more than six impressive decades, was responsible for the flourishing of such artists as Ogata Korin and Ogata Kenzan. In the field of maki-e lacquer (designs with gold-dust and silver-dust), Koetsu and Korin made notable advances.

Nichiren priests were responsible for elevating these unpretentious tea-pavilions used by Koetsu and his friends to the status of a temple, but they wisely retained the informality and rural calm that he sought here in the country.

Nishi Honganji

Nishi Honganji is the headquarters of the Honganji sect of the Jodo Shinshu (Pure Land) sect. A supreme example of Buddhist architecture, it may be seen by joining free Japanese-language tours which start daily at 10, 11, 1.30 and 2.30.

The founder of the sect, which boasts 10,500 temples with twelve million believers throughout the world, was Shinran Shonin, also known as Kenshin Daishi (1173–1262) who abandoned his studies on Mount Hiei in dissatisfaction at the age of 28, and became a disciple of Honen, founder of the Jodo sect. Shinran rejected monastic celibacy, abstinence from meat and other ascetic practices, stressing the 'Name' of Amida Butsu (in Sanskrit Amitabha Buddha) as sufficient in itself for salvation. 'Embodied within the Name', runs the official teaching, 'are the totality of Vows and Practices necessary for deliverance, and thus endowed it becomes the true cause for deliverance into the Pure Land.'

Such was the growing strength of the sect that in 1602 Ieyasu, first Tokugawa shogun, weakened it by the 'divide et impera' principle of authorising a former abbot to found a new school, the Otani, called Higashi Honganji (Eastern Honganji), nearby. Not only is the Western Honganji more imposing, with some of the most massive wooden structures anywhere in the world, but historically it benefits from incorporating parts of Hideyoshi's Fushimi Castle (dismantled by Ieyasu) and parts of Hideyoshi's Jurakudai.

Nishi Honganji (Western Honganji) was first established at Otani Hombyo in Higashiyama, but the headquarters temple moved from pillar to post as civil and ecclesiastical disruptions dictated, and it was only in 1591, with the grant of land by Hideyoshi, that this key situation in Kyoto was finally adopted and the move from Yamashina made. All of the original buildings were burned down in 1617. The Goeido you see today was constructed in 1636, followed by Hyunkaku, Karamon, Taimensho, Shiro-shoin and the Noh stages, and culminating in the Kuro-shoin of 1657, and the Hondo or Amidado of 1760.

After taking off our shoes, we visited the Hondo, with a fine sculpture of Amida Butsu by a sculptor of the Kasuga school. To right and left of the altar respectively are portraits of Prince Shotoku (573–621, the effective patron-founder of Buddhism in Japan) and Honen (1133–1212). Fusuma paintings of phoenixes and peacocks are by painters of the Kano school.

The Founder's Hall (Daishido) contains a carving of Shinran by himself, made when he was seventy-one and offered to his daughter, a nun, surrounded by portraits of successive abbots.

Both the Karamon and the Dai-shoin behind it survive from Fushimi Castle. Breathtakingly gorgeous in size and decoration, the Taimensho served Hideyoshi as a council chamber and is cunningly designed with a reverse

Nishi Honganji

perspective effect, its wooden storks carved by Hidari Jingoro on the transoms striking against the dominant yellow and gold of the chamber. More storks are painted by Watanabe Ryokei against a gold background with green pines adding piquant asymmetry.

After the south Noh stage we come to Gonnoma (Wild Geese Chamber), an eighteen-mat room named for its fusuma paintings, with clematis on the ceiling painted by Ryokei. Kikunoma (Chrysanthemum Chamber) is a masterpiece by the Kano-school painter Yusetsu Kaihoku (1598–1677), with cedar-door paintings by Hidenobu Kino and fans painted by Yusetsu and Koi.

Opposite the north Noh stage stands the Shiro-shoin, three chambers from Fushimi originally used by Hideyoshi and his Cabinet for affairs of state. Paintings are by Koi, Yusetsu and Ryotaku. Next door, the Kuro-shoin is adorned with fusuma paintings by Eitoku Kano.

Sometimes visitors are shown the 16th-century Hyunkaku (Floating Cloud Pavilion), known as one of the Three Pavilions of Japan, the others being Kinkaku and Ginkaku, also in Kyoto. It was transferred from Hideyoshi's mansion Jurakudai in 1630, together with its boat-docking room. Principally a tea-pavilion, with eight views of a Chinese lake by Tanyu Kano and Zensetsu Tokuriki (1591–1680) and Eitoku's charming willows, on the first floor portraits of thirty-six poets have been made by Sanraku Kano (1559–1635), and on the second a painting of Fuji-san by Motonobu Kano created in such a manner that the observer must kneel to see it clearly. The bathroom has paintings by Eitoku (1543–90).

Apart from two attractive pond gardens, Nishi Honganji possesses a fine dry landscape garden which has been variously dated to both Momoyama and early Edo times. The use of palms is unusual, beside a delightful curved bridge and a symbolic waterfall.

Higashi Honganji

A short distance away is the sister-temple Higashi Honganji, headquarters of the Otani branch of Jodo Shinshu, a ten-minute walk due north of Kyoto Station. The temple, founded in 1262 as a mausoleum of Shinran at Otani, in the foothills of Higashiyama, underwent numerous vicissitudes before establishment on its present site as an offshoot of Nishi Honganji on land provided by Ieyasu for Kyonyo Shonin (1558–1614). Repeatedly destroyed, the temple was last reconstructed in 1895, and in 1984 scaffolding was up again around the Founder's Hall and Amidado. The entrance, unclear from the official map of Kyoto, lies on the eastern side of the temple, on Karasumadori. Organized with an efficiency reminiscent of Nissan (which has not had a serious dispute in over 25 years), Higashi Honganji has a head elected to a four-year term of office like any President of the United States, with five appointed members in the Executive Cabinet and sixty-five members of the Legislative Council representing thirty regions. There are more than 9,000 branch temples and several million members in Japan, the United States and South America, where overseas missions carry the word of Shinran Shonin.

Kyoto Tourist Information Office recommends that you apply to visit the temple a day in advance, but this requirement was kindly waived on my visit.

Gigantism is the downfall of Higashi Honganji, and there will be those who prefer the tiny Jakkoin at Ohara to this immense Founder's Hall Gate (Goeido-mon) of 1911 or the huge Founder's Hall (Goeido) itself, completed in 1895, with a seating area of nine hundred mats. The Amidado or Hondo (Main Hall) beside it is almost equally awesome, but the Japanese aesthetic sense does not seem to correspond to Higashi Honganji's extravagance, and I left deflated and disappointed, after securing a free permit at the desk to visit the temple's detached garden due east.

Kikokutei

What an extraordinary contrast! After the purposeful hustle of many silent believers trooping in herds round an enormous temple distinguished only by its size, I found myself the sole visitor to the garden called Kikokutei (Tangerine Pavilion) after its most fragrant trees. One of the few expansive lawns in Kyoto covers an area that in any other Japanese city would long ago have fallen victim to the real-estate developer. The land was given to the temple in 1641 by Iemitsu, and when Abbot Sennyo retired in 1653 he chose this garden as his retreat, commissioning the poet and scholar Jozan Ishikawa to redesign it. This was achieved on the model of Jozan's own garden at Shisendo in north-east Kyoto. The garden mansions fell victim to fires in 1858 and 1864, but a faithful restoration allows one to imagine the scene here as it was more than three centuries ago.

The great pond of Ingetsuchi has two larger and two smaller islands, the latter named Tonoshima (Tower Island) from its nine-storey tower and Matsunoshima (Pine Island). Sochinkyo, a small two-room tea pavilion, stands on the edge of the pond, with a jetty close by: the delicate tea-picking scenes were painted by Yeino Kano. The highest part of the garden is crowned by the tea-pavilion Shukuentei, but my favourite features in Shoseien or Kikokutei are the bridge Kaitoro, the red maple valley called Tampukei, and the gate Bokakaku leading to Onrindo, a family shrine with screens painted by Shiko Munakata.

On the northeastern corner of Kawaramachi-Shichijo there is a net where one golfer at a time can practise driving off a tee; there is barely room to swing the driver and it reminded me of tantalising a racing driver by setting his car down on a track ten yards longer than his vehicle. Nearby, three old ladies laboriously swept all traces of dust and litter from another street corner, emptying the rubbish from the bin with a kind of reverential care that one notices among gardeners of a certain age. I recalled the old ladies I had seen shovelling snow in Budapest, and others picking up débris from Wuhan streets: nothing seems too menial for our grandmothers.

Tofukuji

One glorious spring morning I set off from my minshuku near Sanjusangendo south of Tofukuji, headquarters of the Tofukuji branch of Rinzai Zen, founded in 1236 by Michiie Fujiwara (1192–1252), a son of Yoshitsune, with the priest Shoitsu its first abbot. The temple is well-known outside Japan for the Zen book, written by a foreigner studying there, entitled *Unsui*, which would fascinate anyone desirous to delve into the intricacies of Zen practice. Garden enthusiasts will revel in the modern designs by Mirei Shigemori (1938), who has evoked Zen as it was in the Kamakura period within a framework drawn from modern abstract art: the two are closely related in paradox, immediacy, and simplicity.

Tofukuji. Japanese garden

The 'serious' southern garden is a dry landscape with four islands set in a spiral sandy sea, with five mossy sacred 'mountains' on the west. The western garden is less solemn, with gentle mossy beds and azaleas. Now you emerge on to a covered platform overlooking the northern garden: a deep wooded valley below you and a charming wooden bridge (Tsutenkyo) on the left. Square-cut stones, and moss are arranged in small asymmetrical squares. Seven cylindrical stones thrust out from a mossy ground in the eastern garden to represent stars in heaven.

Three 13th-century gates dominate the entrances to Tofukuji. The two-storey Sanmon is adorned with ceiling paintings by Mincho (called Chodensu, 1352–1431) and his disciple Kandensu. Rokuharamon was once a gate of the local Rokuhara headquarters of the Kamakura government. Gekkamon came from the palace bequeathed to the temple by former Emperor Kameyama in 1268.

Tofukuji's Hondo is a reconstruction of 1932 with a huge dragon on the ceiling painted by Domoto Insho. If you want to see the everyday life of a Rinzai temple, avoid 15 March, when Chodensu's painting of 'Buddha's Entrance into Nirvana' is exhibited.

I marvelled again at the unassuming tolerance which permitted a little Shinto shrine its perpetual existence at the top of the hill; a Japanese Buddhist explained to me that if Shinto-worshippers were ever inclined to desecrate this Buddhist temple, they would be stayed by the presence of a shrine. He fetched a plastic bucket with his name on it and a water scoop, and swiftly cleaned a few specks of dust that had gathered since his last respects to his father's plain gray grave. I recalled how the Korean priest known in Japan as Gyogi (670–749) had sought funds for Todaiji's great Buddha by pilgrimage to the Shinto shrine at Ise, offering there a Buddhist relic as token homage, after which funds poured in from Shinto and Buddhist worshippers alike. A Shinto emblem was later installed at Todaiji and all later Buddhist temples of any size made similarly sure of Shinto protection.

Fushimi Inari

Sauntering due south of Tofukuji, parallel with Japan National Railways' Nara Line, against the flow of one-way traffic, I observed small-town life, with neighbourhood drug-stores on the American pattern, youngsters on bicycles, and diminutive old ladies burdened with heavy shopping bags. At Inari Station I turned left and the trickle of passers-by going the same way swelled into a flood. Garish toy motor-cars and lolling paper lanterns competed for attention with sprawling stalls selling sukiyaki, sweet pastries, piles of apples, and live crabs.

If you are usually conscious in Japan of taking part in a carefully-rehearsed play, where the designer has just completed his stage set, and you have been given a trivial walk-on rôle, it is time to relax at Fushimi Inari. No other foreigners are to be seen, and the Japanese are informally dressed as if for a picnic or carnival rather than a religious ceremony. And no ceremony in the West looks anything like this. While stone foxes with red scarves around their necks look on, a service is going on somewhere but it is inaudible. Worshippers ring bells to remind the spirits of their presence, clapping their hands twice while chanting. Newborn babies cry in their fathers' arms as their infant lives are blessed. Wooden plaques tied on to a large wooden board flap and clack like storks on a nest. A lottery bucket clanks. Shops selling amulets and charms for success in business do a thriving trade. The shrine was erected by the Hata family in 711, originally to the gods of rice and rice-wine, then by extension to

Fushimi Inari. Inside the Shinto shrine (*Photo. Author*)

the gods of agriculture, and as agricultural land diminished with the passing centuries (12% of Japanese are country-dwellers now, compared with 45% as recently as 1945), so the flexible deities of Fushimi began to devote themselves to business, and a notional 'ten thousand' wooden torii painted vermilion form a seemingly endless archway up the hillside over a circuit of at least five kilometres. They stand in some places so close together that they almost prevent light reaching the paved ground. Aston has suggested that the torii first reached Japan from the Asiatic mainland about 770 A.D. Kipling claimed an Indian origin (see an example at Alwar, Rajputana) and comparable structures are recorded by Chamberlain in Korea. The other great source of Japanese importations is of course mainland China, and there too the native *p'ai lou* seem obvious ancestors. Some Japanese believe that the word derives from the Japanese 'tori' (sacred birds) which were maintained as a religious duty at the shrine, but the etymology seems too fanciful for credibility.

Apart from the torii, Shinto shrines are typically bare of images so beloved of Hinduism and Buddhism, but invariably bear a wand with strips of white paper (gohei) to represent cloth offerings formerly tied to trees during festivals.

Inari Shrine's main building (dating from 1499) is guarded by a pair of carved and painted ama inu and koma inu, intended to ward off evil. Fortune-telling by numbers, and the sale of amulets, together with the pantheistic chatting that goes on between silent deities and voluble holidaymakers would seem peculiar in any Western church or cathedral, but the Japanese seem much more relaxed in a religious atmosphere. Stone foxes with red scarves add a strange touch, but this is Inari-no-Jinja, the Shrine dedicated to the Fox-Goddess Inari, one of whose festivals takes place every 8 November. Fires are lighted at Fushimi and other shrines to Inari in honour of the mythical assistance she rendered to the swordsmith Kokaji, as she worked the bellows while he forged a sword for an early emperor. The fox is closely connected with sorcery in the Japanese mind: some people are believed to possess foxes (kitsune-mochi) or in other words forces which can inflict evil on their foes; others are believed possessed by foxes (kitsune-tsuki) which supposedly enter, to quote Dr E. Baelz, 'sometimes through the breast, more often through the space between the fingernails and the flesh', after which 'the fox lives a life of his own, apart from the proper self of the person who is harbouring him. The person possessed hears and understands everything that the fox inside says or thinks; and the two often engage in a loud and violent dispute, the fox speaking in a voice altogether different from that which is natural to the individual.' Jekyll and Fox, indeed.

Uji

From the Shrine I returned at midday to the railway station called Inari on the JNR Nara line and found that the next train to Uji was due at 12.36, so enquired at the adjoining Fushimi Inari station of the private Keihan line and found the next departure for Uji was at 12.04, so I paid two hundred yen for the thirty-minute train ride via Fukakusa, Fujinomori and Sumizomi, each station with spotless toilets and a stall for snacks and cold drinks such as Coca Cola. The comfortable green train sped between the backs of two sets of houses, where an inquisitive Tom can peer without guilt or remorse.

We pulled into Uji Station, and – like hundreds of high-spirited Japanese sightseers around me – I strolled across the famous seventh-century Uji Bridge, with its echoes from the last ten chapters of the eleventh-century novel *Genji Monogatari*, and great battles such as that between the Minamoto and the Taira in 1180 and that between the Minamoto cousins Yoshitsune and Yoshinaka four years later.

If you have plenty of time at Uji, visit the Shingon-Ritsu temple near the bridge called Hashidera ('Bridge Temple') or Hojoin; the oldest shrine buildings in Japan at the Shinto Uji Shrine; the first Soto temple in Japan, Koshoji; and Mampukuji, owing much to Chinese architectural styles.

Byodoin

But Uji is celebrated for three other things: nightfishing with cormorants, green tea reputed the finest in the archipelago, and the Hall of Equality, Byodoin. Byodoin, originally a Tendai foundation, but now supervised by the Jodo sect, has four particular points of interest of which one, the Treasure House built in 1965, is opened only twice a year, when one can see the original bell, with those of Jingoji and Miidera one of the three great bells of Japan. The bell-tower itself is the second notable feature, with a careful copy of the original bell. The third is Kannondo (Hall of the Goddess of Mercy), also called Tsuridono (Angling Hall) because the river Uji once ran below it and through a hole in the floorboards one could catch fish.

The eleven-headed Goddess of Mercy of the 12th century is flanked by two 13th-century figures, one of Jizo (156 cm.) made out of a single piece of zelkova wood and one of Fudomyoo (88 cm.) made of a single piece of Japanese cypress, like the Kannon herself, whose gentle, enigmatic smile is reminiscent of Mona Lisa's.

North of Kannondo is a garden with a fan-shaped lawn (ask for 'Ogi no shiba'). Yorimasa of the Minamoto encamped with his army, including the warrior monks of Miidera, at Byodoin in May 1180 to await the attack of Tomomori of the Taira and his 28,000 men. 'When a battle broke out on the Uji Bridge', *Heike Monogatari* relates, 'their leaders, Yorimasa and his son, fought desperately, holding their sense of loyalty above their lives. Overcome by the greater number of the enemy, the Genji warriors perished. Some of the bodies were left on the moss of the riverbank, and some were left to drift in the waters of the great river, Uji'. Yorimasa, escaping to Byodoin, committed suicide there at the age of 76.

Now for the revelation of the Phoenix Hall, known as Amidado or even more commonly as Hoodo. The site is recorded as having had over thirty buildings, including seven pagodas, during the height of its splendour first as villa, then temple. The villa belonged to 'Hikaru Genji' (hero of *Genji Monogatari*), or Minamoto no Toru, according to the official guidebook of Byodoin, but J.N.T.O.'s *New Official Guide* states that it was 'originally a villa of Prime Minister Michinaga Fujiwara (966–1024)' and converted into a temple in 1052 by Michinaga's son Yorimichi. Of this great temple-complex, only the Hoodo of 1053 remains. Named for the phoenix it imitates in shape, the Hall is surmounted by two facing bronze phoenixes, replicas of the weathered originals. The phoenix (identified for convenience with the *hoo* of Chinese and Japanese legend by such scholars as Newman and Ryerson) is revered in Japan as the symbol of energy and wisdom, and because it is said to have protected the meditating Buddha.

Uji. Byodoin

The Hall was once completely surrounded by the Aji Pond, isolation which protected it from the fires which gutted every other early temple here. Below and above the still pond Phoenix Hall shimmers in warm browns, blues, yellows, then old carp break the surface and the illusion of a mirror shatters. The decorative stone lantern between pond and pavilion may be as old as Phoenix Hall itself: it has certainly been copied by generations of lantern-makers.

Whether you belong to another religion or to none at all, close your eyes and anticipate the ecstasy in the face of death taught by Jodo, the Buddhist school deriving its doctrine of the Pure Land from the Mahayana of Northern India through Chinese priests. By *Namu Amida Butsu*, or invoking the name of Amitabha Buddha, the faithful could achieve salvation in the Pure Land at the moment of death. Yorimichi attempted to recreate the vision of Paradise on earth at Byodoin by beautiful scented flowers, an all-reflecting pond, carefully-selected trees planted in the exact places, the winged hall with its celestial birds, carved angels playing music, painted bodhisattvas of exquisite beauty welcoming the newly-reborn, the central, serene, all-merciful Amida encompassing wisdom, truth and love.

The tenth-century monk Kuya, dancing through the streets with a bell tinkling at his neck, cried out:

Hito tabi mo	*He never fails*
namu Amida bu to	*to reach the Pure Land*
yu hito no	*if he calls*
hasu utena ni	*just once*
noboranu wa nashi.	*the name of Amida.*

'Wings' on each side of the light central hall, with ample space below the wooden struts, impart a feeling of such mobility that one almost imagines the delicate bird-temple taking off, with its pyramidal roof swirling into the beckoning sky.

Inside, brilliant day gives way to velvet dark. Light focuses on the face and breast of the seated Buddha carved in 1053 by the priest-sculptor Jocho, a pupil of the sculptor Kosho whose work has – if it survives at all – not yet been identified.

Jocho, whose name is first recorded in 1022, is responsible for innovations both technical and aesthetic. He repudiated the traditional method of carving from a single block of wood or from an assemblage of blocks, adopting a method of taking separate pieces of wood, carving those to leave a hollow space within, and covering the whole with a thin lacquer to conceal joins. This technique, yosegi-tsukuri, gradually obtained ascendancy over the single-block method. The name of the Byodoin (Hall of Equality) indicates a Shingon feeling for the equivalence of human nature with Buddha-nature, but Jocho's Buddha-image, in the meditation mudra called join, seems closely identified with the paradise cult of the later Jodo sect which came to share this beloved temple with Tendai.

We have seen how the Nara sculptor of the Saidaiji directs his image's gaze outward to the spectator, whereas later figures of the tenth century cast their eyes down and seem indrawn. With Jocho's wondrous Buddha we revert towards the Saidaiji ideal, eloquent eyes nearly upcast once more, and flowing shallow drapery rendered with realistic eloquence. Below Amida juts out a contemporary lotus pedestal, each single petal breathing in its own voice, but the halo (kohai) is later.

Hoodo's central hall ceiling is coved and latticed, with arching girders. Circular bronze mirrors are fixed about a metre apart below the framework of the ceiling and girders. Fifty-two bodhisattvas on clouds, made of Japanese cypress, play musical instruments such as the yokobue (flute) or odaiko (drum), or gesture in various Buddhist mudras, hold a lotus flower, or dance. They inhabit the Pure Land surrounding Amitabha Buddha in his eternal peace. These glorious figures, ascribed to Jocho and his pupils, preserve remnants of their bright colours. Paintings attributed to the 11th-century artist Tamenari on the doors and walls, regrettably but understandably, do not conserve their ancient colours and many of the details are missing or so far faded as to be scarcely intelligible. We can however make out visions of the Pure Land on the wall behind the main image, the contemplation of the sunset (one of the Sixteen Ways of Meditation) on the door of the rear wing, and on each door scenes from the Nine Categories of Rebirth (Kubon Raigo) which are the oldest of their kind in Japan. This is the most precious single collection of Japanese wall paintings *in situ* now that those of Horyuji in Nara have been destroyed. The eight door paintings are reconstructions, the originals being stored in the Treasure House.

Exhilarated at Byodoin as I had been by the tapestries of the Philadelphia Museum of Art or El Greco at Toledo, I made my way back, dazed, to a little restaurant near Uji Bridge, and devoured a bowl of noodles, and then another, listening to the giggles of passing schoolchildren and the sound of clapping wooden sandals on the pavement: the receding clack the Japanese call 'kara-koro, kara-koro'.

Daigoji

At Uji Station I bought a ticket for Rokujizo, the train stopping at Minurodo, Obaku and Kowata. At Rokujizo I caught a bus for the eight-minute ride to Daigoji and there alighted beside the long white wall signifying monzeki status.

The name 'Daigoji' means 'Temple of Milk Essence', deriving from the highest degree of teaching by Gautama Buddha, corresponding to the level of his listeners' understanding. The earliest teachings correspond to fresh milk, the next phase to coagulated milk, then fresh butter, ghee and finally milk essence, in the original Indian tradition the most delicious of all edibles. Local legend records that the priest Shobo of the Shingon sect was seeking for somewhere to practise asceticism and to found a temple, when a five-hued cloud rose above the hill where Daigoji now stands. As Shobo approached the summit of the mountain, he came across an old white-haired man who dipped his fingers into a well, tasted the liquid, and said 'This is the taste of daigo'.

Shobo, later dignified by the title Rigen Daishi, founded the temple in 874, but all the buildings you see today are later, the oldest being the pagoda of 951 forty metres high, with the oldest coloured mandala in the world. To see the latter, you must apply in advance, and even then it is usually not shown. The Treasure Hall (Reihokan), open from early April to late May and from early October to late November, contains 100,000 precious volumes, important screen paintings and scrolls.

In 1470, a fire during the Onin Wars destroyed all the Lower Daigoji buildings except the pagoda. Most of the buildings were eventually reconstructed, but the Main Hall (Kondo) and Guardian Gate (Niomon) were presented by

Daigoji. Five-storey pagoda (*Photo. Author*)

Hideyoshi from the Negoro Monastery in the peninsula of Kii which had vainly rebelled against his power and suffered accordingly.

The Kondo is of roughly 14th-century date, with a central image of the Healing Buddha (Yakushi Nyorai), dated (by Watson) to about 909 A.D., flanked by Nikko and Gekko, and protected by the four heavenly kings (Shidaitenno). The traditional positioning of the Shidaitenno is Tamon, who hears all, to the north, usually carrying cudgel, spear, and miniature pagoda; Jikoku (upholder of the state) to the east, carrying sword and spear; Zocho (the Mighty) to the south, carrying sword and spear; and Komoku, who sees all, to the west, bearing rope, spear, pen and scroll.

Sanboin

Sanboin is the headquarters of the Daigoji school of the Shingon sect. Founded in 1115 by Abbot Shokaku, it is one of the five monzeki sub-temples of Daigoji, and suffered the same fate as the others in the devastating fire of 1470, before being rebuilt in 1601. It gives the impression more of a Toyotomi pleasure villa than a religious foundation. The interplay of mansion and garden strikes the Western visitor as superlatively tasteful, elegant and imaginative, ensuring that functionalism never dominates the aesthetic impulse. The courtyard boasts a cherry-tree of great size and reputation, attracting crowds of visitors each spring.

The first building has three rooms. Aoinoma, the Room of the Aoi Festival, is named for the genre paintings on the fusuma of 1760 by Ishida Yutei. It is extraordinary to see these paintings of the Kano School in the knowledge that Ishida was the first master of Maruyama Okyo (1733–95), founder of the Shijo movement celebrated by Jack Hillier in his marvellous book *The Uninhibited Brush* (Hugh M. Moss, London, 1974). Akikusanoma, the Room of Autumn Grass, dazzles with its fusuma paintings of 'seven autumnal grasses' by Sanraku Kano (1559–1635), overlooked by a cherry tree. Chokushinoma, the Room of the Imperial Messenger, has Sanraku's paintings in the conventional mode of 'kachosansui' (flower-bird-mountain-water).

The messenger's gate along the path is believed to have come from Fushimi Castle; its emblems are the sixteen-petal imperial chrysanthemum and the paulownia affected by Hideyoshi.

Next comes the building called Omote Shinden (Study Hall), again with three rooms. Agebutainoma possesses fusuma paintings of peacocks and sago palms by Ishida Yutei, a portable screen with Ishida's white eagle, and a wooden floor occasionally used as a Noh stage. Chudannoma (Middle Room) is adorned with bamboo and pines painted by Sanraku Kano, who was also responsible for the willow paintings in Jodannoma (Upper Room). Here are the tokonoma (alcove) and splendid asymmetrical shelves (chigai-dana) on the east wall next to the alcove.

You cannot cross to the Junjokan (Very Pure View) without passing a clump of bamboos, inducing a sense of illusion that one is out in a forest while one steps from one building to the next.

The Junjokan was used for blossom-viewing, incense and poetry parties, its views being wonderful at all seasons. It may have been part of Fushimi Castle; at all events it was reconstructed, after typhoon damage, in 1936 with screens painted in the same year by Domoto Insho.

Sanboin's Main Hall shows an image of the future Buddha, Miroku Bosatsu, carved in 1198 by Anami Kaikei, pupil of Kokei, himself descended from the great Jocho. Flanking Miroku (Maitreya in Sanskrit) are sculptures of Shobo and Kukai.

The tea pavilion called Chinryutei, restored in 1950, possesses a delightful dry landscape garden in keeping with its tiny proportions, while the tea pavilion, on the opposite side of Junjokan, named Shogetsutei, takes its mood

Sanboin. Island in the centre of the garden (*Photo. Author*)

from the water in which one of its corners stands. From Shogetsutei (Teahouse of the Moonlit Pines) one could take a boat below Junjokan and out to the pond, for moon-viewing in the open air. The east wall of the pavilion has a round window for viewing the moon on blustery nights, or from a discreet distance. Next to this teahouse stands Okushinden, with paintings attributed to Tohaku Hasegawa (1539–1610). The shelves, chigai-dana, are as celebrated as those at Shugakuin or Katsura.

Sanboin's garden is believed to have been created quickly, without regard to expense, by Hideyoshi himself, with the designer Baishoken Takeda, though improvements were certainly carried out by the priest Junko after Hideyoshi's death in 1598. It is the antithesis of the sober Zen gardens such as Ryoanji or Daisenin. No expense was spared, and the lavish profusion of stones, colours and foliage types, islands and bridges contradicts the spirit of karesansui that you experienced a few minutes earlier at Chinryutei. Horai-san is no longer the paradise island to which one has to sail, but a promontory with access from the bank, allegorically close. Tortoise and Crane Islands are reminders of longevity, as abundant in Japan as the *memento mori* is in Western Renaissance art. If you stand near the dry landscape garden in Omote Shinden and gaze across Tortoise Island (with its pine artificially pruned and shaped – like any bonsai – to represent a tortoise), your eye will come to rest on the largest of the eight hundred or so stones brought from all over Japan. This is called Fujito, and is the subject of a Noh play, having come originally from the locality of Fujito, near Kojima in Okayama Prefecture, first to Ujitsuna Hosokawa's garden in Kyoto and eventually to Hideyoshi's at Jurakudai. The latter offered the then abbot of Daigoji, Gien, the stone Fujito or five thousand bushels of rice. The abbot chose Fujito.

Outside the white wall, back in the everyday world, I caught bus 12 to Higashiyama Sanjo, then bus 206 to Shichijo Ohashi, and fell asleep in my Haiku Room at seven o'clock before rising at eight to dine nearby on beef and rice with noodle soup, to the cacophony of Japanese popular music (as raucous as Western pop) and the excited chatter of Japanese families at their evening meal. The highest price on the menu was ¥700, just over £2 or $4, so the Japanese can and do dine out much more frequently than do Americans or Europeans.

Sculpture

If your main interest in Kyoto is sculpture, there are three more temples which you should visit: Shogoin, Joruriji, and Hokaiji.

Shogoin possesses a Shintoesque carving by Ryosei of the Tendai priest Enchin (814–891) dated 1143. Enchin founded Onjoji and is venerated for bringing back Chinese learning to Japan.

Joruriji has nine Amida images in its Hondo: it is in fact precious as the unique survivor of more than thirty great Amida Halls, each with nine Amida figures, which once existed. The central sculpture (its hands in the raigo mudra) seems similar to the Amida by Jocho in the Hoodo at Byodoin, and it is not unlikely that a disciple of Jocho worked here. Interestingly, the yosegi carving technique seems more advanced.

Hokaiji, south of Daigoji, dates to the ninth century and has an Amida Hall of 1051 with an Amida probably by Jocho himself, who died in 1057. Its murals date from the late 12th–early 13th centuries, when similar work was executed in the Nanendo of Nara's Kofukuji.

Lake Biwa

'Landscape' in Japan, following the Chinese example, is sansui, conjoining 'mountain' (yang, male) and river (yin, female) in a single word. Kyoto has an abundance of mountains, but for water you are restricted to the rivers Kamo and Katsura, ponds like Shinsenen, or lakes adorning the villas and palaces. Until you remember Lake Biwa, the largest fresh-water lake in the country and famous in Japanese literature for the evening bell of Miidera, which you may sound yourself, and for the 'eight views' conventionally accepted as the most beautiful vistas at various times of day, or at various seasons. The eight views are: Flight of Wild Geese at Katada, Sunshine and Breeze at Awazu, Sails Returning to Yabase, Evening Glow at Seta, Evening Snow on Mount Hira, Evening Bell at Miidera Temple, Night Rain at Karasaki, and Autumn Moon at Ishiyama.

To see at least a few of these views, take an hour's train-ride from Kyoto to Biwa, which allows time to see Miidera, the grave of Matsuo Basho in the temple Gichuji, east of the rail station, and the grave of the American Buddhist and critic Ernest Fenollosa (1853–1908) at Homyoin, near Onjoji, preferably by taxi. Then lunch at the small port of Hamaotsu, and take the steamer for an hour's sail or up to five hours. The 'eight views' are at the southern or Kyoto end of Biwa, but there is much to be said for exploring Hikone, a town half-way along the lakeshore, and the northern end of the lake. Take the train from Kyoto to Hikone (45 minutes by express); 1 km. from the station stands the castle, built in 1603 by Naokatsu Ii. Naosuke Ii (1815–1860) was the chief minister of the Tokugawa shogun, and is best-known for his achievement in promoting trade and understanding between Japan and the outside world.

The white three-storey donjon of the castle is designated a 'national treasure' and one of the turrets contains a typically refined museum of bonkei (tray landscape) and scrolls. You can still see the Ii family villa (Rakurakuen) and garden (Genkyuen), the latter a superb example of the seventeenth-century kaiyushiki style, roughly translated as 'strolling garden'.

Ishiyamadera

The most famous Japanese novel of all, *The Tale of Genji*, was supposedly written in Ishiyama Temple, five minutes' walk from the Ishiyamadera station on the Keihan. The temple belongs to the Toji school of the Shingon sect and was founded by the priest Roben in the eighth century, though most of the buildings you see today are of the sixteenth century or later. The Genji Hall (ask for 'Genjinoma') adjoins the main hall: there Murasaki Shikibu wrote part of her epic *Genji Monogatari* in the first quarter of the eleventh century. The elegance and sophistication of the imperial court, 'the world of the shining prince' as Ivan Morris calls it in the title of his classic study, contrasts not only with the rough and primitive life in Europe at the time, but also with the rest of Japan, for the population then is calculated at five million, of whom only one per cent lived in Kyoto, and only one tenth of one per cent belonged to the privileged court hierarchy. Culture, position and rank (though not necessarily wealth and certainly not possession of lands) depended on living at court, and anyone who was appointed to a remote province felt like a Roman senator exiled to the *limes tripolitanus* or a courtier dismissed from Versailles to cultivate his *terres* in Provence.

As you wander from the Todaimon to the main hall of Ishiyama, or from the rocks in the compound that gave the temple its sobriquet ('stony hill') to the belfry, recall the brittle world of gossip and intrigue immortalised by Murasaki, by the authoress of the Sarashina diary translated as *As I crossed the bridge of dreams*, and by Sei Shonagon, writer of the *Pillow-book*. Come back if you can on a moonlit autumn night to view Lake Biwa from the temple grounds.

QUICK ITINERARIES IN TOKYO

If you have only half a day between flights at Narita International Airport, visit Narita City and do not try to get into Tokyo metropolis in that time.

If you have a full day, I suggest you spend it in Tokyo's Ueno Park.

TWO DAYS
Day 1. National Museum in Ueno Park. Asakusa for Nakamisedori and Sensoji, with Denboin. Evening at Kabukiza or Ginza Nohgakudo.
Day 2. Meiji Shrine, Shinjuku Gyoen National Garden, circuit of the Imperial Palace walls. Evening at National Theatre or Tokyo Bunka Kaikan Hall.

THREE DAYS
Days 1 and 2 as above.
Day 3. Yushima Tenjin, Yushima Seido, National Museum of Modern Art, East Garden of the Imperial Palace, Ginza department stores. Round trip outside the rush hours on the Yamanote line.

TOKYO

The Bullet Train

The Japanese travel light, and I felt conspicuous lugging my heavy suitcase into Kyoto rail station one summer morning for the bullet train to Tokyo. The spotless trains are so frequent that you don't really need a timetable and, arriving at the ticket office by 11 a.m., I had bought my unreserved ticket for ¥11,300, and milk on the platform for ¥65 by the time a shinkansen glided up at 11.11. I found a seat, one of five facing the engine, split three and two with the corridor between. Along here come smiling uniformed girls with drinks and lunch-boxes for the 2½-hour journey to Tokyo on this fastest of all the world's trains bar the Paris–Lyons express. Carriages 1 through 5 were all unreserved, and the others reserved, numbers 11 and 12 being the more spacious green cars, requiring an extra charge; carriage 8 is a dining-car. The principal shinkansen line connects Tokyo with Nagoya, Maibara, Kyoto, Osaka, Himeji, Okayama, Hiroshima, Ogori, Kokura and Hakata, covering 1,176 kms. (736 miles) in less than seven hours. For the record, other shinkansen lines connect Omiya (near Tokyo) with Morioka (505 kms. or 315 miles) in 3 hours 17 minutes and with Niigata (303 kms. or 188 miles) in under two hours. You can book shinkansen fares with Japan Air Lines before departure to Japan, reserving seats between two months and two days before the date of shinkansen travel. A Japan Rail Pass is worth buying if you are travelling throughout the country, or at least on the move nearly every day for at least a week. A 7-day pass would cost – as an indication – about ¥35,000 for a week in Green or First Class, or about ¥25,000 in Ordinary Class, with exactly half-price fares for children (defined as aged between 6 and up to and including 11). There are 14-day and 21-day rail passes too, each more economical than the last. Of course, you do not have to travel by bullet train. You can see more of the country on 'limited express', ordinary express and local trains, in descending order of cost. Cheapest of all are the overnight 'dream buses' linking Tokyo with Nagoya, Kyoto and Osaka, a typical Tokyo–Kyoto fare being about ¥8,000 (more than half for a child) departing at 11 p.m. and arriving in Kyoto at 7.45 a.m., returning every evening from Kyoto at 10 p.m., arriving at Tokyo (JNR terminus) at 6.43. Since the buses are run by Japanese National Railways, you can arrange a combined 'dream bus' and shinkansen (valid 6 days) for a price intermediate between return bus and return shinkansen, currently about ¥18,000.

I kept alert for glimpses of Lake Biwa on the left, and as we approached Hikone I made out the white crest of Hikone Castle, and then at 11.40 we stopped for a couple of minutes at Maibara. The stretch to Nagoya takes a further 25 minutes, passing through Ogaki (a cotton town) and Gifu, famous for bamboo, paper and for cormorant-fishing, in which trained cormorants catch river smelt (ayu in Japanese) on the Nagara during the summer months. Before reaching Nagoya we sped over the Nobi Plain. Nagoya, well-known for machinery, rolling-stock, chinaware and wooden goods, is the last stop, and we hurtled through the countryside with the Pacific occasionally in view on our right – through Toyohashi, Hamamatsu, Shizuoka until Mount Fuji came in sight on our left. Inactive since it covered Edo (now Tokyo) with ash in 1707, it can be climbed along several different paths during the summer. At an altitude of 3,776 metres it is not only the highest volcano in Japan, but it stands almost as a national emblem in the minds of the people – an Arc de Triomphe, a Statue of Liberty but unlike those it is significantly a natural feature, not man-made or controllable. Hokusai made 'A Hundred Views of Fuji', and I recalled that this swift crossing of central Honshu was very far in mood and speed from the traditional Tokaido journey immortalised by Hiroshige in his 'Fifty-three Stations of the Tokaido' series of 1833–4, consisting of fifty-five colour prints. This sequence was so successful that he made other prints, altogether over nine hundred, eclipsing the reputation for landscape prints of his older con-

Inside the bullet train from Kyoto to Tokyo

temporary Hokusai, who dwelt more on the travellers than on the countryside they passed through.

Within a few minutes we cruised through the south-western suburbs of Tokyo, and everyone alighted at Tokyo Station, a three-storey red brick and stone building completed in 1914, quite out of keeping with the ultra-modern architectural styles extending southward to Ginza. You can go straight to your hotel or leave your luggage in a locker and explore.

Accommodation

If you want to stay in a clean, comfortable lodging where English is spoken and the room rate is around £10–£15 or US$11–18 a day, even Tokyo still has such

The bullet train seen against Mount Fuji

accommodation, despite the myth that it is the most expensive city in the world. You can pay top rates at de luxe hotels if you so desire, but such facilities are at odds with the Japanese experience of bustle, close contact, and the tradition of simply converting your sitting-room into a bedroom at night.

I stayed my first night in Japan at the Heimat Business Hotel opposite Tokyo Station, so convenient for the shinkansen to Kyoto and the connection for Nara. Other business hotels of equivalent standard are the Asian Center, 8–10–32 Akasaka, Minato-ku, five minutes' walk from Aoyama–1–chome station on Ginza subway line; Hotel Sun Route Shibuya, 1–11 Nampeidai-cho, Shibuya-ku, five minutes' walk from Shibuya station on subway or JNR; Tokyo Green Hotel Awajicho, 2–6 Kanda-Awajicho station on Marunouchi subway line; and Tokyo Green Hotel Suidobashi, 1–1–16 Misaki-cho, Chiyoda-ku, four minutes' walk from Suidobashi station on subway or JNR.

Youth hostels are always a bargain: men have the Tokyo YMCA, 7–1 Kanda-Mitoshirocho, Chiyoda-ku, three minutes' walk from Awajicho station on the Marunouchi subway line, and women have the choice of Tokyo YWCA, 1–8–11 Kanda-Surugadai, Chiyoda-ku, five minutes' walk from Ochanomizu station on subway or JNR (public bath only); and Tokyo YWCA Sadohara, 3–1–-1 Ichigaya-Sadohara-cho, Shinjuku-ku, eight minutes' walk from Ichigaya station on subway or JNR.

Shibuya shopping district

Among the most reasonably-priced ryokan are the Fujikan, 4–36–1 Hongo, Bunkyo-ku, three minutes' walk from Hongo–3–chome station on the Marunouchi subway line; the Kimi, 2–1034 Ikebukuro, Toshima-ku, six minutes' walk from Ikebukuro on subway or JNR; English House, 2–23–8, Nishi Ikebukuro, Toshima-ku, one minute's walk from Mejiro station on JNR; and Yashima, 1–15–5 Hyakunin-cho, Shinjuku-ku, one minute's walk from Shin-Okubo station on JNR.

If you cannot get into the last-named, close at hand is the Ikubo House (dormitory accommodation), 1–11–32 Hyakunin-cho, two minutes' walk from Shin-Okubo station. A guest-house with only four rooms where you breakfast with the family is Tom Oshidari's House, 5–29–3 Shimo-Meguro, Meguro-ku, two minutes' bus-ride from Gotanda station on JNR. I also recommend the 139-room Tokyo Yayoi Kaikan, 2–1–14 Nezu, Bunkyo-ku, four minutes' walk from Nezu station on the Chiyoda subway line. My own preference is for the student hostel for men called Wakeijuku, 1–12–1 Mejirodai, Bunkyo-ku, five minutes' bus-ride from Mejiro station on the Yamanote line (alight at Mejirodai-san-chome bus stop), which normally has a few rooms available for foreigners if booked by telephone or letter in advance (tel. 03–941–5534). A single room cost me about £3 per night, with a communal hot bath and shower facilities, and Japanese canteen-style meals shared with exuberant young university students delighted to practise their English, and to talk about their lives and aspirations.

If you wish to stay in the Ueno area for the Zoo or the National Museum, there are Japanese rooms without private bath in the Ryokan Suigetsu, and Western rooms with bath at roughly the same price in the Ohgaiso Business Hotel, both at 3–3–21 Ikenohata, Taito-ku, three minutes' walk from Nezu station on the Chiyoda subway line or five minutes' walk from Keisei Ueno (take Ikenohata exit). The Ohgaiso will delight those who know the work of the novelist Mori Ogai (1862–1922), who lived in this house for some time.

Shoppers may choose to stay in the fashionable Shinjuku, where reasonable rooms in both Western and Japanese styles can be rented at the Ryokan Inabaso, 5–6–13 Shinjuku, Shinjuku-ku, three minutes' walk from the subway stations Shinjuku Gyoen-mae or Shinjuku 3-chome, so near the lovely Shinjuku Gyoen Park and Hanazono Shrine.

National Museum

Your first day in Tokyo is likely to be spent in Ueno Park. The park itself is attactive, but you will be visiting it for the Tokyo National Museum in much the same spirit as the Japanese in London head first for the British Museum and the National Gallery. Like most (but not all) Japanese museums, the National is closed every Monday. Hours of opening are 9 to 4.30 from 4 January to 25 December and I advise early arrival to give yourself time for leisurely appreciation of the carefully-selected masterpieces. Displays of lacquer, textiles, painting and calligraphy are changed every few months for

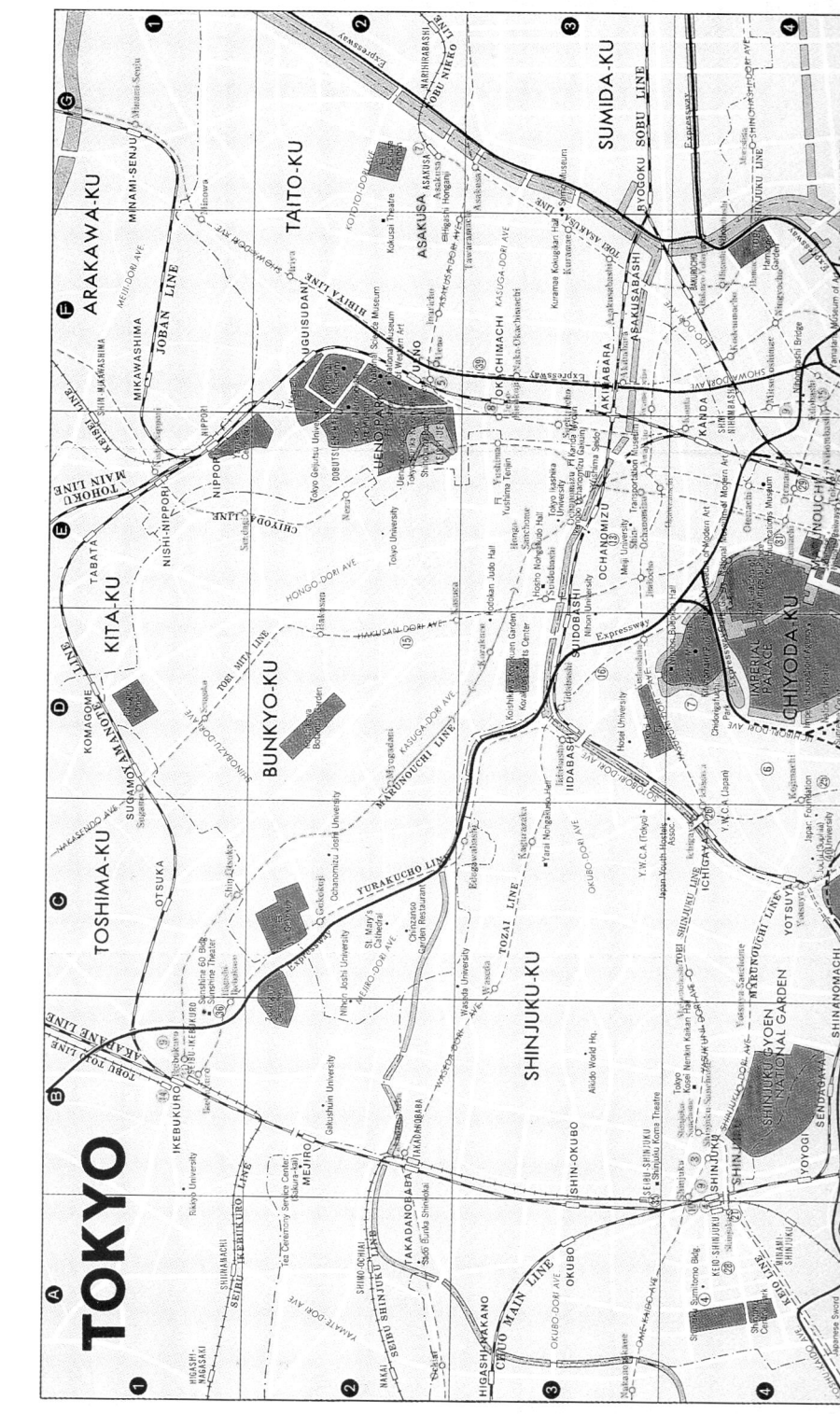

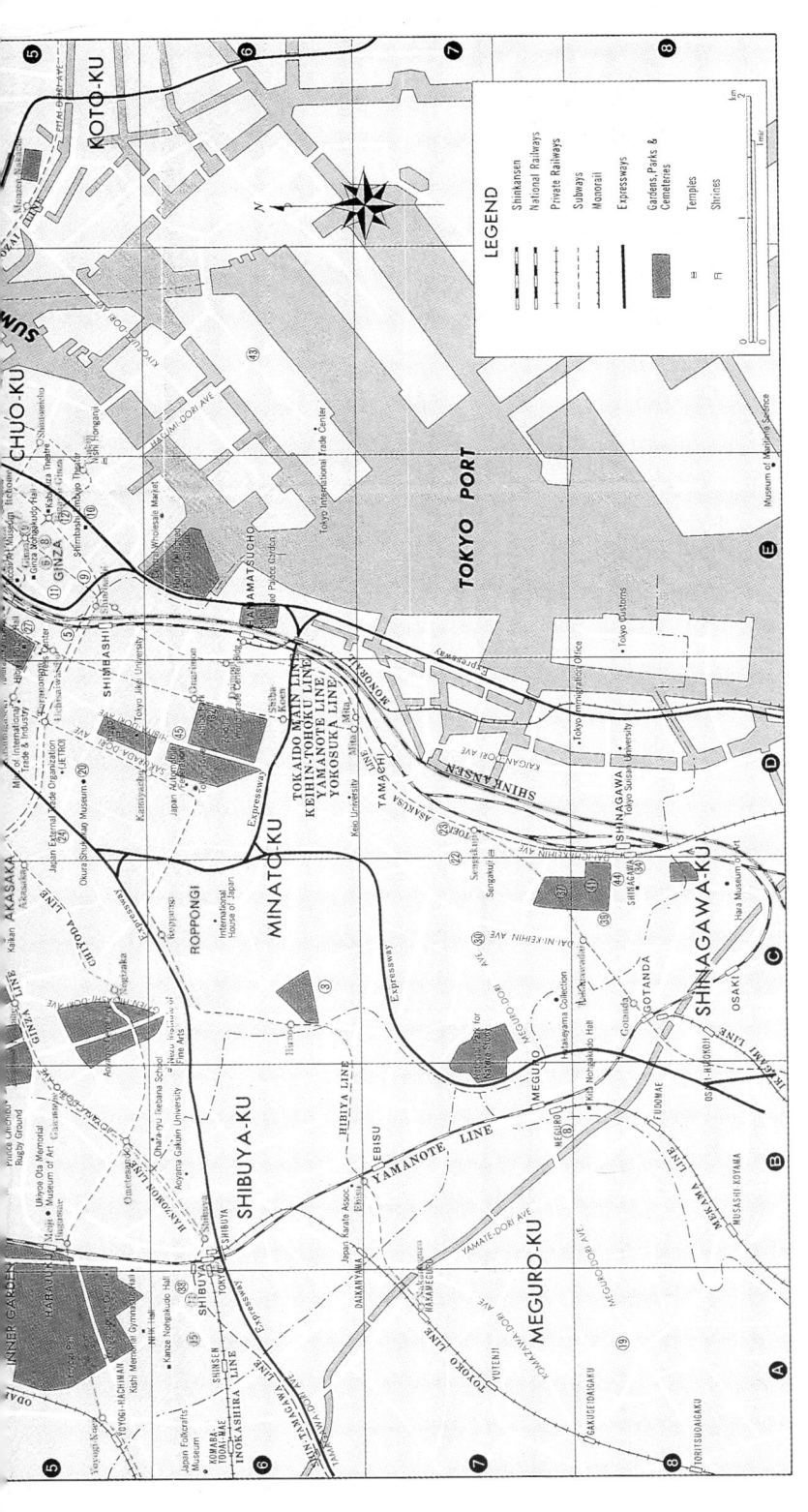

reasons of conservation, and special temporary exhibitions are held in reserved rooms in the Main Gallery or in the Special Exhibition Hall in the Toyokan Basement.

I began with the Hyokeikan Gallery, devoted to Japanese archaeology and prehistory. Useful companions include J.E. Kidder's *Japan* (Thames & Hudson, 1959) in the 'Ancient Peoples and Places' series and Namio Egami's *The Beginnings of Japanese Art* (Weatherhill, 1973), volume 2 in the Heibonsha 'Survey of Japanese Art'. Japanese prehistory had to be rewritten in 1949 with the discovery at Iwajuku of an early Stone Age culture without pottery; similar sites have been discovered since in Hokkaido, mainly dating to the middle and late Palaeolithic. The ground floor rooms 1 and 2 of the Hyokeikan show stone and pottery vessels of the pre-Jomon and Jomon periods, the latter ending in the 3rd or 2nd century B.C.; and Yayoi pottery and bronzes from the end of the Jomon to the 3rd century A.D. On the upper floor, rooms 3–6 present artefacts from the large tombs which give the Kofun period of the 3rd–6th centuries its name. Characteristic of this age of the beautiful, gnomic, amusing and touching baked-clay images, many of men, animals and houses, called haniwa. Their origin is told in the chronicle called *Nihongi* translated by W.G. Aston (Charles E. Tuttle, 1972, p. 178). In the Japanese year corresponding to our 2 B.C., the Emperor Suinin's younger brother died. He was buried at Tsukizaka in Musa. 'Thereupon his personal attendants were assembled, and were all buried alive upright in the precinct of the misasagi (mausoleum). For several days they died not, but wept and wailed day and night. At last they died and rotted. Dogs and crows gathered and ate them. The Emperor, hearing the sound of their weeping and wailing, was grieved in heart, and commanded his high officers, saying: "It is a very painful thing to force those whom one has loved in life to follow him in death. Though it be an ancient custom, why follow it if it is bad? From this time forward, take counsel so as to put a stop to the following of the dead". When the Empress Hibasu died, the official Nomi no Sukune came forward with clay-workers from Izumo, suggesting to the Emperor: "Henceforward let it be the law for future ages to substitute things of clay for living men, and to set them up at tumuli", and the Emperor agreed.'

The weakness of the literary record in purely archaeological terms seems to be proved by the fact that the first human haniwa figures so far known date from the fifth-century site of the Emperor Nintoku's mausoleum near Osaka. Fumio Miki, in his illustrated history of *Haniwa* (1974), shows that the eighth-century annals project contemporary events back to the time of Suinin to lend them an attractively antique aura. He suggests that 'the account of Nomi no Sukune's earning imperial gratitude for devising clay figures to take the place of human sacrifices makes perfect sense if it is viewed as an attempt by the Haji family, who supervised imperial funerals and cared for the mausolea, to manipulate the meritorious service of their ancestor to their own benefit'. This indicates the suspect historicity of the Nara-period annals: the *Kojiki* compiled in

712 and the *Nihongi* in 720; and also how historical literature has constantly turned on the fortunes of those who commissioned it, or those who were in a position to influence its composition. The haniwa are not only attractive in themselves but make a vital contribution to our knowledge of how the Japanese of the third to seventh centuries dressed, ate and built their houses.

Less immediately appealing perhaps are the tiles, urns and caskets of Asuka and Nara age (538–794) on the ground floor on your way to the exit.

The Main Gallery (Honkan) of Tokyo National Museum has ten rooms on each of two floors, and a further five (three of them on the ground floor) reserved for temporary displays. If you choose to follow the route in this book, you will reap the benefit as you enter Room 1, with its great Nara-period Shaka Nyorai from Saidaiji and Yakushi Nyorai, images familiar in style and iconography from Nara. Here is a great standing wooden Juichimen Kannon from Yakushiji, Nara, and a Senju Kannon from Nara's Seinanin. In Room 3 I found the great 13th-century bronze Bishamonten from Kyoto's Kuramadera: a miraculous concentration of stillness and vigour, delicacy and strength. Eison's Amida Nyorai of 1259 stands near the refined Kannon of the same century from Kyoto's Kiyomizudera. Rooms 4 and 5 are devoted to the greatest examples of Japanese metalwork, while Rooms 6 and 7 show arms and armour, including named swords, with the finest objects from the golden age of the Bizen and Myochin schools of the Kamakura period. After Room 8, on textiles, you come to two halls of ceramics arranged chronologically, Room 9 being dominated by a tall-necked jar of Kofun-Asuka (7th century) from Mie Prefecture. In Room 10 I particularly admired the elegant tea caddies by Aoki Mokubei, who died in 1833. Rooms 11–18 are devoted to the various genres of painting: Buddhist tales and images, secular hand-scrolls, folding screens, and prints of the floating world: those ukiyoe so despised until recently in Japan and so avidly collected in the West – partly because so many examples have come on the market and published guides like those of Stewart, Michener and Hillier have stimulated demand in their turn. Room 12 showed 'Wagtails' by Soen (15th century) and a landscape by Shinso; Room 13 flowers and birds of the four seasons by Okamoto Shoko (1807–62). Room 14 sketches the development of ukiyoe from its origins with Moronobu about 1660, to the first addition of colour (vermilion) about 1700, and the use of numerous colours from 1765 initiated by Harunobu; it must be said that this selection is both tiny and unrepresentative. Room 15, devoted to lacquer, offers a fragment dated to the 8th century from Nara's Todaiji. The view down to the pond and trees is delightful. Room 16 displays lacquer treasures such as the writing box of the artist Ogata Korin (1658–1716) with its design of Yatsuhashi Bridge. Rooms 17–18 exemplify the dilemma of 19th and 20th century Japanese art after the Meiji Restoration: where do we go from here? Poor imitations of western art, like 'Maiko Girls' by Kuroda Seiko (1866–1924), seem to offer no better a solution than the tired convention of Japanese art such as 'Heian Shrine and Maruyama Park' by Takeuchi Seiho (1864–1942).

Rooms 19–20 are devoted to exquisite examples of calligraphy, the despair of western 'writers' who are after all so often only 'typists' or 'manipulators of word processors' and have forgotten or never known the contact of fresh black ink with a flowing brush or pen on blank white paper.

Lunch can be procured at a reasonably-priced restaurant beside the Toyokan (Gallery of Eastern Art): I enjoyed a crisp salad with fried fish for ¥600 (£1.80 or US$2) but coffee is as usual in Japan very expensive at ¥250.

The ground floor of the Gallery of Eastern Art and mezzanine provide a sketchy view of objects outside Japan and Korea, beginning with a group of four masterpieces of Gandharan art, that transitional Greco-Buddhist style centred on modern north-west Pakistan; fine T'ang bas-reliefs of the eighth century from the Bao-ching-si Temple in Shensi; a Parthian limestone Hercules of the 1st–2nd centuries from Hatra in Iraq, bronze ibexes from Luristan, Iran; and a marvellous ibis from Egypt. Sculptures from Angkor Thom and Angkor Wat give way to a spectacular array of Chinese bronzes and a small 14th-century hanging scroll of a 'Boat tied up at a Quay' by Lou Luan of the Yüan dynasty.

The first floor is devoted exclusively to Chinese art, from the earliest ritual bronzes and jades of the Shang to stone reliefs of the Han, and paintings of the Sung and Ch'ing.

The second floor covers archaeology and art of Korea (gold earrings of the 5th–6th centuries are of dazzling quality) and Central Asian painting and sculpture, with excellent examples from Khotan, Turfan, Tumshuk and Yotkan.

After your visit to Horyuji in Nara, your appetite will have been whetted for the Treasures of Horyuji (closed on Thursday) in the special gallery in the National Museum. They date from the Asuka Period (522–644) before Nara became the national capital, to the Edo period (19th century) and are particularly strong in painting, sculpture, calligraphy, Buddhist religious objects, and textiles. There is a priceless range of Nara-period Gagaku masks, and a T'ang seven-stringed kin or zither of lacquered wood dated 724. Look out for the silver dragon-head pitcher of T'ang date and an Asuka-period copper incense-burner with a long handle in the shape of a magpie's tail.

More Museums

Another day you might wish to see other museums in Ueno Park. By starting early in summer from Uguisudani JNR station you come after a twelve-minute walk to Kaneiji Temple. The original Kaneiji once owned all the land in present-day Ueno Park. It was destroyed by fire in 1868 (except for the secret Yakushi image) and the main hall of another temple was moved here. Passing the National Museum, which we have seen in detail, we come to a choice of three more museums.

The National Science Museum is open every day but Monday between 9 and 4.30. The National Museum of Western Art, open every day but Monday between 9 and 5, has captions in English as well as in Japanese, and an illustrated catalogue of *Masterpieces* (1983) ranging from Rogier van der Weyden and Joos van Cleve to Tintoretto and El Greco. I found a wonderful 'Village Wedding' by my *pittore dilettissimo* Jan Steen, and a characteristically turbulent 'Landscape with Stormy Sea' by Alessandro Magnasco. If the French Impressionists are on the whole represented by disappointing examples, the same is not true of the works by Hubert Robert and the stunning collection of bronzes by Rodin, the best outside France.

The Metropolitan Art Museum, near the entrance to Ueno Zoo, is open every day but Monday between 9 and 5, free of charge except for any special exhibitions, and is the best place to see a cross-section of contemporary Japanese artists.

Ueno Zoo

Ueno Zoo, open 9-4.30 every day but Monday, must be one of the world's most attractive animal parks. The giant pandas Huan Huan (born January 1980) and Fei Fei (born November 1982) munch unconcernedly amid a barrage of camera flashes and awed exclamations: but then even the Chinese among whom they are native gape at them in wonder in Peking Zoo. (They are not seen on Fridays). The South African Meerkat had just produced three babies, and equally a cynosure for many eyes in the East Garden are the bison, polar bear, scarlet ibis, elephant, and tapir. A three-hundred metre monorail chugs you to the West Garden, where flamingoes lord and lady their aristocratic way amid hippos and rhino, giraffe and Barbary sheep, and a multiplicity of water fowl presided over by neat penguins. Of course I stayed too long among the fennecs and beavers, cormorants and ostriches, imagining this hill when it housed the villa of Todo Takatora, who designed Edo Castle.

Not far from the bisons is the Five-Storey Kaneiji Pagoda, originally dating from 1631 but in its present form rebuilt in 1639 following a fire.

Toshogu Shrine

Toshogu Shrine is open from 9–5 every day of the year, as is its peony garden between 1 January to mid-February for winter peonies, and from mid-April to mid-May for spring peonies in over two hundred varieties. The Shrine itself naturally retreats into the shade of its celebrated namesake at Nikko, north of Tokyo, likewise dedicated to the deified Tokugawa Shogun Ieyasu, named Tosho Dai Gongen, or Great Avatar of Eastern Ilumination. The Tokyo shrine to Ieyasu was designed by Todo Takatora in 1627, but heavily restored in 1650. Wall paintings by Tanyu Kano of the celebrated Kyoto school show Chinese lions in the decorative style of the mid-17th century; dragons are the chief feature of the great gate, like the fence and the paintings of the mid-17th century.

Shinobazu Pond

Shinobazu Pond was the scene of my first and only encounter with that rarity in Japan: the down-and-out. Japan is not yet a welfare state like Sweden or Britain; but reliance on individual efforts to find jobs and solidarity within the extended family are no longer the dependable bulwarks they were in the boom years of the 1960s and 1970s. Unemployment may be much lower than in Western Europe, but its very rarity afflicts the jobless correspondingly more bitterly. The caring family is traditionally so devotedly responsible that those without a family find themselves even more than customarily isolated. There are few hospitals for those outside the network of private and official medical plans, and those few depend on donations to supplement subsidies from the city authorities. Tuberculosis, geriatric ailments and alcoholism are the main hazards of these misfits, who have found out that it can be distressing to find oneself outside a conformist society dedicated to material success.

At the south end of Shinobazu Pond I looked up to Shinobugaoka, as Ueno Hill was once called. It means Mount of Endurance, and Abbot Tenkai of Kaneiji imagined that this expanse of water, then still a stretch of Tokyo Bay, was his beloved Lake Biwa not far from Kyoto and caused an island to be built in the centre, like Biwa's Chikubu, with its temple to Benten and Kannon. Tenkai built his own Benzaiten, dedicated to the Goddess of Fortune. The pond, which became known as Impatient Pond (Shinobazunoike), was made into rice fields during World War II and in 1945 the Benzaiten was destroyed. A new edifice transcends religious frontiers (tenuous as they are throughout Japan), incorporating both a Shinto torii and Buddhist worship. The lotus and lily pond has been restored, and all year round you can glimpse moorhens, egrets, little grebes and cormorants. Five thousand wild ducks (mostly pintails) visit the pond each September, disturbing tramps asleep on benches, and stay in this mild climate until April.

Shitamachi Museum

Southeast of the pond you can find the Shitamachi Museum, open between 9.30 and 4.30 every day but Mondays, national holidays, and between 29 December and 3 January. A folk museum helping residents and visitors alike to picture old Edo from the later Meiji era to the Great Kanto Earthquake of 1923, it presents on two floors the minutiae of a lost epoch before plastic or neon, before computers or the Atom Bomb. The ground floor shows the shops and houses of craftsmen and merchants, while the upper floor displays photographs and material objects of daily life such as tools, clothes, domestic utensils and children's toys. A way of life that has disappeared almost entirely, you might think, yet the particular cultural baggage of the Japanese is not so easily lost. The biggest killer in Japan has always been rampant fire after earthquakes, then war: first civil and later global. Population expanded jerkily over the centuries, then the baby boom of the mid-1960s forced the planners to think about creating more space for a rapidly-increasing population. Planners built downwards: an underground transport system and new shopping centres; they built upwards: skyscrapers for offices, high-rise apartment blocks. They rationalised the use of existing land and expanded into the mountains by excavating into the hillside and flattening barren slopes for new villages and towns. They reclaimed land from Tokyo Bay, turned a blind eye to houses built in back gardens which overcrowded many communities, and they designed and built expressways above rivers and existing roads.

Yet paradoxically Tokyo is not only the electric jungle of Ginza's lights at night and the stolid administrative façade of Marunouchi. You step outside Shitamachi Museum and find yourself in Ueno Park, and claustrophobes can find many other such open spaces.

Yushima Tenjin Shrine

We can find one very close: the Yushima Tenjin Shrine, celebrated all over Japan for its plum blossom from mid-February to mid-March. 'Tenjin' refers to Michizane Sugawara, whom we have encountered in Kyoto, and by extension to the patron saint of students, who come here to pray for success in examinations. They write their name and address on votive wooden tablets, ema, or 'horse pictures' because many contain a picture of a horse, emblem of power and authority in a land where peasants were forbidden to ride. They then hang this tablet in the shrine and presumably blame failure on themselves and credit success to Tenjin. Thus do superstitions rise and prosper: nobody can finally prove that they are always useless. It is something of a surprise, in this ravaged city, to learn that the shrine's main hall is a survival from 1885, quietly overcoming all the menaces of earthquakes and world wars.

Yushima Seido

Yushima Seido, facing Ochanomizu Station across the river Kanda, is a shrine dedicated to Confucius, whose wisdom, scholarship and devotion to learning have made an incalculable impact on Japanese history and culture. A predecessor of the Seido, or Sacred Hall, was built on Ueno Hill (where Saigo's statue now stands) in 1632, when the Hayashi family founded a Confucian college, moved here to Yushima in 1690 by Tsunayoshi, a fervent Tokugawa Confucianist shogun. The present Seido dates from 1935, and is the work of Chuta Ito, architect of Kyoto's Heian Shrine. Admission to the courtyard and main hall is from 10–4 on Sundays.

Imperial Palace

As you might imagine, the greater part of the Palace is private to the Imperial Family, and the curious foreigner is normally restricted to walking around the external perimeter of the walls (2½ hours without any major pause) and visiting the Eastern Garden, accessible through the Otemon, on the south-eastern or Tokyo Station side; the Hirakawamon, on the north-eastern or Takebashi side; or the Kitahanebashi, on the northwestern or National Museum of Modern Art side.

Admission to the Eastern Garden is from 9–4 (last entry at 3 p.m.) daily except on Mondays, Fridays and state ceremonial days. Nothing is payable, but you need to collect a plastic token on the way in, and surrender it again on the way out. If you enter by the Ote Gate, past administrative offices you will eventually come to two barrack-rooms of the 1860s, where the Imperial Guards were accommodated. On the right is the garden of Ninomaru, said to have been designed originally by Enshu Kobori, whom we have met in Kyoto. 'Ninomaru' means 'Second Stronghold', the Main Stronghold being 'Honmaru', where the Shogun lived and kept his staterooms. Edo Castle, constructed from 1590 by the Shogun Ieyasu on the ruins of an earlier fortress, was the residence of the Tokugawa Shogunate for 265 years. The northern stronghold (Kitanomaru) is now a public park. The western stronghold (Nishinomaru) remains, by and large, the private sector of the Imperial Palace grounds. Ieyasu's castle was finished in 1640, but burned down in 1657 despite a moat-system and had to be rebuilt, with walls so high and thick that the power of the Shogunate seemed invincible. But then, the Roman and Aztec Empires seemed eternal too. The palaces were devastated by fire, or pulled down when a new Imperial Palace was built; the latest in the line was completed in 1968, and it was then that the Honmaru and Ninomaru sectors were made public. Rock for building the slope from the Swan Moat up to Honmaru was quarried from all over the archipelago, and brought in ships that all too often sank in bad weather: in one convoy alone more than two hundred ships capsized.

Moat beside the Imperial Palace

Though both Ninomaru and Honmaru have all but vanished, the Fujimi Tower of Honmaru Stronghold is still visible, if you leave the Ninomaru garden, turn right past another barracks, then left at the summit of the hill. The mid-17th century tower can then be seen through a gate.

Otherwise, our picture of the Honmaru must be culled from old plans, which reveal three building complexes: state halls, where the Shogun would receive homage from his vassals; the private chambers where the Shogun would retire for a few hours free from the restrictions of etiquette; and the inner chambers, a euphemism for the harem, with its hundreds of concubines available to the Shogun in addition to his official wife. This vanished palace-castle (Kyujo as the Japanese say) was protected by 66 gates, 36 barracks or guardhouses and 19 towers called yagura. It must in its heyday have resembled Peking's Forbidden City.

Edo was thus the political and military heart of Japan, but the most celebrated early literary reference to the town on the Sumida was by a courtier whose first priority was to get back to Kyoto. What was Edo famous for? Dried sardines and salted crackers, perhaps. But when the West discovered Japan, it was the portable colour prints of the 18th and 19th centuries that defined Japan, rather than the great murals and screen of Kyoto. In a people tactful, discreet and modest, it is only in Edo–Tokyo that boasts of 'the largest city in the world', 'the tallest skyscraper in Japan' can be heard, and perhaps we should do well to look for the true heart of the country elsewhere. As you are about to leave by the Hirakawa Gate, look for the great mass of boulders, part of the foundations of the castle. Volunteers anxious to offer their lives for the eternal strength of Edo Castle came forth to be buried alive. As the Frenchman François Caron wrote in the seventeenth century: 'If a lord cause a wall to be built, either for the king or for himself, his servants oftentimes beg they might have the honour to lie underneath, from a belief that what is founded upon a living man's flesh is subject to no misfortune. This request granted, they go with joy to the designated place and, lying down there, allow the foundation stones to be laid upon them, which by their weight immediately bruise and shiver them to pieces'. If this appears to be a tall story, it must be remembered that when the Edo walls were repaired after the 1923 Kanto earthquake skeletons were found with their hands in prayer, and gold coins on their head and shoulders.

The Shoguns, known throughout Japanese history as usurpers of the power originally vested in the Emperor, eventually had to give way, and when the old edict forcing daimyo lords to live part of the year in Edo was rescinded in 1862, many left the capital, until within a few years its population had fallen to fewer than 600,000 inhabitants and in 1868 power was restored by Shogun Tokugawa Yoshinobu to the Emperor in the form of a boy of 16 called Mutsuhito Sukenomiya, named subsequently like his reign Meiji ('Enlightened Rule'). Edo's name was dropped as another link with a past to be forgotten in the wake of intended modernization, and replaced by 'Tokyo', eastern capital, while Kyoto was officially renamed 'Saikyo', western capital. The Meiji era which followed saw the growth of Japan as an industrial, financial and commercial power comparable in some ways to Victorian England, with the same stress on middle-class values such as probity and hard work, and vigorous expansionism. Because of the Kanto earthquake of 1923 and the aerial devastation caused by bombs in 1945, little survives from Meiji Tokyo – or the Tokyo of his son Taisho, who reigned for fourteen years, until 1926. Despite the effects of World War II, which left the capital flattened, dazed and empty, Japan has emerged if anything even more resilient, the old values intact, and the new values (such as a greater rôle for women, and more allowance made for individualism) cautiously seeking compromises.

As I strolled round the old castle moats encircling the Imperial Palace, I reflected on the series of internal and external events which had led from the decision to settle in Nara in 710 to the tumult of vigorous, chattering modern Japanese in western clothes leaving Marunouchi's Mitsubishi Building or Sumitomo Bank.

National Museum of Modern Art

From the Hirakawa Gate I made for the National Museum of Modern Art, divided between so-called 'fine arts' and 'crafts', a western distinction to which Japanese museum-planners here conform.

British Embassy

The Craft Gallery, Kogeikan, is at 1–1 Kitanomaru Koen, with opening hours like that of the Main Hall 10–5 daily except Mondays. You can buy a combined ticket to both museums for ¥500; individually the two fees total ¥750. The Craft Gallery opened in 1977 to display pottery and porcelain, lacquer, basketry, textiles, metalwork and other leading crafts. If this gallery is closed for administrative reasons, you can see a similar display at the Japan Folk Crafts Museum, 4–3–33 Komaba, Meguro Ward, five minutes' walk from Komaba-Todaimae station on the Keio-Inokashira line (10–5 except on Mondays and during February).

The Main Hall (Honkan) of the National Museum of Modern Art is at 3 Kitanomaru Koen, stressing twentieth-century Japanese artists such as Takamura Kotaro but also featuring special exhibitions by painters of international stature such as Picasso and Edvard Munch. Emerging on the main road outside Chidorigafuchi park, you soon come to a grey stone building which is the British Embassy, as strategically close to the Imperial Palace as its counterpart in Moscow is to the Kremlin.

Yasukuni Shrine

Instead of continuing along the circuit of the walls in the same direction, I headed back for Yasukuni Shinto Shrine, on the opposite side of Yasukunidori. The shrine's name, 'Peace to the Nation', stands for the usual euphemism familiar from Orwell – 'Peace means War', for here are enshrined the spirits of those millions of Japanese who have perished in combat. Allied soldiers who fought against the Axis may be deterred from visiting this place, but in a spirit of reconciliation I urge everyone to do so. There is nothing ancient about Yasukuni, erected in 1869, except for the fact that here stands the first bronze statue erected in Japan (dating to 1888): Masujiro Omura (1824–69), the first Meiji War Minister, to be seen in the outer precinct. And except that Noh plays are performed on shrine festivals falling annually on 21–23 April, 14–16 July, and 17–19 October. Sumo matches are held here at the same time. Naturally enough, only Japanese worshippers are permitted to enter the inner sanctuary.

The Palace Circuit

Returning down the majestic Uchibori Avenue past the British Embassy, with the National Theatre also on my right, I saw the National Diet Library – Japan's equivalent of the Library of Congress – next to the National Diet itself, the Congress or Houses of Parliament of Japan. The next crossing of the imperial moat is called Sakurada Bridge, and the next Nijobashi ('Double Layer' because of the extra strengthening required to support it). Next comes Sakashita Bridge, where you enter to request permission (with your passport an absolute necessity) from the Imperial Household Agency to visit the Imperial Palace itself on a 1½-hour tour in Japanese between 9 and 4.30 on Mondays to Fridays or between nine and noon on Saturdays. The Palace itself is however intrinsically uninteresting, dating from 1968 and being made of ferro-concrete.

Idemitsu Art Museum

Not far from the Imperial Theatre, and designed by the same architect, Taniguchi Yoshiro, the Idemitsu Art Museum (Idemitsu Bijutsukan) is an interesting private gallery, open daily from 10–5 except on Mondays. It is to be found on the ninth floor of the International Building, with breathtaking views over the Imperial Palace. The central hall is customarily devoted to masterpieces of Chinese and Japanese ceramics, including work by Ogata Kenzan popularised in the West by Bernard Leach. Among the prints, drawings and

National Diet Building

paintings selected for show are pieces by the Zen master Gibon Sengai (1750–1837), subject of a monograph in English by D.T. Suzuki (1971). You may also be lucky enough to see one of the special exhibitions held five or six times a year at the Idemitsu.

St Mary's Cathedral

If you were intrigued by Kenzo Tange's Olympic stadia for swimming and basketball in Yoyogi Park, you may well wish to see an equally bold conception carried to fruition: his Roman Catholic Cathedral at 16–15 Sekiguchi 3-chome, Bunkyo Ward, near the Chinzanso Restaurant. From above it looks like a paper kite; from floor-level the walls seem to rush up with quite a Gothic, heavenward feeling. Light is skilfully conveyed from above and, instead of using European stained-glass techniques, Tange adopted veined marble, through which a softened light streams into the vast interior, its steep roof emulating the vaults to which prayer may ascend. All the walls seem at first to be flat, as in the case of the separate bell-tower, but they are in fact hyperbolic.

Jimbocho

The 'Town with God's Protection' is as famous for its bookshops as is Akihabara for discounted electrical goods. About two hundred bookshops are crowded into six hundred metres of Yasukunidori centred on Jimbocho crossroads and ending at the Surugadai intersection. You are near five private universities (Chuo, Hosei, Meiji, Nihon, Senju) and many student lodgings – and not too far from Tokyo YMCA Hotel.

Japan's largest bookshop is Sanseido in Jimbocho, displaying a million volumes on about 4,000 square metres throughout eight storeys. For advice, ask at the Customer Information desk. You will not be alone: when it opened in March 1981 it attracted 103,600 customers and the daily average for its first month was 65,000. The pride of the area's many antiquarian bookshops is Isseido, not far from Sanseido and on the same side of the road, with a worldwide clientele and books in fifty and more languages.

Yet the joy of Jimbocho is its proliferation of tiny specialist bookshops, like the good old days of London's Charing Cross Road before it became infected with remainder mania: one shop has books only from the USSR, another specialises in Chinese literature, a third antiquarian movie magazines, a fourth fortune-telling, a fifth maps, and a sixth comics, that curiously ubiquitous genre which infests many Japanese coffee-shops. Look for ceramic cats in bookshop windows holding up one paw in a gesture of welcome. This is the area, too for records, cassettes, and the sporting equipment currently favoured by students, from skiing to baseball.

Russian Orthodox Cathedral

Which Russian Orthodox Cathedral was built by a British architect? Why, Tokyo Fukkatsu Daiseido, affectionately known as Nikoraido (Nicholas' Hall) not after the saint of that name, but after the priest Ivan Kasatkin Nikolai (1836–1912). It took eight years to build (1876–1884) under the architect Josiah Conder. Earthquake damage was made good in 1929, and the Cathedral remains, much like the Russian Church in the Czech spa of Karlovy Vary, a curiosity faintly touching in its quiet incongruity. It is open daily between 1 and 4 p.m.

Paper Museum

If you take the Keihin Tohoku line north of Ueno and alight at Oji you will come to Kami no Hakubutsukan, the Japanese Paper Museum, open 9.30–4.30 except for Mondays, national holidays and from 30 December to 4 January. Japanese handmade paper still leads the world, and Japan was one of the first countries outside China to produce it in sufficient quantities for the spread of religious and literary classics. Invented in Honan about the year 105, paper had spread to Turfan in Central Asia by 399, and to Japan in 610 – before its first recorded appearance on the Silk Road to Samarkand in 751, Baghdad in 793 and Cairo in 900. It is about 1100 before paper is known to have been made at Fez, 1150 in Spain, 1189 in France and 1494 before it was made in quantity in London. Japan ranks ninth among the world's leading consumers of paper per capita (175 kg per capita in 1983, compared with 250 kg per capita in the USA) and paper is used for many purposes in Japan which are unknown in the West, such as for umbrellas, cups, tea-caddies, windows, doors, and clothes (though I found bark-cloth in Sumatra and Mexico). Oji has been connected with paper since the first industrial papermill began operations here in 1875, using the conveniently near Sumida river for transport. Nowadays the papermill's operations are centred in Hokkaido, but many villages throughout Japan remain well-known as paper-producing co-operatives, and a glance at the distribution map on p. 434 of Sukey Hughes' *Washi* (1978) reveals the spread of paper-makers from Kagoshima to Aomori, with particular concentrations (worth visiting if you are nearby) in Shimane and Kochi, respectively north and south of Hiroshima.

You can buy sheets of mulberry paper called kozo at the Museum, as well as a history of Japanese papermaking in English, revised by the Museum in 1980. This is helpful – as is the guidebook in English – because the Museum's captions are only in Japanese. Room 1 shows raw materials and machines, and Room 2 some of the many types of paper for such various purposes as cigarettes, nappies, egg cartons, stencils, cups, folders, magazines and tissues. Room 3 is devoted to origami, the Japanese art of paper-folding, and Room 4 to historical papers such as papyrus, parchment, papier-mâché, and kites. Room 5 is for special changing displays and Room 6 for the history of machine-made papers and mills. Room 7 is for connoisseurs of washi, Japanese hand-made papers, including poem-sheets, woodblock papers, stencil patterns, exquisite wrapping papers, and thick decorative papers used as wall partitions. Room 8 shows the raw materials and processes in manufacturing handmade papers, including poem-sheets, woodblock papers, stencil patterns, exquisite wrapping papers, and thick decorative papers used as wall partitions. Room 8 shows the raw materials and processes in manufacturing handmade paper. In 1901 there were 68,000 people engaged in making handmade papers, but the figure has dropped to a few hundred in 1985.

I tiptoed past a women's club busy in Room 8 with cutting paper and designing flower pictures on every available inch of table-space and found the plants in the garden outside from which papers are made: not only kozo, but also gampi and mitsumata. An astonishing find too: Edgeworthia, an old British steam engine. Outside the gate again I was overwhelmed by the sheer exuberance of activity and noise, from the trains entering and leaving Oji to the blunt bop of tennis balls swatted by youngsters playing in full tennis gear against walls where the other half of the court should have been. In the west we should have halved the number of courts so that fewer people could have a full game; in Japan they double the number of courts so that more people can play a new game: semi-tennis.

Tokyo Bunka Kaikan

At 6.30 I settled down in the Tokyo Bunka Kaikan for the fiftieth anniversary performance of Fujiwara Opera. It was the Japanese première of Donizetti's *Maria Stuarda*, conducted by Armando Gatto and sung in Italian by Yasuko Hayashi (Mary Stuart), Maria Luisa Nave (Queen Elizabeth), and Ottavio Garaventa (Earl of Leicester). The auditorium was packed, the acoustics highly effective, and the production and lighting up to top western standards, the audience as discreetly quiet as in Germany. This opera house, used also for concerts and recitals, is as narrow as the National Theatre is wide, and side seats suffered from limited visibility. The cheaper seats in categories D and E were already sold out, and I could only obtain a C seat in the circle for ¥7,000 (£21), the top price for that performance being ¥12,000.

Gardens

Tokyo as a garden city? What a peculiar notion, in the opinion of many. But a great green swathe of gardens dominates central Tokyo, from the Meiji Shrine's Inner Garden on the west to Shinjuku Gyoen, the Meiji Shrine's Outer Garden, and the moated Imperial Palace on the east. We shall find so many gardens in fact that it will be difficult to justify the label 'concrete jungle' once applied to Tokyo. I remember reading – and taking a note for some unimagined future reference – that in *Encounter* many years ago Edward Seidensticker of all people (author of *Low City, High City*, one of the most evocative of Tokyo books) said 'It does not take long to become an Old Resident of Tokyo: only a little more than the two years considered standard by the diplomatic corps and foundations. Then the years begin of trying to show newcomers the city. There can be few cities in which this particular duty of the Old Resident is more trying, for there is almost nothing to show'. This may be relatively true in comparison with Nara and Kyoto, or Florence and Venice, or Bukhara and Samarkand, or Sabratha and Leptis Magna. But if one ignores the more odious comparisons, Tokyo is still a thrilling city, and it becomes more exciting day by day, as you discover the Tsukiji Fish Market, Suntory Museum, atmospheric Sengakuji, or Rikugien Garden.

Meiji Jingu

For me, I suppose the overwhelming shock of delight came with the unexpected sea of irises in the Meiji Inner Garden. I had alighted at Harajuku on the Yamanote line and joined a throng of strolling families. Eight million people visit the Meiji Shrine and its forest every year, many of them during the New Year festivities, and others on the day of the Grand Festival of the deified

Meiji Shrine. Garden in Spring

Meiji, 3 November. Both Emperor Meiji and Empress Shoken are enshrined and worshipped at Meiji Jingu, not least for their achievements in leading an agrarian feudal society into industrial democracy without sacrificing the central traditions of Japanese culture. Compulsory education paved the way for a modern nation, the National Diet or Parliament was established, and the country opened to the world after centuries of isolation. Emperor Meiji died in 1912 and the Empress Dowager in 1914, after which the pattern of deifying former rulers – Shomu, Shotoku, Ieyasu are examples already noted in these pages – was followed by designating Yoyogi as the site of a new Meiji Shrine. Work on the Shrine began in 1915 and was completed in 1920, the buildings being surrounded by 120,000 trees of 365 varieties, predominantly evergreen. Demolished by air raids in 1945, the Shrine was completely rebuilt by 1958 in the nagare-tsukuri style.

Do not miss the Iris Garden, off the main avenue of the inner gardens to your left, which is at its loveliest in May and June but remains open between 1 March and 3 November from 9.00 to 4.30, and every other day from 9 to 4. Their range of glorious yet subtle colours runs through every shade of violet and purple above a sea of green stems, below a canopy of green trees. A decorously tiny rough tea pavilion (Kakuintei) enhances the sweeping, riverine views rather than interrupting them. A legend by the well of Kiyomasaido, which feeds the South Ponds, reads 'the pure water gush out with a rush all the year round. This well is famous for the ingenious way of sinking and the superiority of water'. Equally timeless is the graceless, flowing curve of the shrine's many curves. Nobody is admitted into the inner courtyard, but the outer courtyard frequently offers spectacles of bells, drums, and the waving of symbolic paper streamers to cast out evil. A long, relaxing walk, free of any traffic, brings you from the shrine to the Homotsuden, or Treasure Museum, built in azekura style, but of concrete 'logs' rather than the historic wooden logs we have seen at Todaiji in Nara. The museum (open 9–4.30 from March to October and 9–4 from November to February) shows the imperial robes, furniture, books (his favourite being the annals called *Kojiki* and *Nihongi*) and carriage. White and red arrows laid permanently on the floor ensure that you walk round only in the approved manner; you maintain a reverent silence, and it is possible that you may not be admitted if your apparel is too informal.

Shinjuku Gyoen

You can leave the Meiji Shrine by the north-east corner, in the direction of Yoyogi (another exit on the west side will bring you out near Sangubashi station on the Odakyu line, not far from the Japan Sword Museum), for the Shinjuku Gyoen.

The Sendagaya entrance is the nearest to the Meiji Shrine, but there is a main entrance at the east of the garden not far from Shinanomachi station, a third (with parking) at the north-east corner, and a fourth very close to Shinjuku Gyoenmae station. Open every day of the year except Mondays from 9 to 4, the garden presents two worlds in one: a western garden in the French style and a Japanese garden, with the traditional wooden bridges, islands, ponds, cherry blossoms in spring and chrysanthemums in autumn. I wandered in the splendid greenhouse built in 1958, with its selection of orchids and thought back nostalgically to those unrivalled orchid houses at Bogor in Java where specialists produce orchids that smell of tobacco and chocolate, cheese and spices.

The present Shinjuku Gyoen was created between 1901 and 1906 to designs by Henri Martinet of Versailles, and extends to an area of 180,000 tsubo, equivalent to 147 acres. The Shinjuku Imperial Garden includes the land granted by the Tokugawa Shogunate to the feudal Lord Naito of Takato, Shinshu, which subsequently became state property and has developed into a scientific centre for research into horticulture. The lawns, rare in Japan, can be used for picnics, sunbathing, and parties. It is a place to relax away from the city bustle.

Southwest from Shinjuku Gyoen you come to the Outer Garden of the Meiji Shrine, access being from either Sendagaya station or Shinanomachi. Beside the gymnasium, swimming pool, National Stadium, two baseball stadia, rugby park and tennis courts stands the Meiji Memorial Gallery. The Meiji Memorial Hall faces the palace of the Crown Prince. Wedding ceremonies and receptions are organized here (as well as at Meiji Jingu) and it is said that the dressing-room can accommodate ten brides at once, though I cannot personally vouch for this.

Asakusa

Most visitors – irrespective of their special predilections – are rightly taken to Sensoji, otherwise known as the Asakusa Kannon Temple, headquarters of the Sho Kannon sect of Buddhism. Take the Ginza subway or Toei Asakusa line to the relevant Asakusa station, then turn away from the Sumida River towards the Kaminari Gate leading towards the main street of souvenir stores called Nakamise. Dolls and sweets, paper lanterns and plastic ducks, lady bootblacks charging ¥400 (more than £1): the noise and colour are infectious, and we gaze at the plethora of consumer goods willy-nilly, no matter how keen we are to reach Sensoji. Try the fried broad beans at Bairindo (the first shop of all): ask for hajikemame. Amid the postcards and fancy boxes look out for the ivory shop of Hyotanya, the kimono accessory shop of Matsugaya, and the cake-dolls of Kimuraya.

If your notion of religion is Quaker silence or Zen meditation, it will be difficult to adjust to the noise of Sensoji, once you have walked the tantalising length of Nakamisedori. Two old ladies are chuckling over old times. Pigeons flutter and coo. A businessman in a smart grey suit fixes a fortune-telling paper wish to an iron stand. A young housewife, on her way home from the shops, shakes a fortune-telling drum. And accompanying the din of children chasing each other the constant chink and thud of coins falling between the bars of the largest offertory box I have seen. Hands are clapping to draw the attention of benevolent deities. Bells ring out of unison and sweet smoke permeates the whole open-air arena from the incense bowl in the centre.

The legend of Sensoji's founding dates to 628, when two brothers called Hinokuma dredged in their fishing net a tiny statuette to Kannon (in Sanskrit Avalokiteshvara) and presented it to the nobleman Haji no Nakatomo who worshipped it in his house. Twenty years later a shrine was built for it by Shokai, and the original figure was kept hidden, being replaced by a copy. Excavation after the ravages of World War II brought to light materials dating to the seventh century, some of Korean provenance, which indicate that there may be an element of fact behind the pious fictions.

The fascination of compassionate Kannon resembles the cult of the Blessed

Asakusa. Nakamisedori

Virgin Mary in Roman Catholic countries, and there is a similar preponderance of women devotees. This cult fostered the development of Asakusa district, together with its strategic position by the Sumida river. After the destruction of successive temples, the Main Hall you see today was built of ferroconcrete in 1958 to convey the same impression as its predecessors, with a steeply sloping roof covered by seventy thousand tiles. The outer part has a dragon painted on the ceiling by Kawabata Ryushi and angels and lotuses by Domoto Insho. Three colossal lanterns were presented by geisha unions. It is worth spending some time with the votive tablets painted by important artists, beginning at the right with Zesshin Shibata's 'Demon Ibaragi', by a 19th-century Asakusa artist famous mainly for his lacquer. The 18th-century Edo painter Sukoku Ko was responsible for the 'Killing of the Nue Monster', the hero being the 12th-century hero-poet Minamoto no Yorimasa, and the slain demon having a monkey's head, raccoon's body, tiger's claws and snake's tail. Look too for the 'Surprise Attack at Horikawa' a 12th-century scene by Kikuchi Yosai (1788–1878), artist of the portrait-collection known as *Zenken-kojitsu*.

The heart of the main hall is Gokuden, the gold-covered altar enshrining the hidden image of Kannon. On one side of Gokuden is Fudodo, enshrining the god Fudomyoo who represents strength and justice; and on the other Aizendo, enshrining Aizenmyo, god of love and prosperity.

You can explore for a whole day in the precincts of Asakusa, but in any event do not miss the oldest surviving Edo Bridge, built in 1618, to Awashimado. Small it may be – even unobtrusive, with its weathered timbers – but the calligraphic tablets hung around it tell of its great popularity ever since the 17th century. It is dedicated to a daughter of the scholar-statesman Michizane Sugawara, whom we have already encountered deified as the patron god of learning. Infected while serving in the Sumiyoshi Shrine, she was cast away to sea but managed to reach the shore at Awashima, where she spent the rest of her life in prayer for the relief of women from disease. Since then Awashima shrines have proliferated, and women of all ages come to pay homage there and beg release from their own ailments, putting a needle into a plate of beancurd on her altar.

Now apply at the temple office beside the pagoda for permission to visit the garden of Denboin, created about 1650 by Enshu Kobori or one of his school. It adjoins the abbot's living quarters, so permission is by no means automatic and if granted it must be honoured by quiet and respectful behaviour. The main entrance is always closed, so turn right past Hozomon (Sutra Library Gate) as if leaving Asakusa by Nakamisedori, and enter by a gate on the right-hand side opposite the Public Hall.

The pond is in the heart-shape (kokoro or shin in Japanese, from Chinese hsin) familiar from Kyoto; its carp and turtles to symbolise longevity are watched over by evergreen pines, and the ancient bell near the entrance dates from 1387, so even in the vortex of noisy Asakusa you can experience 'the still centre of the turning world' and go back in time six hundred years by the tap of a knuckle.

Asakusa Shrine is also called Sanja-Sama ('Three Shrines') in honour of the two fishermen who rescued the Kannon figurine and their noble lord who enshrined it. The shrine dates from 1649, when the third shogun Iemitsu erected it for the worship also of his grandfather Ieyasu. The Sanja Matsuri is held on 17–18 May every year.

Other festivals held within these precincts on New Year's Eve and New Year's Day, 3 February (Bean-Scattering), 18 March (Rescue of Kannon with Golden Dragon Dance), 8 April (Buddha's Birthday), 18 June (Water Sprinkling), 9–10 July (Festival of Kannon), 15 August (Lanterns), 18 October (Chrysanthemums and Golden Dragon Dance), 15 November (Children aged 3, 5 and 7), and 17–18 (End of Year Market).

The water-bus stop is just by the police box near Azumabashi, next door to Asakusa station.

Asakusa. Sensoji, with Five-storey pagoda

Sumida Cruise

I am not one of those who enjoys the Sumida river cruise as much as those on the canals of Bruges or the Seine or Thames. But every visitor should at least stroll down to the river from Asakusa in token homage to the waterways that provided Edo with its chief means of transport. Land transport of goods was inhibited by the shortage of bridges over the many rivers, canals and mere streams that nevertheless provided a great obstacle to road traffic. The early Tokugawa shoguns feared bridges as a strategic weakness and authorised only one across the lower Sumida, at Senju: the road to the deep north. This – admittedly dreary – stretch of the river has been immortalised by the Noh play *Sumidagawa* by Kanze Motomasa set in 976 on the banks of the Sumida. A patrician boy, Umewakamaru, has been snatched from Kyoto and is being taken into slavery when he dies, being buried by the pious villagers. His mother pursues the kidnappers, but commits suicide on learning of her son's fate. And this story has no mere literary postscript, for a small hall sacred to the boy's memory still exists – and can be found in Mokuboji, at 2–36 Teitsu. Evocation of mood is characteristic too of the stories and articles by Nagai Kafu (1879–1959), lovingly introduced and edited by Edward Seidensticker in *Kafu the Scribbler* (1965). Kafu's novella 'The River Sumida' is evocative of the waterway and its environment around Asakusa, Honjo and Fukagawa, rather than of any memorable character or dramatic plot.

If you ask the meaning of the first bridge you can see, as you start your cruise down the Sumida, Kototoibashi, you may be no wiser for learning it is 'Asking for News'. This is in fact a reference to the autobiographical miscellany *Ise Monogatari* by Ariwara no Narihira (823–880), who saw at this point on the river a seagull and 'asked it for news' of his sweetheart in Kyoto. The bridge itself is only sixty years old, replacing a ferry. Next comes Azumabashi, 'Bridge of my Wife', dating from 1887 in this form, followed by Komagatabashi, named for the Foal-Shaped Hall (Komagatado) nearby.

Umayabashi is the Stables' Bridge, so-called because the shogun's horses were stabled in the vicinity. Kuramaebashi is the Bridge at the Warehouses. Ryogokubashi, Bridge of Two Provinces, was once called the Great Bridge, Ohashi, because at one time it was the major link between Musashi Province, on the West Bank, and Shimosa, on the East Bank, whereas all the territory concerned was ultimately to fall within Musashi.

Now you cruise below the Syuto Expressway before reaching Shin Ohashi, the New Great Bridge, the third of that name. The first, built in 1693, was used gratefully by Matsuo Basho; the second, of 1912, has been transferred to the Meiji Village near Nagoya.

Kiyosubashi is a portmanteau word deriving from the districts of Kiyosumi and Nakasu on the banks. Eitaibashi, Everlasting Bridge, was the first single-span bridge over the Sumida, and dates in its present form from 1925. Tsukudabashi and Kachidokibashi are passed before the boat ties up at

Hamarikyu Garden. Much of this garden has been opened for a fee to the public (except on Mondays) since 1946, when it became Tokyo civic property. Two ponds are now nature reserves, but you can wander peacefully among cherry trees, pines, and on the shores of a lake spanned by three bridges shaded by wisteria trellises.

Tsukiji Fish Market

If you get up before dawn another day and head for Tsukiji, just north of Hamarikyu, you can experience one of the most exciting and novel of life's many pleasures. It is a ten-minute walk from Tsukiji subway station to the Wholesale Fish Market. At four in the morning (every day but Sundays and holidays) buyers congregate to bid for a hundred species of fish sold in this enormous market from about 5 a.m. The market of Tsukiji (which means 'Reclaimed Land') has operated here since the 1930s and employs more than fifteen thousand people directly, though about seventy thousand come here to do business – not only wholesalers but 1,270 stallholders and their thousands of customers such as restaurateurs and fishmongers. Tourists in groups no larger than four are permitted, and can enjoy the dozens of restaurants, the local shrines, and shops selling tea, books, and all else. Remember to wear waterproof boots and coat against the constant spray. Ten million dollars wholesale pass through Tsukiji daily, and you might well think that much of it is spent on the gigantic tuna (in fact the figure is closer to 10%) when you realise that the Japanese eat 450,000 tons of tuna every year.

Shiba Garden

I left the cruise boat at Takeshiba Pier, and made for Hamamatsucho. On the way you can explore the Shiba Detached Palace Garden (9 to 5 daily), in the Japanese style called 'a strolling garden with man-made hill and spring'. If you can ignore the hectic bustle of Tokyo all around you and (because of the sky-scrapers) also above you, you will be enchanted by the spring blossoms and rural pond, by the artificial hills which offer their own still and subtle defiance to industrial expansion. From this green haven I confess I wandered illicitly through the World Trade Center as bemused as K in Kafka's *Castle*, a financial and commercial labyrinth with hundreds of doors marked as if in some multi-national farce 'Government of Ontario', 'Delaware Port Authority', 'Malaysian Rubber Bureau', 'Australian Meat and Livestock Corporation'.

Zojoji

Continuing along this same road, punch-drunk now as usual with the multiplicity of impressions that Tokyo forces upon every sense, I passed through the Sangedatsumon, or Gate of the Triple Release, leading to Zojoji. The gate, dating to 1622, is the oldest part of the Jodo temple, which acts as the eastern counterpart of Kyoto's Jodo headquarters Chionin. At one time this zone boasted more than forty temples with more than three thousand novices training for service within the Jodo sect, but Zojoji is virtually all that is left, and that little is not intrinsically very beautiful or important, if you except the historic bronze bell (of 671) on your way from the gate to the Main Hall and the graves of several shoguns and some of their womenfolk, in the northwest corner of the grounds, behind the Ankokuten with its blackened image of Amida Butsu shown to the public only three times a year. The temple itself was rebuilt in 1975, with an underground car park for visitors.

Tokyo Tower

Going to the top of Tokyo Tower I spent ¥600 to gawk from the first viewing platform 150 metres up, and missed by ¥400 the last 100 metres not so much because of the risk of vertigo, as because I had already sped up the world's fastest elevator in Ikebukuro's Sunshine City sixty-storey tower the day before. Tokyo Tower, built as a television transmitter, has a splendid aquarium (¥600) on the first floor, with exotic plants, the tanks being cap-

Zojoji and Tokyo Tower

tioned in both Japanese and English. Some fish are also on sale.

To Haneda

Having enjoyed the short monorail ride at Ueno Zoo, I wanted to take the Hamamatsucho monorail to Haneda, the domestic airport. It is located just by the Yamanote line station. Departures between 5.50 a.m. and 11.15 p.m. range from every seven minutes or so between 10 a.m. and 4 p.m. to every fifteen minutes at the less crowded times. We passed above Hamamatsucho's multiple railway lines, Tokyo roofs, expressways, and the port. The first stop, after ten minutes, is by the container port Oikeibajomae. The second stop, two minutes later, is at Ryutsu Senta. The third, three minutes later, is Haneda Seibajo, and the last, two minutes later, is under Haneda Airport.

Sengakuji

Another day I took the Yamanote line from Hamamatsucho south to Shinagawa, then changed to the Keihin line, alighting at the first stop north called Sengakuji, for the temple and burial-place of the 47 masterless samurai, or ronin, whose feats are narrated in the greatest of all plays in the Kabuki repertoire, *Chushingura* (Collection concerning Loyal Subjects), based on actual events of the year 1702. To find Sengakuji, out of the station of that name turn right, continue past Genseiji on the right and at the traffic signal

From Tokyo Tower

turn right. The temple closes at 4.30, and I was there for the last hour of a day darkening with stormclouds which seemed to be in tune with the doomladen scent of grey revenge hanging around the swept slabs on the ground and the almost featureless tombstones. You will count 48, not 47, because another samurai is thought to have been vowed by his father to inactivity until the vendetta was complete, and only then became free to commit ritual suicide. The retainers were followers of Naganori Asano, a young noble. He was to receive imperial envoys and was taught court etiquette for this purpose by Yoshinaka Kira. Kira anticipated payment for this and when offered nothing began to insult Asano who, goaded into retaliation, drew his sword within the Castle of Edo, a rash action punished by condemnation to ritual suicide here at Sengakuji, his family temple. The outraged retainers bided several months, lulling Kira and his bodyguard into thinking that revenge was daily less likely, then descended on Kira's protected home, decapitated their enemy and presented the bloodied head before Asano's grave at Sengakuji, where they too committed ritual suicide.

Sengakuji's main gate is later than the story, dating to 1836. Incense still burns at the graves, visitors will come to bow and pay tribute to the passion for loyalty, and not far to the north you can see their drama re-enacted, whether at the traditional Kabukiza by Higashi-Ginza subway station or at the new National Theatre (Kokuritsu Gekijo) overlooking the Imperial Garden and not far from Hanzomon subway station.

National Theatre

The National Theatre was completed in 1966, in a concrete variant of the traditional azekura (storehouse) style, and has a large and small theatre so that you will almost invariably find something of interest. The large hall, very broad and shallow, may offer a schools performance at 11.00 a.m., another at 2.30 p.m., and a public performance in the evening at 5.30 or so, ending at 9.30. The theatre performs Gagaku musical dance drama (over a thousand years old), Noh plays (more than six centuries old), and Kabuki (with a tradition spanning 350 years), together with other forms of music and drama such as Kangen (classical orchestra), Bunraku (puppets) and Shomyo (Buddhist chanting). Expenses for staff and artistic personnel are borne by the Japanese Government, while production costs are financed from box office income and other revenue earned independently by the National Theatre.

Of the two auditoria, the larger is used for Kabuki, Gagaku and traditional dance and drama, while the smaller accommodates Noh, Bunraku, Kyogen, Shomyo, and Kangen. I saw the fifth and sixth acts of *Kanadehon Chushingura*, with Kankuro as the samurai Kanpei and Kotaro in the onnagata (female impersonator) rôle of Kanpei's beloved Okaru. Shogun Ieyasu decreed that each class should have its own music and its own theatre: Kagura for shrine festivals, Gagaku for the Emperor and the Court, Noh for the samurai, and Kabuki for the common townspeople. Each type of theatre (except for certain folk dances created for the geisha) is nowadays exclusively the preserve of men though this was not always so; each play is at once ritual and an escape from ritual in a paradox familiar to anyone who has seen a carefully made-up and costumed maiko drinking Pepsi-Cola. Gagaku dance drama arrived from China in the eighth century and became fossilized in Japan with the severance of Chinese contacts in the ninth. The best period of Bunraku was the eighteenth century, and some connoisseurs would argue the same for Kabuki, though each succeeding generation has recreated the repertoire, stressing some classics and neglecting others. The star system endemic in Kabuki ensures that the favourite plays of great actors are performed relatively frequently.

There is absolutely no reason why you should not enjoy Kabuki nearly as much as does the Japanese family sitting next to you. A plot summary is invariably available in English; the action is slow, stylized and consequently easy to

National Theatre

follow; poses are held for greater effect to allow those unfamiliar with Kabuki make-up, costume and stage-sets to absorb both detail and ensemble. The Japanese themselves have difficulty in following the Edo-period dialogue.

One Kabuki genre (exemplified by *Chushingura*) is the historical drama, in many instances – again like *Chushingura* – based on a Bunraku original. Another is the domestic drama of plebeian origin, such as *Kagotsurube* ('The Courtesan') where realistic scenes are enlivened by startling costumes of gorgeous colours and fabrics and comic or heightened diction. A third is the dance drama (shosagoto) such as *Musume Dojoji* ('The Maiden of Dojoji Temple'), which may derive from a Noh or Kyogen original.

Ennosuke III, a great Kabuki actor still in his 40s, has claimed that Kabuki should emerge from its chrysaloid stasis to become the renewed 'people's theatre', enticing young people away from western pop music, rock music and jazz. He demonstrated the versatility of Kabuki and its seminal creativity by directing a Paris production of Rimsky-Korsakov's *Le Coq d'Or* in 1984, instilling into a great Russian fairy-tale opera an authentic frisson of Japanese fantasy. Though Kabuki actors are not singers, anyone who enjoys Western opera will appreciate the conductorless group of vocalists and instrumentalists who match their artistry with the action on stage beside them. They are in full view of the audience, as are the stage-hands or kurogo ('men in black') conventionally 'invisible' to the audience because of their costume, contrasting with the brilliant red, gold, blue and green robes of the principal actors.

Kabukiza

Since Kabuki is probably the central dramatic experience of your stay in Tokyo (where *Cats*, *Godspell* or *South Pacific* are just as likely to be on offer in garish pastiches), it is recommended to head straight for Ginza and its Kabukiza Theatre, just by the Higashi-Ginza station on the subway lines Hibiya and Toei Asakusa.

The 11 a.m. show included a new play, *Togashi* by Tatsuji Noguchi, starring Karoku, Kasho, Shinjiro and Shibajaku; the famous Noh-inspired dance drama *Musume Dojoji* of 1753 performed by the great onnagata Tamasaburo; and *Natsu Matsuri Naniwa Kagami*, three scenes from a drama first performed as a puppet play in 1745. Tickets at ¥10,000 down to ¥6,500 (first floor) and ¥8,500 down to ¥6,500 (second floor) are on sale at one box office; from ¥3,000 down to ¥1,500 (third floor) at another, and specially restricted in time for those seeing only a small part of the performance with a guided tour or for a flavour of Kabuki (fourth floor) at a third. For ¥600 (plus ¥1,000 deposit) you can hire a useful English-language 'Earphone Guide' which not only explains the action and characters but adds background information about the work you are seeing, stage properties and other aspects of Kabuki.

Shouts from members of the audience at entrances, specially-held poses or moments of heightened drama are normally the unique 'house names' such as 'Nakamuraya' for Kanzaburo Nakamura.

The Kabuki profession is controlled by twelve main guilds, the oldest going back to 1650. Each guild is run by one or more leading actors who pass on their names to direct male heirs or to actors adopted into their theatrical family. Only five new actors on average are allowed to enter the profession annually, following intensive tests. The appeal of Kabuki may be worldwide and permanent, but the average age of audiences is steadily increasing, and Kabuki as a genre must clearly continue to produce new plays and new actors of a calibre equal to those of the past if it is to flourish as more than a state-subsidised curiosity.

Riccar Art Museum

Not far from Kabukiza is the Ginza Nohgakudo, where you may be lucky enough to be able to see a performance of Noh plays, and five minutes' walk from Ginza railway station is the Riccar Art Museum (Rikka Bijutsukan), specializing in ukiyoe, those colourful woodblock prints so familiar to westerners from our own collections. On the 7th floor of the Riccar Building, it is nor-

Kabukiza

mally open between 11–6 (closed on Mondays). During my stay there was a temporary exhibition of modern woodblock prints by Awazu (1984) on the themes of cow and bull, collages by several other artists, and no traditional ukiyoe at all. These can be found in changing displays at the Ota Memorial Museum, 1–10–10 Jingumae, Shibuya-ku, one minute's walk from Meiji-jingumae subway station and thus combinable with a visit to the Meiji Shrine. Opening hours are 10.30–5.30 except on Mondays and from 25th to the end of every month.

Suntory Museum of Art

Another museum that you might enjoy is the Suntory Museum of Arts on the 11th floor of the Suntory Building, three minutes' walk from the Akasaka Mitsuke subway station, and thus combinable with a stroll towards Akasaka Palace. It is open from 10–5 every day but Mondays, with a special two-hour prolongation on Friday evenings. While I was in Tokyo the Suntory was displaying 'Animal Sculpture from Prehistoric to Modern Times' and generally you can see there a variety of glass, costume, ceramics and lacquer. There is, as you might expect, a breathtaking view over Tokyo from the windows.

Nezu Institute of Fine Arts

I caught the Ginza line subway from Akasaka Mitsuke to Omote Sando and walked ten minutes to the secluded Nezu Institute of Fine Arts at 6–5–36 Minami-Aoyama, with its elegant garden and teahouses. Opening hours are 9.30–4.30, but it is closed every Monday, during August, and on the days following national holidays. Its private collection formed originally by Nezu Kaichiro has been augmented by other collections since it first opened in 1941, and now contains masterpieces in most genres of Japanese art and craft. As there is currently no English-language guide or brochure to the Nezu Institute, it is worth mentioning that a permanent exhibition of choice Chinese ceramics, Yin bronzes and T'ang Buddhist sculpture is supplemented by a changing display from the seven thousand objects in the Institute's collection. I was lucky enough to see the folding screens of wisteria by Maruyama Okyo (1733–95), well visible also from the gallery above; a splendid standing painted wooden Jizo Bosatsu of the Heian period; four sliding doors with flowers painted by Yamaguchi Soken (1759–1818); a Korin sword with prunus blossom; *Genji* illustrations by Tosa Mitsuoki (1617–91) and Sumiyoshi Gukei (1631–1705); and exquisite hanging scrolls by Sumiyoshi Hiromori (1705–77) – a Court Lady viewing snow – and by Tosa Mitsunari (1646–1710) – a quail and millet.

Home Visit

A pleasant variation from museumgoing in Tokyo is a home visit. Apply a day or more in advance at the Tourist Information Center in Tokyo (and also in Hiroshima, Kagoshima, Kobe, Kurashiki, Kyoto, Nagoya, Narita, Osaka, Otsu, Sapporo and Yokohama, for that matter) either in person or by telephone (in Tokyo this is (03) 502–1461) and ask to visit a typical Japanese home.

The address of your host family will be written in Japanese on a card or map for use by a taxi driver, because you may experience difficulty in trying to find your own way.

Remember to take off your shoes at the entrance, changing into slippers which are probably provided by the family, and removing the slippers when you step on to tatami floors. The Japanese are astonished by the proliferation of Western methods of cleaning floors; their method is not to get floors dirty by walking over them in outdoor shoes. When shown into the guest room, sit on the cushion (zabuton) placed in front of the alcove (tokonoma), which is the place of the honoured visitor. You will be offered traditional green tea with small sweets or cakes. Alternatively, a Western-style dining room with chairs may be used for entertaining. The time chosen on weekdays will be after you and your hosts have eaten, and the visit will normally last two or three hours. At weekends you may be lucky enough to join the family on a visit to a neighbourhood shrine or festival. Whatever happens, you will have a rare chance to speak English with a family whom you could otherwise never have known.

Always take one or more small gifts, as the Japanese are punctilious about offering presents to guests, and you would be embarrassed if you had forgotten this gesture. Never offer a bouquet, of course. In *Glimpses of Unfamiliar Japan*, Lafcadio Hearn summed up the Japanese view of a bouquet as 'a vulgar murdering of flowers, an outrage upon the colour sense, a brutality, an abomination'.

Home Stay

If you would rather stay for a week as a paying guest in a private home, you could try Experiment in International Living, Upper Wyche, Malvern, Worcs WR14 4EN (tel. 06845–62577). The cost is very much lower than you would pay in any hotel and your introduction to the intricacies of Japanese family life will be eased by knowing that at least someone in your host family will speak some English. A week in 1985 cost £135 and six to eight weeks' notice was required for the necessary arrangements to be made.

Sport in Tokyo

Many westerners are intrigued by Japanese sports and would like to see them practised. Sumo, wrestling between giants over 90 kgs, can be seen six times a year: fifteen days at a time in January, May and September (Tokyo), March (Osaka), July (Nagoya), and November (Fukuoka). The winner of any bout is the wrestler who forces his opponent out of the circle or forces any part of his body but his feet on the hard clay floor. Bouts may last only a few seconds as there is a repertoire of seventy different tricks to defeat your man. In Tokyo, obtain your ticket at play guides in department stores or on busy street corners for matches at Kokugikan Sumo Hall, 2–1–9 Kuramae (near Kuramae subway station). By the time you read this, however, it may be that the sumo head-quarters will already have made its planned move to the district north of Ryogoku station, so check in advance.

Kyudo (the Way of Archery) can be learnt on application to Shinjukuku Taiikukan, 3–1–2 Okubo, Shinjuku, fifteen minutes' walk from Shin Okubo station (9–8 except Fridays).

Martial arts such as judo (self-defence) and kendo (the Way of the Sword) can be seen free of charge between 5 and 9 p.m. daily except Sundays at Nippon Budokan, near Kudanshita subway station, the address being 2–3 Kitanomaru-koen, in Chiyoda Ward. A year's tuition (6–7 p.m. on weekdays from April through March) currently costs about ¥48,000, and of course it is training for spiritual power as well as for physical strength. Karate (self-defence) can be seen at several places, but try first the headquarters at 1–6–1 Ebisu-Nishi, Shibuya-ku, which is near Ebishu JNR station.

Aikido is much more recent than Chinese karate or Japanese judo, being

Sumo

evolved by Morihei Ueshiba (1183–1970) to combine those sports with kendo concepts; it may be watched at Aikido Hombu Dojo, 102 Wakamatsucho, Shinjuku Ward, about ten minutes' walk from the western exit of Shinjuku station, any weekday evening from about 5.30 to 8 and on Sundays from 9 to 11.30 a.m.

Despite all of this, the delights of skiing and skating, and the snob value of belonging to a golf club, there is one sport that ranks above all others in Japan, and that is baseball, professionally played in two leagues of six teams each between April and October, and followed as avidly on television as it is in the United States. Korakuen Baseball Stadium (near Korakuen subway station) seats fifty thousand people (most supporting Tokyo Giants) and is as near as you will get to Madison Square Garden or Wembley for heady sporting excitement in Japan.

Baseball has become Japanese as besuboru, and if you think there is something very familiar about some of the other Japanese words you hear, you will be right. Page 148 of Obunsha's *Essential Japanese–English Dictionary* prints the following eleven consecutive Japanese words: diditi, Dikkenzu, dina-pati, dipi-i, direkuta, direttanto, disukasshon, disukaunto, disuku-jokki, disutenpa, and dizeru-enjin. However exotic they may look, once you start to pronounce them they become astonishingly familiar: D.D.T., Dickens, dinner-party, D.P.E. (in photography, development, printing, enlargement), director, dilettante, discussion, discount, disc-jockey, distemper, and diesel-engine.

That is not to say that the grammatical structure of Japanese or the subtle intricacies of its colloquial style may be approached with anything but trepidation. With Burmese and Thai, Japanese may claim to be one of the most fiendishly difficult languages on earth.

Korakuen

Near Korakuen subway station are Kodokan Judo Hall and the famous landscape garden called Koishikawa Korakuen, now only a tiny part of a much greater garden planned on land given by Ieyasu to his eleventh son, first Lord of Mito. I entered by the west or Iidabashi gate, paid my two hundred yen, and obediently pursued the recognised route laid down for visitors past a cherry tree to a series of imitations (vague, not slavish) of well-known Chinese and Japanese landscapes real and imagined, from the steep mountainsides of Lu Shan to Hangchow's West Lake, and two Kyoto landmarks: Kiyomizudera and Tofukuji. Next you find Tokujin Hall, the only original 17th-century building remaining in the garden, and you amble round the lake past the waterfall and cross the Chinese stone bridge named for the Full Moon before entering woods, passing plum-trees and a pond with irises, then a country tea-house, the lake island of Horai-san. A mountainscape mimics Kiso (in Nagano) and then you find maples that flame in autumn. Korakuen is open from 9 to 4 or 5 according to season except on Mondays and on the last three days of the year.

Botanic Garden

Koishikawa Botanic Garden (in Japanese Koishikawa Shokubutsuen) is some distance north from Korakuen, and I suggest taking a taxi there, or you could walk back to Suidobashi subway station and travel two stops northward, alighting at Hakusan. This botanic garden was created by the Shogun Tsunayoshi and now belongs to Tokyo University, labels being both in Japanese and the international language of botany, Latin. The building in the northwest corner is the old main hall of Tokyo Imperial University's medical department, a Meiji building of anachronistic charm in this garden constructed for the most part for scientific ends, though you can find a lovely traditional Japanese garden in the style of Enshu Kobori. Opening hours are 9 to 4.30 except on Mondays; you buy your entrance ticket at the little shop opposite the gate.

National Park for Nature Study

Another botanic garden for connoisseurs can be found in Chofu City, but much closer at hand, not far from Meguro on the Yamanote line, is the National Park for Nature Study (9–4.30, but the last admission is at 3 p.m.; closed on Mondays). It now belongs to the National Science Museum, and in some ways forms a fascinating contrast to a botanic garden because everything grows wild, and visitors are permitted to intrude only along well-worn paths (and no more than three hundred may be allowed in at any one time) to preserve the untamed nature of this city jungle. 'Nature study' takes the form not of carefully-introduced specimens and meticulously-tended greenhouses but of labels to identify the genera and species of plants indigenous to the garden, which has been kept free of human interference, to all intents and purposes, from prehistoric times, if one ignores the twentieth-century imperial palace now used for events such as weddings and receptions.

I suggested earlier than one could spend a week in Tokyo enjoying only its gardens and parks, like Hibiya, with its lunchtime concerts in summer and chrysanthemums in November.

Chinzanso

One of my favourite Tokyo gardens is that of the Chinzanso Restaurant (Mansion on the Camellia Mountain), so called by Prince Aritomo Yamagata, who created here on the heights overlooking Tokyo from Mejirodori a rolling garden of seventeen acres. The three-storey pagoda dating from the ninth century stood originally in the Takamura San Chikurinji temple, Hiroshima Prefecture, until it was re-erected here in 1924 by Baron Fujita, the next to acquire Chinzanso. At the same time Baron Fujita transferred from Kyoto's Shimogamo Shrine the oratory of Inari. Strolling in this garden, which dips and curves to reveal new aspects of itself and Tokyo's skyscrapers below and beyond, one feels far removed from the physical presence of a metropolis. The address is 10–8 Sekiguchi-machi, Bunkyo-ku.

Happoen

Much the same is true of Happoen, another expensive garden restaurant, 1–1 Shiroganedai 1-chome, Minato-ku, where you have a choice of a barbecue meal in Rokumeikan or a charcoal-fire meal cooked in the traditional irori. Happoen's natural ponds are visited by heron and teal, while kite build in the taller trees. Of the thirty-odd stone lanterns scattered throughout the grounds, the most celebrated is that of Midaroku, carved more than eight hundred years ago, while the pagoda on the top of the hill behind the tea-pavilion dates to the tenth century. While on the subject of restaurants, I pay tribute to the charming Indonesian restaurant run by a husband and wife: the little Sederhana, 5–4 Kami Osaki 3-chome, Shinagawa-ku, in the Tanaka building on the corner of Expressway no. 2 not far from Meguro station, open 12–2 and 5–10 daily.

Rikugien

As you travel between Sugamo and Komagome on the Yamanote line, more than half of the distance overlaps the length of the Rikugien Garden, probably the most enchanting in Tokyo. It owes its present aspect to Iwasaki Yataro, the founder of the Mitsubishi commercial empire, who in the 1870s set to rights a garden which had been left to go wild after the death of its original owner, Yoshiyasu Yanagisawa (1658–1714). It constitutes a major example of an eighteenth-century strolling garden with man-made hill and spring, in Japanese kaiyushiki chikusan sensui teien. It is open daily except Mondays from 9–5 for a small charge, and should properly be contemplated without crowds early in the day at unpopular seasons. Almost entirely man-made, the garden has a winding path encircling a large pond with a great island densely wooded with pines and its own teahouse, and small rocks named for the mythical Horai islet of eternity. Rikugien has its own Mount Fuji, and several bridges with constantly-changing views represent the microcosm of the universe to which every garden aspires overtly or covertly.

Kiyosumi Garden

And if you thought that all Tokyo gardens were to be found on the western or city side of the Sumida, you have only to cross Kiyosu bridge and within five minutes you will have reached another garden donated to the citizens of Tokyo by Mitsubishi's founder, Iwasaki Yataro. He bought this land reclaimed from Tokyo Bay in 1878 and created a new suburban mansion, using Sumida water for a new pond, and a choice of rocks from all over Japan. The splendid Kiyosumi garden is open daily except Mondays from 9 to 4, except for evening extensions in the summer months.

Department Stores

Many visitors will spend a great deal of their time in the department stores of Shinjuku (Isetan, Mitsukoshi, Odakyu, Keio), Shibuya (Tokyu, Seibu) and above all Ginza (Matsuya, Mitsukoshi, Hankyu, Meitetsu Meisa, Matsuzakaya). But even if you don't want to spend much money it is still an important feature of any Japanese holiday to examine the huge range of familiar and unfamiliar wares offered, and to marvel at the exquisite courtesy shown by all sales staff.

Narita

If you have a limited amount of time at Narita International Airport, or an extra half-day before your flight leaves, take the half-hour bus ride from the airport to the Japan National Railways Station at Narita. There is an information point between the bus stop and the station itself, so if you need reassurance, get it here. (And remember on going back to the station not to use the Keisei–Narita station nearby unless you want to go to Ueno in Tokyo).

Mitsukoshi Department Store, Ginza

Your destination is the temple called Shinshoji, about eight hundred metres to the north, founded in 939 and dedicated to Fudo (in Sanskrit Acala), the God of Fire. Taxis and buses are available, but strolling there, and stopping whenever something catches your eye, forms half of the pleasure. If you can spend a night in Narita City, as opposed to the fiercely expensive and western-ised airport hotels (Holiday Inn Narita, Narita View, Nikko Narita), why not try the small and friendly ryokans like the Ohgiya, Oonoya, Umeya or Wakamatsu? The Kirinoya is farther from the centre, and less convenient but quieter.

Shinshoji is a Shingon temple unashamedly commercial, with its brand-new buildings and its burning-off of worshippers' anxieties, when the wooden plaque on which your worries are written is held over a sacred fire. Whenever I stay in Pompeii, my hotel balcony overlooks a side-passage of the Santuario della Madonna del Rosario, where priests – for a fixed sum – are usually blessing the cars. 'La benedizione delle macchine' works out rather more expensively at Shinshoji (¥3,000 per vehicle), but there is a special discount if you buy a blessing from a vending machine.

The image of Fudo in the temple is attributed – like too many others, alas! – to the hand of Kobo Daishi, founder of Shingon. In one hand he holds a rope and in the other a sword, to destroy evil and to distance evildoers. The earlier temple was moved to its present site in 1705, but many of the buildings are recent due to the temple's enormous popularity. On 3 or 4 February is the bean-throwing ceremony called Setsubun, when beans are scattered to the crowds by a priest or famous public figure, to cries of 'Fuku wa uchi', (In with good luck), omitting as he is on sacred ground the customary sequel 'Oni wa soto' (Out with devils) which is recited when the ceremony is carried out in private homes.

Six million visitors a year teem within Shinshoji, so you will expect to find (and be lucky) sideshows, stalls of cakes and sweets, soft drinks a-plenty, toys, fruit and souvenirs of every description.

As a contrast to the crowds at Shinshoji, the equally vast Naritasan Park, adjoining it, could hardly be more relaxing and welcome. From late February to early March you can enjoy the Plum Blossom Festival, with its open-air tea ceremony. Early April is the time for cherry-blossom viewing in Shinshoji. Naritasan Historical Museum (entrance charge levied) is near the lovely park, at Narita Koen-nai, and specialises in crafts and bygones, with panels relating the life of Sogo Kiuchi (1612–53), who took the fatally unprecedented step of complaining direct to Shogun Tokugawa Ietsuna about illegal and unjust acts committed by the Sakura daimyo family. Sogo knew that it was criminal to approach the Shogun direct, and paid for his audacity by being crucified, while his wife and four children were decapitated, 'pour encourager les autres'. Yet the oppression of the Sakura ended by shogunal decree, and since that time the local people have felt profound gratitude towards their hero, building a Sogo Mausoleum, and a Sogo Memorial Hall. Sogo's own house, reconstructed in 1820, is still inhabited by his descendants. Sogo-Reido can be reached by bus in twenty minutes from Narita JNR station, or in 5 minutes by train from Keisei-Narita station, then a ten-minute walk. You may well feel that this half-day has yielded more vivid impressions of Japan than those you received in Tokyo.

Envoi

Rural peace may be congenial, but the Japanese have always seen that serenity may be as easily achieved in the midst of urban noise. The writer Matsuhiro expresses this view thus: 'if you keep calm and untroubled by anything in creation, making your friends of the flowers of springtime and the tints of autumn, and taking a drop of liquor when you feel inclined, you need not regard the world as such a bad place. Just sit down quietly, and arrange a flower or two, burn a stick of good incense and sip a cup of fine tea, with some old books for company; and if a congenial friend happens to drop in, you may find it very comforting to chat with him about all sorts of people from ancient times to the present day. Some say this kind of life is best achieved by retiring to the hills, but however far away you live you will find no peace of mind if you still harbour egoistic thoughts of honour and profit. So you may just as well live right in the middle of the city, without changing your style or choosing any particular locality'.

The small town life of Nara, the miraculous rural calm so easily found behind many a façade in the city of Kyoto, and the oases of green soothing Tokyo's hectic megalopolis: each environment, so distinct from the others, harbours an essential facet of the Japanese diamond. Tranquillity and tradition are still discovered in past and present Japanese capitals.

USEFUL INFORMATION

When to Come

Businessmen will generally not have a great deal of choice as to time and place when visiting Japan. Serious travellers, on the other hand, will choose to find conditions at their best in spring (March, but preferably April and May) or autumn (September, October, but preferably not November). In June (except for Hokkaido) there is a brief period of torrential rain, with a longer period generally between early August and mid-September.

Winters are cold, with winds blowing from Siberia and picking up moisture over the Japan Sea which they deposit as snow, often heavy, over most of Japan. Pacific-facing cities enjoy bright, cold weather in winter. The Japanese prefer winter cold to summer heat and, since they cannot build houses to offset both extremes, in the south and east build to neutralise as far as possible the humid heat of summer.

Southern Japan is frequently ravaged by typhoonal winds, rains, and tidal waves. Minor earthquakes happen every day and are mostly disregarded, just as they are in southern Italy. Volcanoes have traditionally caused much less harm than one might have thought, if one recalls that most of Japan comprises a chain of volcanoes, from the active Aso in Kyushu to Fuji on Honshu.

How to Come

With all the time in the world, one can take the Trans-Siberian express (described in Michael Pennington's classic *Rossya*) via Moscow to Nakhodka and Yokohama. The 'Mospak' tour operated by the Japan Soviet Tourist Bureau is economically priced and highly entertaining. Ships also run weekly services between Keelung in Taiwan and Naha in Okinawa, and three times a week between Pusan in South Korea and Shimonoseki. For 'Mospak' or other Soviet services contact the Japan Soviet Tourist Bureau, Kamiyacho Bldg., 5–2–21 Toranomon, Minato-ku, Tokyo. For the Taiwan service contact the Arimura Sangyo Co., Echo Kyobashi Bldg., 3–12–1 Kyobashi, Chuo-ku, Tokyo. For the Korean service contact the Kampu Ferry Co., Ginza Asahi Bldg., 3–8–10 Ginza, Chuo-ku, Tokyo.

If you intend to follow Michael Pennington's route from Japan to England or in the reverse direction, the cost by rail from Harwich and Hook of Holland or

Dover and Ostend to Hannover, Berlin, Warsaw and Moscow (Byelorusski Station) is about £120 first-class single and about £90 second-class, departing daily in summer, and between two and four days weekly in winter, arriving 2½ days later. The Trans-Siberian Express leaves at 10.10 a.m. and passengers must pay extra for the night's hotel in Moscow. The more convenient route is 82 hours by train to Irkutsk, 3 hours by plane to Khabarovsk, and 16 hours more by train to Nakhodka, the cost being about £340; the less convenient is by train Moscow to Nakhodka with a change and overnight stop in Khabarovsk, taking about 166 hours and costing over £360.

Alternatively, you can fly from Moscow to Khabarovsk (non-stop, 8 hours) then take a train (16 hours) to Nakhodka, costing about £345; or fly from Moscow to Bratsk (non-stop 7 hours) and then to Irkutsk (1 hour) then a train to Khabarovsk (67 hours, with stopover) and to Nakhodka (16 hours), costing about £380.

Sailings from Nakhodka to Yokohama take about 52 hours. Schedules can be obtained from your local Intourist office, but as a rough guide there is one a week on average from mid-April to late October. Some sailings leave Yokohama for Hong Kong (about 175 hours).

Should you choose an organised tour, like those arranged by Japan Air Lines? In 1985 a Thomson's 'Japanese Experience' costing £1,153 for eleven nights bed and breakfast in western-style hotels comprised Tokyo, Kamakura, Hakone, Kyoto and a day in Nara, the latter concentrating on Todaiji and Kasuga. Domestic travel was by coach out from Tokyo and by bullet train back. Main meals were excluded, thus making the holiday much more expensive than it looked at first sight.

I strongly advise that, irrespective of your budget, you go it alone. For a budget holiday, use a cheap return flight (I was offered Egyptair via Cairo, Bangkok and Manila) booked well in advance saving more than £400, and stay in Japanese-style shukubo or minshuku (£7 a night on average). Meals out can be cheap if you avoid de luxe restaurants, and there is no danger of food poisoning because restaurant hygiene is either as reputable as in Northern Europe and the USA or better. The man in the Japanese street, unlike his counterpart in Singapore or India, can usually understand English, and delights in practising his skill, offering aid without any reluctance. Japan can be very expensive if you prefer all possible creature comforts, but Australians and New Zealanders I met were economising during two-month or three-month stays very successfully even in Tokyo, and elsewhere it can be much easier.

Public transport will get you anywhere quickly, courteously, cheaply, and cleanly. You can use any toilet without worry, and many of the more frequented sites are equipped with western-style pedestal toilets, though you may occasionally find a 'squat' variety.

Most American, Australasian and European visitors will arrive by air. Remember that Kyoto and Nara are much more easily reached from Osaka

International Airport (about 1½ hours to central Kyoto as opposed to about 15 minutes to central Osaka). There are, however, far more flights worldwide through Tokyo, and if you prefer to sample the shinkansen (bullet train), the stretch between Kyoto and Tokyo will be an unforgettable experience, and as quick as by air, centre to centre.

Cut-price fares booked far enough in advance will halve the cost of your journey to Tokyo: check current offers in the classified advertisements in the travel section of your newspaper.

Tours and Excursions

Many tours are available, but they cover only a tiny fraction of interesting places, which are consequently tiresomely overcrowded. Since the Japanese experience is predominantly calm and beauty, it seems perverse to join a crowd where only your own language is spoken, and never have time to meditate on anything you see. So my advice is to go it alone, with this book and the excellent Japan National Tourist Organization maps of Kyoto/Nara and Tokyo, available free of charge from the Tourist Information Centers at Tokyo's Narita Airport, Central Tokyo (6–6, Yurakucho 1-chome, Chiyoda-ku), and by Kyoto Station (1st floor, Kyoto Tower Bldg., Higashi-Shiokojicho, Shimogyo-ku).

JNTO offices can be found in Brazil, France, West Germany (Frankfurt), Hong Kong, Mexico, Switzerland and Thailand. The Australian office is situated at 115 Pitt Street, Sydney, N.S.W. 2000; the Canadian office at 165 University Avenue, Toronto, Ont. M5H 3B8; the English office at 167 Regent Street, London W1; and there are American offices in Chicago, Dallas, Honolulu, Los Angeles, New York, and San Francisco.

Taxis, Buses, Trains

You can call a radio taxi or limousine by telephone (only Japanese spoken), or find a taxi stand at railway stations or hotels or on busy city streets, or hail one of the numerous cruising cabs. Taxis are convenient, efficient especially if your destination is written down for the driver to read in Japanese, but the most expensive form of travel, starting at ¥470 in Tokyo for the first 2 km., with ¥80 for each successive 370 m. If a cab is free, it will display a *red* light on its left (right as you face it). If it stops for you, stand well away because the automatic doors could strike you when they open; similarly, allow the driver to open the doors before you alight. Extras you may be called upon to pay include waiting in traffic (currently ¥80 for every 2½ minutes) and 20% between 11 at night and 5 a.m.

Buses are complicated to use in Tokyo unless you possess a precise route plan, but in Kyoto and Nara they are simple, convenient, practical, and cheap. Your free JNTO 'Tourist Map of Kyoto–Nara' has a clear subway and bus plan of Kyoto, from which you will see that most shrines and temples, museums and gardens, palaces and castles are close to frequent services. The underground system runs in a straight line north from Kyoto Station, under

199

Karasumadori, to Kitaoji, passing Higashi Honganji (which is however near enough to walk to), Sento Gosho, and the Former Imperial Palace (Gosho), with a minimum fare of ¥120. If you intend to travel by bus five or six times a day it is easier to buy a daily bus pass (¥770) at Kyoto Station or Kyoto City Tourist Information Office (8.30–5) across the square from the Karasumadori exit of Kyoto JNR station. Otherwise the buses cost a minimum of ¥140 per trip. You get on at the front and pay the driver in coins, waiting for your change to rattle down the slots. Longer-distance buses are entered from the rear. You take a ticket showing the fare stage from the machine by the back door, and as you leave you correlate the fare stage in question with the changing fare shown above the window near the driver and pay the exact fare if you can. Most buses start from Kyoto JNR station, but there is another bus terminal at Sanjo-Keihan served by buses 11 (to Arashiyama), 12 (to Kinugasa, for Kinkakuji) and 59 (to Yamagoe, for Ryoanji).

Trains are available in abundance. In Tokyo you will become familiar with the Yamanote line, looping around the city; it became the peg on which Jean Pearce hung the useful observations of *Foot-loose in Tokyo*. Circling Tokyo clockwise or anti-clockwise in 62 minutes, the green trains should be avoided only in the rush hours, say 7–9 a.m. and 5–7 p.m. Orange Chuo trains bisect that circle, running between Tokyo Station in the east and Shinjuku via Kanda, Ochanomizu and Yotsuya. The minimum fare on these Kokuden (JNR) trains is ¥120. Tickets are obtained in advance from vending machines in Japanese. If you have no friend who understands them, and do not want to ask for help, just buy the cheapest ticket and pay the difference when leaving your destination. Private lines proliferate all over the capital, as well as in Kyoto and Nara, making your travel arrangements easier than in any other country in the world.

At JNR stations, you can obtain tickets for long-distance trains, including the shinkansen (bullet trains), at windows or counters with green signs or stripes. Remember to specify economy or first-class, limited express or ordinary express, and one-way or round-trip ticket. The Hikari shinkansen on the Tokaido line from Tokyo to Shin Osaka stops only at Nagoya and Kyoto, whereas the Kodama shinkansen makes eleven stops.

Hotels and Restaurants

There is the widest range of Western-style and Japanese-style hotels in **Tokyo** and **Kyoto**, being the major travel destinations. Just ask the JNTO for a list.

Nara by contrast offers only two large hotels: the Nara Hotel, 1096 Takabatakecho (5 minutes by taxi from Nara Station); and the Yamatosanso, 24–1 Kawakamicho (5 minutes by taxi from Kintetsu Nara Station).

Anyone who thinks that Japanese hotels must be expensive because the service is faultless and the rooms spotless would be quite wrong. You have a choice of 75 public youth hostels and 465 privately-operated youth hostels, hundreds of minshuku (guest houses), ryokan (Japanese-style inns), kokumin shukusha (people's lodges), kokumin kyukamura (holiday villages), camping sites and temple lodgings. Wherever you decide to go – and a mixture of lodgings is the obvious recommendation for those keen to see all facets of life in Japan – you can be assured of its cleanliness, and that you will not be swindled: indeed it is not polite to bargain, as you would elsewhere in Asia.

When booking a room, be careful to ask for the price and whether it includes meals. You will never be cheated, but you might be misunderstood. When filling in your residence form, you will often be asked to state when you are leaving; if you cannot be certain, at least advise your host on the day before eventual departure and pay the full amount requested (no tipping) in an envelope, which is more delicate to the Japanese sensibility than handing over yen notes. This embarrassement over receiving cash does not apply to modest transactions such as paying for restaurant meals or entrance-tickets to museums, but I still suggest that it is more discreet to offer money gently, with a smile and slight bow, and never count it out ostentatiously.

The Tokyo Tourist Information Center will currently not make reservations for you, but those in Kyoto (Kyoto Tower) and in Nara (Kintetsu Nara Rail Station) will be glad to do so.

The hotel and some ryokan are highly-priced and widely advertised. The minshuku, by contrast, is so economical that it often cannot or need not advertise: there are over 30,000 of them throughout Japan, so you will never be far away from one. The biggest cities, where land is at a fantastically high premium, offer the budget traveller the so-called 'business hotels', with small rooms and miniature private toilet and bath or shower. Business hotel rates are comparable to those of minshuku.

In the same price range are kokumin shukusha (people's lodges) and temple lodgings. The people's lodges are intended principally for Japanese, and Westerners are uncommon. You can book in advance (and must do so in summer, when they are packed) through Japan Travel Bureau, who supply you with a green coupon in exchange for your cash. Most temple lodgings are in communal rooms, all Japanese-style with tatami (mats) and low tables in the daytime, and roll-up bedding at night. These shukubo offer vegetarian meals, and quite often there will be a guest-master able to speak English. Youth hostel directories will show many shukubo, but there are dozens of temple-lodgings around Kyoto and Nara not listed in the youth hostel guides because they are not affiliated, so take the trouble to ask at the Tourist Information Center.

Those accustomed to Western youth hostels will find those in Japan excessively disciplined, noisy and boisterous: this is not where the spirit of Japan is best sought.

National vacation villages have something of the atmosphere of Western holiday camps, catering for the gregarious, and are found in national parks and similar holiday spots. Reservations are difficult to make at the last moment, and should be planned as far in advance as possible through the Kokumin Kyukamura Association, Tokyo Kaikan Bldg., 10–1 Yurakucho 2-

chome, Chiyoda-ku, Tokyo.

The European pension idea has started to spread in Japan during the last decade, and you can obtain a list of pensions throughout the country from Pension System Development, Inuzuka Bldg., 4–11 2-chome, Suragaku-cho, Tokyo.

Cycling is neither easy nor convenient in a country with such crowded roads and excellent mass transit systems, but if you must take or hire a cycle, make it a folding jitensha acceptable on passenger trains. There are twenty-three purpose-built cycling inns in Japan, offering roughly the same facilities at roughly the same prices as youth hostels. Information from the Nihon Jitensha Kaikan Bldg., 9–3 Akasaka 1-chome, Minato-ku, Tokyo.

Camping is not as popular as youth-hostelling, and indeed there are still some national parks without camping sites. By all means obtain a list of campsites from the Japan National Tourist Organization, but be warned that all are situated a long way from the city centres where you will expect to spend most of your time in the three Japanese capitals.

A single man could spend one night at a sauna bath in a western-style hotel if you make it obvious to the sauna manager that you want to stay overnight and you agree to leave by 9 a.m. You can sleep in a rest room after the sauna, orange juice and snacks are often obtainable, and you will be loaned a yukata with a bag containing soap, a disposable razor and toothbrush, and toothpaste. No ladies!

Restaurants are even more varied in type, price-range, size and luxury than are hotels, for it seems that most Japanese eat out at least once a day, and schoolchildren are often to be seen taking a meal on the way morning and evening, since many restaurants stay open all day and offer a full menu at all hours.

Misconceptions about Japanese food in the West include: it is all raw, it is fiendishly expensive, and it will make a westerner ill. You may *ask* for raw food, but meals will generally be hot. You may eat at picturesquely 'Japanese' restaurants which cater to expense-account clients and Western snobs, but the vast majority of Japanese eat nutritious cheap meals at smaller places easily found as you amble from garden to temple. Kobe beef will *always* be expensive. And finally, all strange food is likely to make you ill if you have too much too often. But if you sensibly temper experimentation with familiarity, you will enjoy the best of both worlds. Japanese water is absolutely safe, and will be brought to your table when you sit down, as will oshibori, flannel cloths provided to wipe your hands and mouth before, during and after eating.

Don't be worried about using chopsticks. Ohashi are the cheap, disposable chopsticks split partway down the middle. Pull them apart, removing by rubbing any splinters remaining. Then hold the upper stick between thumb and first two fingers, keeping the lower stick still with your second and third fingers. Both ohashi are held with two thirds of their length below the hand. A marvellous souvenir to take home is a set of warabashi: reusable lacquer chopsticks that grace any meal and come in an infinity of designs. The age of the plastic chopstick is with us, but luckily most restaurants have not yet succumbed.

It is perfectly acceptable to make noises while eating appreciatively in Japan, whether noodles or soup. What is unforgivable is to blow your nose in public or to demonstrate a soiled handkerchief: use the nearest toilet.

If you refuse for some reason to use chopsticks, you can ask for a knife and fork (*naifu to foku*) followed by *o motte kite kudasai* ('Could you please bring me?'), a phrase you will want on many another occasion. If you are not brought a spoon (*supun*, pronounced 'spoon') for your soup, just raise the bowl to your lips by the edges. If you require your noodles hot in the summer, you will usually have to ask.

The most common restaurant is the shokudo, with a restricted choice of dishes displayed in permanent plastic form in the window for the foreigner to point out, no words being necessary. Western food such as hamburgers are available with rice and noodle dishes.

Restaurant display

A ryoriya by contrast is an oriental-style restaurant without any western dishes; it may have some private tatami rooms, counter service or tables and chairs.

A sobaya is a noodle-house, which is ideal for the budget traveller in search of a quick and nutritious meal.

Fast-food restaurants may not appeal at first glance, but if you are uncertain about how much unfamiliar food and drink you can absorb, the Kentucky Fried Chicken or McDonald's are not only fast and friendly, but cheap, like the Japanese chains called Yoshinoya Gyudon, Hoka-Hoka Bento, and Italian Tomato.

Shopping centres and department stores (depato) all offer a variety of quick, inexpensive meals. The stores are normally open only between 10 and 6, while shopping centres may be open to 8 or 9 p.m.

Coffee-shops called kissaten make a high charge for 'kohi', but you are paying for comfort, relaxation, music and conversation, so if you want a quick coffee go to a fast-food chain, where you will pay less than half. 'Morning service' is not a religious ceremony, but a kissaten snack including toast, fruit juice and possibly an egg with your coffee until about 10.30 a.m.

Sushiya are small restaurants almost solely confined to sushi and sashimi. Sushi are portions of seasoned rice topped by vegetables, omelette or raw fish. Sashimi are the slices of raw fish, which taste much more subtle to the Japanese palate than the overcooked fish commonly eaten in the West. The counter in a sushiya is filled by customers trying different kinds of raw fish and rice. If you sit at a table you will be expected to choose one dish.

Vending machines are as widespread as in the USA and far more so than in Europe. You can buy cartons of delicious pasteurised milk, iced beer, or even whisky, as well as the whole range of soft drinks, tea and coffee from machines in the street, in parks, temples, shrines and gardens, so always keep loose change for these machines, which accept only coins.

Passports and Visas

You must be equipped with a valid passport on entering and leaving Japan. Visas are required for all except transit passengers and for the following: citizens of New Zealand staying up to 30 days; citizens of Austria, West Germany, Ireland, Liechtenstein, Mexico, Switzerland and the United Kingdom staying up to 180 days; and citizens of the following countries staying up to 90 days: Argentina, Bahamas, Bangladesh, Belgium, Canada, Chile, Colombia, Costa Rica, Cyprus, Denmark, Dominican Republic, Finland, France, Greece, Guatemala, Honduras, Iceland, Iran, Israel, Italy, Lesotho, Luxembourg, Malta, Mauritius, Netherlands, Norway, Pakistan, Peru, Portugal, San Marino, Singapore, Spain, Surinam, Sweden, Tunisia, Turkey, Uruguay and Yugoslavia.

Visas are usually valid for four months and are good for only one visit. Reciprocal multiple-entry visa arrangements have been agreed with Australia,

Canada, France, West Germany, Iceland, Ireland, Mexico, New Zealand, Sweden, the UK and the USA.

If a visitor wishes to stay in Japan for 91 days or longer, it is necessary to apply at least ten days in advance for an Alien Registration Certificate. Ask for appropriate details at your nearest Tourist Information Center, and remember that renewal is not automatic.

A visa does *not* entitle you to obtain work from a Japanese employer. Working in Japan is an ideal way to enjoy the full Japanese experience, and is highly recommended, provided that you follow all the proper procedures, outlined in John Wharton's *Jobs in Japan* (The Global Press, 2239 East Colfax Ave., Suite 202, Denver, Colorado 80206). Japan is a rich country, so a hardworking teacher of English can be paid very well, but it is also highly-disciplined, and if you break rules and regulations you can expect the same treatment as if you were a Japanese.

Customs and Currency

You are allowed to take into Japan up to 400 cigarettes or 100 cigars or 500 grams of tobacco, 3 bottles of alcohol, 2 ounces of perfume and a total of three watches, including the one you are wearing.

Prohibited articles include opium and other drugs, counterfeit coins and banknotes, pornographic books or pictures, articles infringing on copyright, patent rights or design rights, certain fruits, vegetables, plants or animals. Permission for entry must be obtained in advance before you bring in plants and animals which are not contrary to the Plant Quarantine Law or the Animal Infectious Diseases Control Law.

Currency may be imported or exported without restriction, providing it is declared to the customs officials. Coins are available in denominations of 1, 5, 10, 50, 100 and 500 yen. Banknotes are available in denominations of 500, 1,000, 5,000 and 10,000 yen. Airport banks are open 24 hours a day, but elsewhere you might find it very time-consuming to change money, so my advice is to take as many yen as you think you will need for the whole trip, plus travellers' cheques for emergencies. Banking hours are 9 a.m. to 3 p.m. (9–noon on Saturdays and closed on Sundays). It is illegal to use anything but yen in Japan, and there is no black market so whatever rate is quoted will be fair and just. Always keep 2,000 yen (or more, as the figure may well rise) to pay at Narita for 'using the airport facilities' on departure.

Luggage and Clothing

Japanese travel very light, and many arrive at a ryokan without yukata (a loose kimono used as nightwear), soap, towel or toothbrush. It follows that you could travel equally light. The trouble is that you will be attracted to ceramics, lacquer, toys, paintings, paper wallets, bamboo bowls, lanterns, books (the list is endless) and that you may have gifts pressed on you which you cannot possibly leave behind. So take a light but roomy suitcase, with strong and roomy polythene bags for your overflow. Your airline will accept only one large suitcase for the hold, and two in theory for the cabin, but in practice cabin staff and check-in staff will turn a blind eye to two or three extra polythene bags which look as though they might contain duty-free goods.

Clothing should also be kept to an absolute minimum, especially if you are travelling daily and wish to minimise weight and bulk. Remember that the Japanese travel light, rinse out their clothes daily, and regard with some amused bewilderment the sight of a gaijin lumping great cases or trunks around. Wear heavy clothes for the winter and light clothes for the summer, with a pullover for spring and autumn evenings. Temple interiors may be chilly even in summer.

Shopping

After Hong Kong and Singapore, I doubt if there is a shopper's paradise more remarkable than Tokyo. Tax-free items, to be noted on the shopkeeper's *Record of Purchase of Commodities Tax-Free* and attached to your passport for checking by customs staff on your departure, include jewels such as pearls, coral, amber, tortoiseshell, cloisonné and ivory, furs, radio and television sets, cassette-players, cameras of all kinds and projectors. Tax exemption ranges from 5% to a massive 40%.

Discount shops flourish in the Ameyoko Shopping Arcade near Ueno Rail Station; Shinjuku (Yodobashi and Doi are well-reputed names here) and Ginza for cameras; and Akihabara for electrical and electronic appliances of all kinds. The best flea market is in the Komingu Kottokan Market, Jimbocho, open every day.

Woodblock prints make wonderful souvenirs, partly because they were the first Japanese art-form to be fully appreciated in the West. Prints pulled in the mid-eighteenth century by the greatest masters such as Harunobu fetch astronomical prices, and even later artists such as Utamaro, Hokusai, Kuniyoshi and Hiroshige are now prized to exaggeration, where once they were despised as illustrators pandering to the low taste of the masses. Bargains are however to be found in the output of younger painters and engravers on show in department stores. Try also Uchida Art, Sukiyabashi Shopping Centre, 5-4 Nishi Ginza, Chuo-ku, Tokyo, and the Kyoto Handicrafts Center, Kumano Jinga Higashi, Sakyo-ku, near the Heian Shrine, in Kyoto.

Ceramics has been called the Japanese art *par excellence*, though much of the tradition was brought over by Korean masters, with Chinese influence. Department stores have a wide selection of pottery, and often charge little more than you would pay at the producing kiln or village. Near Tokyo, the most famous pottery centre is Mashiko. Take a 90-minute train ride from Ueno to Utsunomiya, then a 60-minute bus to Mashiko, where the great English potter Bernard Leach studied. In Kyoto, the study of ceramics alone can occupy you for a week or more. There is a potters' village, Kiyomizu-yaki Danchi, Yamashina-ku (a 10-minute taxi ride from Kyoto Rail Station); the house of the potter Kawai Kanjiro, 569 Kaneimachi, Gojozaka, Higashiyama-ku (2 minutes walk from Gojozaka bus stop also in east Kyoto; open 10–5 except on Mondays and from 10–20 August); the Raku Museum, Aburanokoji, Nakadachuri Agaru, Kamigyo-ku (4 minutes walk from Horikawa Nakadachuri bus stop, open 10–4 except on Mondays); the Kyoto Handicrafts Center, Gion-machi, Kitagawa, Higashiyama-ku (3 minutes walk from Gojozaka bus stop, open 11–7 except Wednesdays); and the Ceramics Hall, Gojodori-Higashioji-Higashi-iru, Higashiyama-ku (3 minutes walk from Gojozaka bus stop, open 9.30–5).

If you want pottery classes in English, a term of 3 months at Nippon Togei Club in Tokyo costs 56,000 yen including registration, tuition fees for 2 hours a week, firing and clay. Classes are held in Togo Shrine near Harajuku station on the Yamanote line.

A pottery class may also be arranged on application to Shimpo Kyoto Togei Centre on the fourth floor of the Marutaka Bldg., Shijo-Horikawa-agaru, Nakagyo-ku, Kyoto.

Kyoto pottery fairs include the Kiyomizu-yaki village fair on the outskirts of Kyoto between 15 and 17 July, and the Gojodori fair between the Kamogawa river and Higashi-Ojidori between 7 and 10 August.

Holidays and Festivals

Festivals are divided in Japan into national and local. Twelve national holidays listed below are celebrated on a Monday if they happen to fall on a Sunday.

January 1	New Year's Day.
January 15	Adults' Day.
February 11	National Foundation Day.
March 20 or 21	Spring Equinox Day. All Buddhist temples hold special services in the *Higan* week centred on this day.
April 29	Emperor's Birthday.
May 3	Constitution Memorial Day.
May 5	Children's Day.
September 15	Day of Respect for the Old.
September 23 or 24	Autumn Equinox Day.
October 10	Day of Health and Sport.
November 3	Day of Culture.
November 23	Day of Labour Thanksgiving.

Additional country-wide festivals, during which work continues as normal, include the following:

February 3 or 4	*Setsubun*, the bean-scattering festival to celebrate the last day of winter. In temple grounds, Japanese throw beans at invisible devils, and yell 'Good luck in!'.

March 3	*Hina Matsuri*, the doll festival especially for girls.
April 8	*Hana Matsuri*, the flower festival to commemorate the birthday of Gautama Buddha. Sweet tea is poured over a small image of Buddha at each temple as a sign of devotion.
July 7	*Tanabata*, the festival of the star Vega, when children tie coloured paper strips with poems to specially set-up bamboo branches.
July 13–15	*Bon*, the festival for All Souls' Day, with rituals for the dead, and lanterns lit for the souls which are supposed to revisit Earth.
November 15	*Shichi-go-san*, the 'seven-five-three' festival when children are taken to shrines by their parents to thank the deities for good health in the past and to pray for good health in the future.

Local festivals are held all over the country.

Nara

January 15	Fireworks Festival at Wakakusa Hill, eastern Nara, to celebrate the turf-burning ten centuries earlier which ended a boundary dispute between two temples.
February 3 or 4	Lantern Festival at Kasuga Shrine, eastern Nara.
March 1–14	*Omizu-tori Matsuri*, Water-Drawing Festival. Each evening young men whirl flaming torches around the temple of Todaiji, and shake off the burning pieces, which are snatched by worshippers to protect them from evil. The climax is on March 12, followed at 2 a.m. on March 13 by the drawing of water, to classical Japanese music.
March 13	*Kasuga Matsuri*, the Festival of Kasuga Shrine, features ancient ritual and dances.
December 17	*On Matsuri*, at Kasuga Shrine, has as its centre-piece a gorgeous procession of Nara people in costumes of courtiers and commoners reflecting earlier periods.

Kyoto

May 15	*Aoi Matsuri* is a pageant celebrated at the Kamigamo and Shimogamo Shinto Shrines. The name means 'Hollyhock Festival'.
May	On the third Sunday in May, the *Mifune Matsuri* or Boat Festival takes place on the Oi river near Arashiyama, in western Kyoto. Local people and visitors, often elegantly dressed, take pleasure-boat trips along the river.
June 1–2	Open-air performances of Noh and Kyogen plays are held half in daylight and half in torchlight at the Heian Shrine.

July 16–17	*Gion Matsuri*, the Gion Festival, is held at the Yasaka Shrine in eastern Kyoto. It has been celebrated for over eleven hundred years, invoking divine protection against plague. The floats parade through the streets on the 17th.
August 16	Mount Nyoigadake Bonfire, in the shape of the Chinese character 'Da' (Japanese 'Dai') meaning 'great', in east Kyoto, above the temples of Nanzenji and Eikando.
October 22	*Jidai Matsuri*, or Foundation Anniversary Festival, commemorates the founding of Heian-kyo in 794. Many groups in period costume parade through the streets to portray various epochs in the twelve-century existence of Kyoto. On the same day the Fire Festival takes place at Kurama, north of Kyoto. Boys cleanse themselves in the upper Kamo river's icy waters, then carry torches through the streets to celebrate the transportation of the deity of Yuki Shrine from the Imperial Palace in 940.
December 31	*Okera Mairi*, the Sacred Fire Festival, takes place at Yasaka Shrine, Gion, in eastern Kyoto. Worshippers take embers home from a fire lit here at midnight with which to prepare the first breakfast of the New Year.

Tokyo

January 6	*Dezome-shiki*, the New Year's Parade of the Fire Brigade, in Harumi Chuodori. Firemen perform acrobatics atop bamboo ladders.
May	In mid-May in odd-numbered years the *Kanda Matsuri* consists of two elaborate palanquins from the Myojin Shrine in Kanda which parade through the streets. On the third Saturday and Sunday in May, the *Sanja Matsuri* consists of three elaborate palanquins from the Asakusa Kannon Shrine in Asakusa which parade through the streets.
June 10–16	*Sanno Matsuri* consists of elaborate palanquins from the Hie Shrine, near the Sannoshita bus stop, on the hill called Hoshigaoka or Sanno-dai, which parade through the streets.
October 12	*Oeshiki Matsuri* consists of a popular march to Hommonji Temple to commemorate the Buddhist Nichiren (1222–82). Pilgrims carry large lanterns decorated with paper flowers.
November	In mid-November the *Tori-no-ichi* or Cock Fair is held on days attributed to the cock in the oriental zodiacal calendar. The best-known *Tori-no-ichi* is at the Otori Shrine in Asakusa.

December 17–19 *Hagoita-ichi* or Battledore Fair is held at Asakusa Kannon Shrine in Asakusa. Worshippers buy New Year decorations, toys including battledores, and presents at stalls near the Shrine.

Words and Phrases

Excuse me!	Sumimasen
Thank you (very much)	(Domo) arigato
Please	Dozo
Yes	Hai (often repeated)
No	Ie (*ee-eh*) (Avoid, if possible)
Don't mention it	Do itashi-mashite
Hello!	Harro!
Good morning	Ohayo gozaimasu (drop final 'u' here and below)
Good afternoon	Kon-nichiwa
Good evening	Kon-banwa
Goodnight	Oyasumi nasai
Goodbye	Sayonara
How are you?	O-genki desu ka?
Fine	Genki desu
Would you please help me?	Onegai shimasu?
Excuse me	Shitsuri shimasu
Where is . . .?	. . . doko desu ka?
When?	Itsu?
What?	Nani?
This/that	Kore wa/Are wa
What do you call this?	Kore wa nanto iimasu ka?
What does that mean?	Are wa do yu imi desu ka?
Do you speak English?	Eigo o hanashimasu ka?
I don't understand	Wakarimasen
I do understand	Wakarimashita
Just a minute	Chotto matte kudasai
May I have . . .?	. . . a kudasaimasu ka?
It is . . .	. . . desu
There is . . .	. . . ga arimasu
There isn't . . .	. . . wa arimasen
My name is . . .	(name) desu ga
I'd like a single room	Shinguru rumu ga hoshii ne desu ga
Is there air conditioning/heating?	Reibo/danbo wa arimasu ka?
Is there hot water/running water?	Oyu/suido wa arimasu ka?
Can you get a taxi?	Takushi o yonde kudasai?
It's been a very enjoyable stay	Tanoshii taizai deshita
We hope to come again	Itsuka mata kimasho

210

Breakfast/lunch/dinner	Choshoku/chushoku/yushoku
Bottle of beer	Biru ippon
Bread/butter	Pan/bata
Chips	Furenchi furaido potato (yes really!)
Coffee/tea	Kohi/o-cha
Dessert	Dezato
Fruit	Kudamono
Ice-cream	Aisu-kurimu
Meat	Niku
Milk	Miruku
Soup	Supu
Sugar	Sato
Water	Mizu
Wine	Budoshu
Open/shut	Aite iru/shimatte iru
Right/wrong	Tadashii/machigatte iru
Good/bad	Yoi/warui
Large/small	Okii/chiisai
Cheap/dear	Yasui/takai
Near/far	Chikai/toi
Early/late	Hayai/osoi
Hot/cold	Atsui/tsumetai
Easy/difficult	Yasashii/muzukashii
How much is that/this?	Ikura desu ka?
Where are the toilets?	Te-arai wa doko desu ka?
Please help me	Tasukete kudasai

Numbers

1	ichi	11	ju-ichi, etc.
2	ni	20	ni-ju
3	san	21	ni-ju-ichi, etc.
4	shi, yo	100	hyaku
5	go	101	hyaku-ichi, etc.
6	roku	200	ni-hyaku, etc.
7	shichi, nana	1000	sen.
8	hachi	1100	sen-hyaku
9	kyu, ku		
10	ju		

1st   ichiban   2nd   niban   3rd   sanban

Days and Months

Sunday	nichiyobi	January	ichigatsu
Monday	getsuyobi	February	nigatsu

211

Tuesday	kayobi	March	sangatsu
Wednesday	suiyobi	April	shigatsu
Thursday	mokuyobi	May	gogatsu
Friday	kinyobi	June	rokugatsu
Saturday	doyobi	July	shichigatsu
		August	hachigatsu
		September	kugatsu
		October	jugatsu
		November	ju-ichigatsu
		December	ju-nigatsu

Books

Considering the crucial importance of Japan in the world today, there is a rather small range of authoritative books. The best books are often dated, and new books often superficial.

G.B. Sansom's *A History of Japan* (3 volumes, 1958–63) can be recommended, as can his *Japan: a Short Cultural History* (2nd rev. ed., 1952) and the anthology compiled by Tsunoda and others, *Sources of Japanese Tradition* (2 vols., 1964).

The best general travel book is Fosco Maraini's *Meetings with Japan* (1959), if one excludes the dull *Official Guide* published every five to seven years by the Japan National Tourist Office, which provides no atmosphere or individuality, and is useful only for a wide range of maps. The most up-to-date is J.D. Bisignani's *Japan Handbook* (1983).

I still like Ruth Benedict's *The Chrysanthemum and the Sword* (1946) for its insights into the Japanese mind and character, but forty years on it should be treated with caution. A more modern view of *The Japanese Mind* (1983) has been written by Robert C. Christopher.

For Tokyo, the best companions were Jean Pearce's *Foot-loose in Tokyo* (2nd ed., 1983) and *More Foot-loose in Tokyo* (1984) until the appearance of Paul Waley's magisterial *Tokyo Now and Then* (1984).

For Kyoto, *The World of the Shining Prince: Court Life in Ancient Japan* (1964) by Ivan Morris is a splendid introduction to Heian culture. Despite its infuriating and eccentric omissions, I still enjoy Gouverneur Mosher's *Kyoto: a Contemplative Guide* (1964). *Kyoto* (1974) by Edwin Bayrd is the best-illustrated album on Kyoto in English, with a useful text. True enthusiasts for Kyoto will particularly enjoy Harold Stewart's *By the Old Walls of Kyoto: a Year's Cycle of Landscape Poems with Prose Commentaries* (1981). The most recent monograph is H.E. Plutschow's *Historical Kyoto* (1983).

For Nara, I recommend H.E. Plutschow's *Historical Nara* (1983), and four volumes in the Heibonsha Survey of Japanese Art series: Seiichi Mizuno's *Asuka Buddhist Art: Horyu-ji*, Takeshi Kobayashi's *Nara Buddhist Art: Todai-ji*, Ryoichi Hayashi's *The Silk Road and the Shoso-in*, and Minoru Ooka's *Temples of Nara and their Art*.

INDEX